SUPER!

SUPER!

The Raiders In Their Finest Hour

Edited by Murray Olderman

To Carla:
Keep rooting
for the Silver
and Black

Al Davis

Published by
The Oakland Raiders and Murray Olderman
Oakland, CA

COVER PHOTO:

Cliff Branch (21) wrestles a touchdown pass away from Roynell Young of the Eagles

BACK COVER PHOTO:

Jim Plunkett (16) sets up to throw a completion in Super Bowl XV

Printed in the United States of America

ISBN 0-9606558-0-8 (Case)
ISBN 0-9606558-1-6 (Paper)

First Edition

CONTENTS

ACKNOWLEDGEMENTS

Just as in football, where teamwork is an essential ingredient, the execution of a book such as this is the product of cohesive effort by many talented people. First, gratitude must be expressed for the cooperation and support of the Oakland Raider organization, particularly Al Davis and Al LoCasale. The guiding thrust in converting the words and pictures into a graceful product and ultimately a book was provided by Hal Silverman. For their writing contributions, I extend my appreciation to Frank Cooney of the *San Francisco Examiner,* Win Currier of the *Alameda Times Star,* Ron Borges of the *Oakland Tribune,* Terry Moore of the *San Francisco Examiner,* Chuck Nevius of the *San Francisco Chronicle,* Dave Payne of the *San Jose Mercury News* and Dave Beronio of the *Vallejo Independent Press.* They were the men who chronicled the success of the Raiders on a continuing basis and transferred their experience to these pages. Finally, a debt is due to the 45 men who comprised the roster of the Oakland Raiders of 1980, champions of the world of professional football, for their exploits made this ultimately a worthwhile project.

The photographs in this book were provided by the Oakland Raiders, through the following photographers—Fred Kaplan, Mike Zagaris, Russ Reed, Dan Honda, Norm Fisher.

Murray Olderman
June 1981

FOREWORD

By Al Davis
Managing General Partner

For two memorable decades, the Oakland Raiders have had the greatest players, some of the greatest coaches, the greatest plays and performed in the greatest games ever played in the history of professional football. During the same period, the Oakland Raiders have also had the best record in professional football.

I feel that achievement is more than coincidence.

When we came to Oakland in 1963, we wanted to build the finest organization in professional sports. We felt that more important than any single event was that a will to win permeate the organization, top to bottom, including the secretaries (which is not to be interpreted as chauvinistic).

We had a commitment to excellence.

I've always felt that way. I was influenced from my earliest days in athletics by the power inherent in success. To go with it, I chimed the words, Pride and Poise. It's a belief in what you're doing, and doing it with total control and confidence.

I felt we could create an environment which would inspire the players to feel the same way, at the same time giving them a philosophy and a strategy which would make them adhere to us.

The key to that environment is treating people the way they want to be treated and yet having rules and regulations they have to observe. Let's face it, that also means a benevolent dictatorship, a para-military situation, but yet not taking away their individual rights as much as possible.

It is accompanied by a football philosophy that advocates attack and pressure. I'd rather be feared than respected. Even defensively, the stress is on attack.

We want to be the most feared. I want teams to come into that Coliseum and see those black shirts and feel the pressure. I love to go to other stadiums and they're sold out, and they boo us when we come on the field. On a personal level, I still feel a chill of excitement running through me when I hear the roar of the spectators as the Raiders come sprinting out on the field. The atmosphere in San Diego for the championship game of the 1980 season, the intensity of the crowd, the booing—it was based on fear as well as respect. I believe in a tough team. And the Oakland Raiders are.

The colors of silver and black, which they wear, were derived from watching Army, the dominant college football team at the time, and the Detroit Lions, successful in pro football in the 1950s. I wanted those colors to be preceded by adjectives, like the FAMED silver and black. I wanted the men who wore that uniform to feel proud of it, even when they gave it up.

To get sentimental, it's more meaningful than belonging to a college with its famous and hallowed traditions. I wanted all our players to feel that way about the Raiders. I wanted people to look at the Oakland Raiders and say we have the best and smartest elements. If there were organizations better in one or two areas, at least no one would equal us in all of them put together. We would have the finest leadership, the finest coaches, the greatest players, playing the greatest games; and then they could all march to a personal Hall of Fame after their five years of retirement.

In short, I wanted us to dominate pro football, and I think we've come close to it. We've done it in terms of consistent victory. We've held the record for most winning seasons in a row. We've achieved everything conceivable except the Super Bowl record of four victories held by Pittsburgh. Yet I would take our history over that of Pittsburgh, without minimizing the Steeler accomplishments of the last decade.

Through all our years of glory, we have managed to remember the days of defeat most. And that makes all the more memorable the fact that the 1980 season was truly "our finest hour." I thoroughly believe that.

There was much involved. In my mind, it was an even more difficult feat than 1963, when we took a 1-and-13 team, an organization that reportedly was being moved every week, that was laughed at and ridiculed, and came up with dynamic football at the advent of the game as a phenomenon on national television, which embraced us because we were exciting and scoring points and not afraid to be innovative. We did a lot of technical things that first year in Oakland which rouses memories in me. We played the 3-4 on defense before most dared to, the stack defense which was later given wide publicity by Kansas City—oh, so many flourishes which became synonymous with the Raider way of football and which bring me to the men who made them come alive.

I feel great appreciation for the response from all the men who've worn the Silver and Black. Jim Otto and George Blanda were voted into the Professional Hall of Fame at Canton, Ohio. That's a great tribute to our organization. We always wanted the Raider organization to feel it could never forget these players who performed for us. We owed them a debt of gratitude which we could never relinquish. The Raiders themselves should encompass a small Hall of Fame. People talk about the reclamation of Jim Plunkett. He was just one. I remember Art Powell, Blanda, others. I remember Frank Youell Field, which was derided for its makeshift stands. I was not ashamed to have the Raiders play there. Because it was a symptom of our progress.

I think the toughest game in our history was the second game of the season in 1977. We played Pittsburgh back in Pittsburgh after beating them in the championship game in 1976 (prior to winning Super Bowl XI) when they were without Rocky Bleier and Franco Harris. People said, "Now Pittsburgh will teach you a lesson." We dominated them, 16-7. The team of 1977 might have been our greatest—until we got some of our key players hurt. We lost to Denver in the championship game on a fumble, but we were really banged up. We couldn't overcome the handicap of the regulars we lost.

But it never affected our spirit and pride. I can remember Marv Hubbard, our fiery fullback of the early 1970s, sitting in the locker room after games and saying to himself, over and over, "I'll never take this uniform off."

Players such as Hubbard symbolized the spirit of the Oakland Raiders. But they were abetted by some fine leadership, too. I want to pay tribute to the vision of a man such as Ed McGah, who was one of the founders of the team back in 1960 and whose confidence in the destiny of the Raiders never waivered. Ed still plays a quiet but strong role as a general partner. Without him, the Raiders wouldn't be what they are today.

The winning of Super Bowls also derives from strong men within the organization. Al LoCasale, the executive assistant, has been a powerful force in the administration of the team behind the scenes. As a master of detail, thoroughly reliable, unbendingly loyal, he has insured the smooth operation of the team in the many facets that modern professional football demands. Ron Wolf came out of the University of Oklahoma with an amazing scope of knowledge in the area of player talent, and that expertise was a corner stone for the building of the team right from the start in 1963, when he joined Oakland as a talent scout. He progressed to become the director of personnel operations and continues to provide the kind of input that insured the Raiders' continuing success.

In their two Super Bowl triumphs, the Raiders were also fortunate to have coaches the caliber of John Madden and Tom Flores. Madden's record is self-explanatory; his 103 victories in a decade of coaching parallels the best in the history of the game. And after his retirement in January, 1979, he remained with the organization to help in special projects. Tom Flores was a natural to succeed him, as a Raiders' original star player who had progressed through the coaching ranks, showing maturity in his handling of the players and sound football knowledge. Tom is less flamboyant than John but no less effective, with a Super Bowl triumph in his second year.

All the men who've been a part of Oakland's success have contributed to a legacy that transcends just winning football games.

When John Robinson left Oakland in 1976 to take over as the head coach of the University of Southern California, I asked him, "What's the biggest thing you learned with the Raiders, outside of football?"

He answered, "To be positive on everything; find the good in everything."

A motto of the Oakland Raiders always has been: "We'll get it done."

If fits the spirit of this book, which is dedicated to the development of the Oakland Raiders as a professional football power.

One word, I believe, most adequately describes the team which took us to the pinnacle on January 25, 1981. Magnificent. It was a team over which hung a cloud of uncertainty, at least in the minds of outside observers, in every area of performance. Our team was supposedly suspect at every position other than our punter. The quarterback, running backs, wide receivers, offensive line, defensive line, linebackers, defensive backs—all were downgraded. Every aspect of our organization was subject to criticism from without—the projected move to Los Angeles which incurred so much emotion, the picking us to finish last in our western division of the American Football Conference.

With all the vivid memories of the AFL, its great teams and its rivalries, it's fair to say I'm proudest of this 1980 team. In 1963, no one expected us to be successful; they were willing to give us time. So the pressures weren't there. Whatever pressure we had was self-induced from our obsession to win.

But this team and its players, they were amazing when you stop to analyze what they accomplished. Their performance in the playoffs and the Super Bowl was, under the conditions, the greatest in National Football League history.

I think you'll find this book reflects the scope of that accomplishment.

The digital electric clock on the mezzanine level of the Superdome—a quarter-of-a-billion-dollar edifice in the heart of New Orleans—flashed inexorably and silently down to the final seconds . . . :05 . . . :04 . . . :03 . . . :02 . . . The Philadelphia Eagles didn't even bother to take the last time out which remained to them as Derrick Jensen of the Oakland Raiders ground into the middle of the line, the football hugged to his stomach. Claude Humphrey was draped over him on the Eagle 16-yard line, a tableau of frustration, as the numbers above them flicked on . . . :01 . . . 00!

And the final score was fixed permanently for the record books: Oakland 27, Philadelphia 10. Finis to Super Bowl XV!

That's when Coach Tom Flores, stoic almost to the last, cut loose with a broad, exultant smile and bear-hugged those nearest him. First Sam Boghosian, the coaching aide at his elbow. Then, running out on the field, Jim Plunkett, the quarterback. Rod Martin, on the sideline with the other Oakland Raider defenders, raised both fists in a gloating salute to victory.

Up in the press box, where he had kept his emotions patiently under control, Al Davis said with excitement, "Boy, they did it. These kids are something!" Not the most historic choice of words, but for him they were significant because they meant achievement such as few teams in sports are privileged to reach.

The Oakland Raiders—derogated, maligned, castigated and sometimes reviled prior to and during 1980—once again dominated all of professional football, the most dynamic and passionate sport in the second half of the twentieth century. They proved their superiority before 75,500 spectators who paid forty dollars each to see them live, and on television before more than 100 million viewers across the nation and in various parts of

the world. It was, everything considered, an incredible feat.

The excitement of such a football game didn't dissipate quickly. It carried over immediately into the locker room, where the gladiators, a term that aptly fits these men who replay the ancient rites of Rome, let their feelings of exhilaration spill out freely. Huge men grappled warmly with each other, ignoring the grime and the clutter and pervasive crush of the media trying to get at them. And they embraced with a private elation that none of the crowd jamming the cramped quarters could really fathom. The Oakland Raiders had won their war, and the acceptance of that victory was unique.

It could have been awkward, for it meant that Pete Rozelle, the commissioner of the National Football League, would have to give the Vince Lombardi Trophy, the symbol of a Super Bowl victory, personally to Davis, the major owner and managing general partner of the Raiders.

They were not friendly. On the Friday before the Super Bowl, in his annual, carefully orchestrated press conference with 500 of the nation's leading sports writers, Rozelle had bluntly branded the Oakland owner an "outlaw." Davis in turn had called the commissioner "corrupt" but now, preferring to concentrate on the game, refrained from commenting on the issue that had divided them for the last year—the Raiders' avowed intention of moving their franchise to Los Angeles, the NFL's rejection of that proposal and the resulting serious litigation. Speculation over the feud became a sideshow to the buildup of Super Bowl week.

When the possibility of Oakland reaching the championship finale first became apparent, which could mean a contretemps involving the two if the Raiders won, Rozelle had blithely stated, "I'll have to consult with Bowie Kuhn (commissioner of baseball) to see how he handled it when Charlie Finley (and the Oakland A's) won the World Series.''

But when it came time for the actual presentation, with Rozelle mounting a platform set up for NBC television, announcer Bryant Gumbel standing in the middle, and Davis joining them after a trip several flights down through the stadium throng, the accomplishment of the Raiders as a football team was paramount.

Handing over to Davis the bright silver trophy, a replica of a football in metal on an elegant pedestal, Rozelle said, ''I think it's a tremendous compliment to the organization because you had to win four post-season games. Today, of course, was the big one—the Super Bowl. I think it's a great credit to you for putting them together, and I think that Tom Flores clearly did one of the great coaching jobs in recent years.'' The commis-

sioner paused briefly. ''All season and particularly today,'' he continued. ''It's a credit to some marvelously dedicated athletes, especially Jim Plunkett and that offensive line today. You've earned it. Congratulations.''

Al Davis, with a proud smile fixed on his face, responded simply and emotionally: ''Thanks very much, Commissioner. You know, when you look back on the glory of the Oakland Raiders, this was our finest hour.

''To Tom Flores, the coaches and the great athletes, you were magnificent out there; you really were. The years will go on. We owe a great tribute to all our alumni all over the country and to our great fans. And we want to welcome back the hostages to the United States. Take pride and be proud,'' and in this Davis was addressing himself directly to the Raiders who clustered around the platform. ''Your commitment to excellence and your will to win will endure forever.

NFL Commissioner Pete Rozelle, right, hands the Vince Lombardi Trophy for winning Super Bowl XV to Al Davis, managing general partner of the *Oakland Raiders. Bryant Gumbel of NBC holds the microphone, with Tom Flores at his right, in the Raider dressing room.*

"You were magnificent."

In the truncated playoff system of the National Football League, the Oakland Raiders were the first legitimate wild card team ever to win the Super Bowl. They were the first ever to endure four arduous playoff games to reach that apex. In succession, they had defeated convincingly the Houston Oilers in the first round (or wild card) playoffs; they had persevered in sub-zero weather to edge the dangerous Cleveland Browns in divisional playoffs; they had outscored the potent San Diego Chargers for the American Football Conference championship; and now they had shown that all of it was done on merit as they dominated the Philadelphia Eagles in the final, most important test.

In all four games, the other teams had been favored by those who establish the odds on football.

The Raiders also forced a revision of all the adjectives that had been used on them in the most controversial season in the team's history. Bawdy, brawling gave way to courageous, committed. Which is what led Davis, with his sense of history, to borrow from Winston Churchill and label the climactic victory in Super Bowl XV "our finest hour."

In the 18 years Al Davis has been with them, first as coach and general manager, now as managing general partner, the Oakland Raiders have been the most successful team in pro football. Their winning percentage of .725, highest in the NFL, was fashioned from a regular season record of 179 wins, 68 defeats and 11 ties. They had 17 winning seasons, the last 16 consecutively.

They won nine division championships outright and in the resulting 24 additional games they played in post-season playoff competition, they were victorious 15 times, including triumphs in Super Bowl XI and XV.

Yet the figures alone are a meager measure of the pulse of the Raiders. Their strong heartbeat as a team stemmed from an attitude. Their management called it Pride and Poise. Also a Commitment to Excellence. Which may be pretentious and even sound like cliches but which embody the philosophy of sports that the Raiders felt was absolutely necessary for winning.

Those phrases were emblazoned on billboards, 16 of them, spotted around New Orleans along routes the Raider players were most likely to travel — to their practice field, to their interview sites and, of course, to the French Quarter. Panels with the same words were also placed propitiously on 100 buses that took routes through the heart of the city, because the Raiders wanted to get their message across. It keynoted their mental approach to the game against the Philadelphia Eagles, who had beaten them during the regular season and were established as 3½-point favorites for the Super Bowl rematch.

The march on New Orleans started formally on Sunday, January 18, 1981, with an advance party flying by commercial airliner out of San Francisco. It consisted of the coaching staff and assorted aides. For a week, they had been assiduously studying films since winning the American Football Conference title over San Diego, and now their game plan was virtually set. Coach Tom Flores and his assistants wanted to get on the scene a day early to make sure the preparations for the main party were finished.

National Football League rules specify that the contestants in the Super Bowl must arrive at the playing site six full days before the game. On Monday morning, a gray day, the players straggled into the Oakland International Airport from their homes spotted around the East Bay area. Generally they were dropped off by their wives or friends because there was no point in keeping a car at the airport a full week. Also in the travelling party on the chartered United Airlines DC-8 plane were members of the press, radio and television who habitually accompanied the team on its road trips, a group of the Raider front office staff and selected guests.

Herb Caen, the oracle of the *San Francisco Chronicle,* had been delegated by his publisher to cover the Super Bowl, since the Raiders were in his circulation area, and was delighted to be in the Monday contingent, particularly since space was allotted to him in the first class section that normally is reserved for the coaches and owners (they were already in New Orleans). Herb, with his *bon mots,* refrained from saying, "On the whole, I'd rather be in Washington."

Billboards carrying the slogans of the Oakland Raiders were strategically placed around New Orleans during Super Bowl week.

It is true that the inauguration of Ronald Reagan as President of the United States was taking place that same week in Washington, D.C. Before the weekend was over, the American hostages would be released by Iran.

The 10 a.m. departure was held up because one player was missing. Derrick Ramsey, the reserve tight end behind Raymond Chester and a clutch contributor in several games, was delayed, it turned out, because of automobile trouble on the Nimitz Freeway leading to the airport.

Moving a team is, logistically, like transporting an army division—a complex, detailed endeavor with all kinds of check lists and sophisticated arrangements, down to making sure the entourage's bags are delivered right to the assigned hotel rooms. The airline crew is invariably the same for all road trips, under the direction of sports representative Red Klaren. The stewardesses—or flight attendants, to be euphemistic—have virtually become a part of the Raider family. And they were all on this trip to New Orleans—Jill Kleinheinz, Michelle Kinchlow, Ginger Mundy, Myra Ming and Leslie Larson.

The movie shown was "Hopscotch," with Walter Matthau and Glenda Jackson. The flight went smoothly, and buses awaited the team on arrival at the New Orleans International Airport. The National Football League had selected the Gateway Motel, in the vicinity of the airport, as the team's headquarters for the week of the Super Bowl. But it wouldn't be big enough to hold all 400 people who would eventually arrive for the Super Bowl as part of the Raiders' official group. So some were placed at the LaQuinta across the road, and at a couple of Holiday Inns and even downtown in French Quarter hotels.

That first day, after being met at their quarters by the inevitable inquiring press and submitting to impromptu interviews, the players were free, and soon clusters of them invaded the French Quarter to become part of the festive atmosphere already pervading the city.

At Pat O'Brien's two contingents of Raiders indulged in a Hurricane contest. This was to see which could swig down fastest the contents of a three-gallon special glass filled with the Pat O'Brien rum potion called a Hurricane. The Gene Upshaw team reportedly outlasted the Ted Hendricks team. ("In a throwup," quipped Caen.)

Tuesday morning provided a clue to the personalities and operational methods of the Raiders and the Eagles, who had also arrived the previous day and were lodged at the Airport Hilton. It was picture day, with the Eagles coming out first on the field at the Superdome in full battle regalia, including bulky shoulder pads. It was after they had already worked out in private for an hour and a half. The Raiders on the other hand showed up in simple white jerseys, with no pads, completely rested and relaxed, at ease with the hundreds of newspapermen who cluttered the artificial turf.

"Then," recalled John Matuszak, their big defensive lineman who relished the whole scene, "we had a crisp, hard, quick-moving, get-used-to-the-lights practice, ran some sprints, and we were ready for the intensive work the rest of the week."

Tooz, as Matuszak referred to himself, definitely left an imprint on Super Bowl week. The Raiders had an 11 p.m. curfew after the first night on the scene, but in the early morning hours on Thursday, Tooz was very much in evidence on Bourbon Street and at such bistros as the Old Absinthe House. And when the Raiders showed up for their daily interview-breakfast at the Fairmont Hotel, with round tables designated for each player, Matuszak's chair was noticeably absent until just before the team was ready to return to its hotel. He showed up with slits for eyes and a sheepish smile.

"I was just checking the spots out," explained Tooz, "to make sure the other guys weren't there. I know what kind of a party town this is."

Later, he said, "Four nights before a game, I go out—no matter where we are. It happened to be after a very hard, brutal defensive practice. I realize I made a mistake and I apologized and paid my fine."

Told of Matuszak's brief delinquency, Coach Dick Vermeil of the Eagles said that if it had been one of his players, he would have sent him home and out of the forthcoming Sunday game. Coach Tom Flores took a more pragmatic approach. The fine for missing curfew was one thousand dollars, and when the score was totalled at the end of the week, some fifteen thousand dollars, it was rumored, had been accumulated. But the lineup was intact, and the Raiders were ready to play football.

Also on Thursday, the rest of the Oakland party—families of players, coaches and officials, plus the Raiderettes, their spirited cheerleaders—arrived in New Orleans. A party for the owners was held at the Hilton Hotel, where managing general partner Al Davis was staying at the special invitation of Barron Hilton. And there was a party for the Raiderettes.

Parties are an integral ritual of Super Bowl week. The Raiders held a special pre-game brunch at the Superdome for their limited partners. They also hosted a post-game party at the Fairmont which was attended by 1,377 guests. The NFL commissioner held his annual Friday night party for 3,000 people with entertainment provided by the big bands of Doc Severinsen and Count Basie. Barron Hilton held a Sunday brunch for 1,500 invitees, and a college marching band that paraded around the ballroom added to the din. Gladys Sargent, one of Oakland's limited partners, entered the spirit of the occasion by moving in with the band and leading its foray around the stacked buffet tables. There was a myriad of private parties all through the city.

"It was New Year's Eve and the Mardi Gras wrapped up into one beautiful mess," said Herb Caen. "It was the Super Bowl of laughing, drinking and lurching from lamp post to lamp post. All of us who were there deserve most valuable player awards. I have never played harder on a more beautiful turf than New Orleans."

Ironically, the man most talked about in the buildup to the Super Bowl skipped all the festivities. Party-going was not the way of Al Davis. His continued determination to move the Oakland Raider franchise to Los Angeles, with the NFL equally determined to block him, intrigued the 1,500 members of the media who had flocked to New Orleans. Speculation over the one-man revolt—some called it a crusade, some branded it a maverick action, some even labelled it anarchy—shared equal billing with the game and made him the cynosure of national attention, particularly because his Raiders, who should have been distracted by the swirl of controversy, had proceeded in almost miracle fashion to within one step of the world championship.

Many adjectives were used to describe the Raiders' leader: clever, scheming, bright, secretive, loyal, shady, egotistic. None of them hit the mark completely. The natural conclusion was to categorize him as complex, but that would also be off target. He was in fact a man with simple tastes and a simple direction in life—the ambition to win consumed it.

He didn't use Vince Lombardi's phrase—"winning isn't everything, it's the only thing"—which really originated with Gen. Douglas MacArthur. But he very well could have. Toward that end, he isolated himself completely in his job. For his entire adulthood, football has been his total absorption, with one brief respite of six weeks in 1979 when his wife, Carole, suffered a severe heart attack.

"I told Caroli [sic] when we were married 25 years ago," he related, "the only thing that would take me away from football is life or death." He grinned slightly. "And she put me to the test."

Even in nursing her back to health, he demonstrated the intense, insular drive that is the key to his personality. He never left Carole while she was in a two-week coma, and when the doctors attending her were most pessimistic he never despaired.

With the single-minded ardor that pushed the Raiders to the top of pro football there was also a boyish naivete and flashes of charm when he was away from the public.

His break with Wayne Valley, the brusque, gregarious man who plucked him from obscurity and made him the Oakland coach and general manager, then later a part-owner, was due primarily to the fact he didn't want to be around Valley, who can be garrulous socially. Valley sued him for control of the club, lost, and bowed out.

Davis, as he showed against Rozelle and the NFL, could be a tough, unrelenting opponent. Larry Merchant, writing a sports column in New York, fostered an image of him as a "gutter fighter." Although he was raised in Brooklyn, a fact sometimes hidden by a pseudo-Southern accent, Davis was not a product of privation. His family was well off. He chose football as a career not for the opportunity but genuine dedication to the game.

The strategy, the assessment of talent, the direction in which football is going proved to be his forte. After all, the Raiders made it to Super Bowl XV with a quarterback who threw a total of 15 passes the two previous years. Their leading rusher gained nine yards in 1979. Their defensive signals were called by a rookie who was a tackle in college. Fourteen men, more than a fourth of the roster, were in their first year with Oakland.

So it was interesting to see Super Bowl XV through the eyes of Davis, which became possible for those who reported the game because he shunned the private box usually reserved for the owners of the competing Super Bowl teams and chose a perch in the press box, where his spontaneous words and actions could be recorded and observed.

For the previous week, a stubble of beard had been sprouting on Davis' face, and national columnists had translated this into a meaningful gesture by the Oakland boss to emulate the late Rocky Marciano, another fighter of renown—they were born in the same city of Brockton, Mass. Rocky habitually stopped shaving a few days before battle.

"I don't shave during the week," Davis leaned over to a writer and explained, "to give my face a break. It gets sensitive if I shave every day, so I wait till the day of the game."

Now he was dressed in customary white and gray—he shuns pastel colors in his wardrobe—and was clean shaven. He watched intently as the starting lineup of the Raiders was introduced to the basically hostile, pro-Philadelphia crowd in the Superdome.

As No. 21 raced past the waving tassels of an archway of scantily clad Raiderettes, Davis said, "Here's my man. Cliff Branch. You got to have one of those to win."

Branch, still a remarkably swift and elusive wide receiver at the age of 32, was to score two of the three Raider touchdowns and catch five passes, keeping the Eagle defenders tentative and on edge for the entire game. The cover picture on this book shows him leaping for a touchdown pass against rookie Roynell Young of Philadelphia.

As Ray Guy of the Raiders kicked off sharply at 5:16 p.m. CST to start the action before 100 million television viewers and a sold-out stadium, Davis exhorted, "Go, baby. This is a big one."

He sized up the Eagles professionally as they put the ball into play on the opening sequence of the game: "They're using two tight ends on first down. They're giving us different formations every down to see how we play it." On the third play, linebacker Rod Martin intercepted a pass by quarterback Ron Jaworski of the Eagles to put Oakland in scoring position on the Eagles' 30-yard line.

"The only thing I don't know about us,"

Wide receiver Cliff Branch lines up for a standing start before the snap of the ball. His speed kept the Eagles on edge.

mused Davis, "is how Jim Plunkett will do in this game." It was pointed out to him, as the veteran quarterback led the offense out of the huddle, that Plunkett had been a star in the Rose Bowl as a collegian.

"But it's not big like this," he shrugged. "Of course, you don't know about Jaworski, either." Plunkett briskly moved his team to the Philadelphia 2-yard line. He stepped back to pass, moved up when the Eagle lineman circled to pressure him, then threatened to run, freezing Herman Edwards, the cornerback, and John Bunting, the linebacker. In the end zone, Branch curled back, and Plunkett quickly zipped the ball to him for the first score of the game.

"That threat of him running," noted Davis, "helps us. The linebackers had to come off their coverage."

By the second quarter, the Raiders had firm control of the game, scoring again on an 80-yard pass play from Plunkett to halfback Kenny King. Plunkett once more had scrambled, stepping nimbly to his left, coming off his primary receiver, Bob Chandler, and locating King on the sideline to start the longest touchdown play in Super Bowl history.

Meanwhile the Oakland defense was putting extreme pressure on Jaworski and forcing him to hurry his pass. "So far," observed Davis, "he's jumpy in the pocket. They're using [halfback Wilbert] Montgomery as a third wide receiver to make us keep our linebackers in the game." His first question of his own team came when Coach Tom Flores elected late in the second quarter to try a 45-yard field goal by Chris Bahr. The Raiders had a yard and a half to go for a first down on the Philadelphia 27. The placement attempt was short and to the right. "I wouldn't have gone for it," said Davis. "I was watching Bahr in practice. He wasn't kicking long."

Contrary to some belief among football people, from his press box seat, Davis didn't dictate strategy to his coaches, although his executive assistant, Al LoCasale, sat at his side with a two-way radio connection to liaison people on the sidelines. No plays were transmitted. Instead, the Raider brass found out quickly that when Reggie Kinlaw, the nose tackle in the 3–4 defensive align-

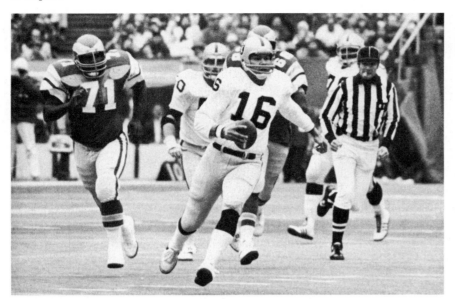

Jim Plunkett (16) on the run evades Eagle defenders Ken Clarke (71) and Dennis Harrison.

ment, vanished for a few plays and was replaced by Dave Pear, it was because Kinlaw had suffered a slight concussion.

The Raiders, with a firm 14–3 halftime lead, scored again in the third quarter on a Plunkett-to-Branch pass of 29 yards, the one in which he outmaneuvered the Eagles' rookie corner back. Then Philadelphia, a strong second half team, moved from its own 10-yard line into Oakland territory. "Look for the tight end," whispered Davis. "They're going to go to him." On third down and 3, Rod Martin stepped in front of Eagle tight end John Spagnola and intercepted his second pass of the game to swing the game back to the Raiders again.

Moments later, when Bahr lined up to try a field goal from the Philadelphia 46, Davis cried out, "Hey, that's out of his range." Bahr put the ball squarely through the uprights, and Oakland's lead had stretched to 21 points.

From the first minute of the final quarter, Davis exhorted the clock on the Superdome scoreboard to keep moving. "C'mon, clock," he pleaded after Jaworski fired a bullet to tight end Keith Krepfle in the end zone to put the Eagles within two touchdowns. The "ratpack" of sports journalism crowded around his seat, checking his every emotion, occasionally interrupting his concentration with questions—David Israel of the *Chicago Tribune,* Mike Lupica of the *New York Daily News,* Pete Axthelm of *Newsweek,* Dave Anderson of the *New York Times*—and they hung on to him until his clogged trip to the Raiders' dressing room to pick up the Super Bowl trophy.

With seven minutes to go, Jim Heffernan, the public relations director of the NFL, came over and asked if Davis would like security protection after the game.

"C'mon, Jim," Davis protested. "This game's not over yet. Can't you see that?"

"Sorry, Al," said Heffernan, backing off.

With five minutes remaining, Willie Jones of Oakland recovered a fumble on the Oakland 42-yard line, and everyone in the stadium knew the game's outcome was decided. The Raiders on the field pointed to a symbolic No. 1. Davis' right fist shot into the air. It was the most emotional he became during the entire game.

As King swept around left end for six yards, Davis yelled, "Go, Kenny! Hit it! They got to dog to cut us off." Arthur Whittington dropped a third down pass and Davis moaned, "He should have caught the bleeping ball."

It was a minimal bleeping day for the Oakland owner, whose casual conversation is pithy. But even with time running out, he concentrated on the technical part of the game: "The flybacks aren't getting deep enough . . . Get off that line . . . He's going to a three-man line orange . . . Hey, quick huddle—get ready . . . Chandler ought to work back in case of a fumble . . ."

Heffernan approached again. This time, Davis said, "Hey, I'm sorry. I didn't mean to chase you."

"I know how it was, Al," said the NFL publicist.

The writers around Davis asked him to describe how he felt, what his emotions were at that moment. "Let Tom and the players have it," he waved them off. As the clock ran down, the Eagles didn't even bother to use their last time-out.

In the radio booth, Bill King, calling the game for Station KGO in San Francisco, intoned the final countdown: "Ten, nine, eight . . . . The prince came calling. Prince Pete Rozelle. He had a silver slipper. He tried in vain, and the only man it fits is Al Davis. . . . The Oakland Raiders are Super Bowl champions."

They also joined the legend of professional sports' miracle teams. The Miracle Braves of Boston in 1914, who came from last place in mid-July to win the National League pennant and sweep the Philadelphia Athletics in the World Series. The New York Giants of 1951, who achieved the Little Miracle of Coogan's Bluff when Bobby Thomson hit the most dramatic home run in baseball history to win the National League playoff over the Brooklyn Dodgers. The New York Mets, who had never finished higher than ninth in their seven years of existence, astounding the world with a pennant and World Series triumph in 1969.

Professional football had featured other wondrous teams, too. The 1934 Giants, with an 8–5 record, upsetting the undefeated Chicago Bears (13–0) for the NFL championship because Coach Steve Owen had the perspicacity to dig up sneakers for his players to wear on the frozen turf. The 1960 Philadelphia Eagles riding to the NFL heights on the arm of Norm Van Brocklin—two years

earlier they had been a last place team. The New York Jets in 1968, capitalizing on the arm and bravado of Joe Willie Namath to shock the Baltimore Colts in Super Bowl III and finally prove the American Football League was as good as, if not better, than the staid NFL with whom it had made peace. Equally unexpected was the feat of the Miami Dolphins in 1972, going undefeated through 17 games, an arduous task, to win Super Bowl VII. And now the Oakland Raiders, the first bona fide wild card team to win a Super Bowl under the toughest of conditions—four playoff games—since a first round test between playoff teams had been instituted in 1978.

Although they didn't come up from the depths—after all, the Raiders had finished with 9–7 records the two previous seasons—their feat in Super Bowl XV was unusual confirmation of the ability of a team to overcome adversity.

"The Oakland Raiders winning the Super Bowl is kind of like an orphan getting elected president," commented columnist Jim Murray of the *Los Angeles Times*. "Or the pauper that became prince. They had a young coach, a controversial owner, a team in ferment. I don't know how they ever found time to play football. And they wound up clobbering Philadelphia, which I think was the least of their accomplishments."

"I thought it was fantastic; I really did," said Frank Gifford, the Hall-of-Fame halfback who now anchors the *ABC-TV Monday Night* tele-

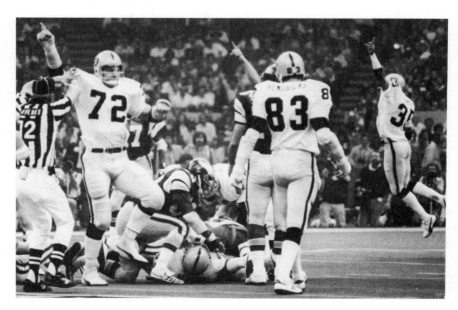

John Matuszak (72) does a jig of joy, and Dwayne O'Steen, far right, completely leaves his feet in jubilation at the recovery of an Eagle fumble by Willie Jones of the Raiders.

casts. "It was one of the best put together jobs I've ever seen in football—the way they got through the season with all the bullbleep that was flying around them. The Raiders remind me of the way we were on the old Giants of the late 1950s. Everybody's got a paw in it. We had some rascals and we had some good, steady players. Everybody seemed to be a contributor.

"None of them are really outrageously good. Vince Lombardi and Tom Landry got the most out of our talent. They did the same thing out there, and I don't think the coaches got enough credit for it because of all the other crap that was going on.

"It takes a lot of character to go through a season never knowing which guy's going to be in jail the next day. They seemed that way to me. They said the furor over moving to Los Angeles didn't bother them, but they had to be answering questions and listening to fans booing them."

Coaches in the NFL also paid tribute to the Raiders.

"They were clearly the better team the day we played them," said Dick Vermeil of the Eagles. "I give the credit to the Oakland Raiders. They didn't allow us to turn it all loose. We were never allowed to jump up and down and get excited. They stayed in charge. I respect the job they did— that they started out slow and nobody gave up and jumped ship on them, which is what happens on losing teams. They battled and came on and became the world's champions."

"They surprised everybody because I don't think many people really and truly thought they were going to be the kind of team they turned out to be," noted Hank Stram, the former Kansas City and New Orleans coach and a keen football commentator. "They didn't play well enough defensively the previous year to merit the kind of consideration they earned during the 1980 season.

"When you look at it, it was a tremendous accomplishment. I think they gave up one less yard per try in 1980 over what they gave up the year before. [Editor's note: the Raider defense allowed 4.7 yards per play in 1980, 5.3 yards per play in 1979.]

"They did a magnificant job of using people. Matuszak, for example, sometimes on the out-

Coach Tom Flores surveys the scene in the Superdome before Super Bowl XV.

side, sometimes on the inside; the way they used [Ted] Hendricks in a lot of ways. People have the mistaken impression they were a totally undisciplined team defensively. But that's not true at all.

"You have to give Tom Flores an awful lot of credit as the young coach who put the whole thing together, and to go back to a philosophy that I think Al Davis has always felt very strongly about. He has always been a very strong advocate of the forward pass. He likes to take the jet rather than take the bus. He doesn't like to travel slowly in certain parts of the field. It's been his personality."

Tom Landry, the astute coach of the Dallas Cowboys, who defeated the Raiders in a late season game, stated, "The key to their success was their defense. They were able to make the big plays, and Lester Hayes ended up with a lot of interceptions that really help from an offensive standpoint.

"The thing they used, and very effectively, was the wild card blitzer, with Hendricks. This is a characteristic of Oakland. Hendricks was smart enough and experienced enough to know where the weakness of the pass protection would be on certain sets. He came from almost any area, which was a little different and which your pass protection had to worry about."

There were other encomiums. But eventually no one appreciated more what had been achieved than the Raiders themselves. Ted Hendricks, who had completed a dozen seasons of pro ball, summed it up for all of them a month later as he accepted the Seven Crown Trophy (plus five thousand dollars) for being the defensive player of the year:

"Gradually, through talks with people, we finally realized long after the season was over what we had accomplished.

"On the field, you know, we have a limited view. We're only interested in our private little world, what the next play is going to be. I felt apprehensive the whole season. We really didn't have the confidence going in. And then every game was close.

"But there is the Raiders' tradition, always with you. 'Come from behind . . . the game doesn't end until the clock shows zero.'

"And now at the end, there is an extremely proud feeling. The best."

Ted Hendricks, as a wild card blitzer, had NFL teams perplexed all season.

This is the play on which Cliff Branch caught a 29-yard pass at the goal line to score against the Philadelphia Eagles in the Super Bowl.

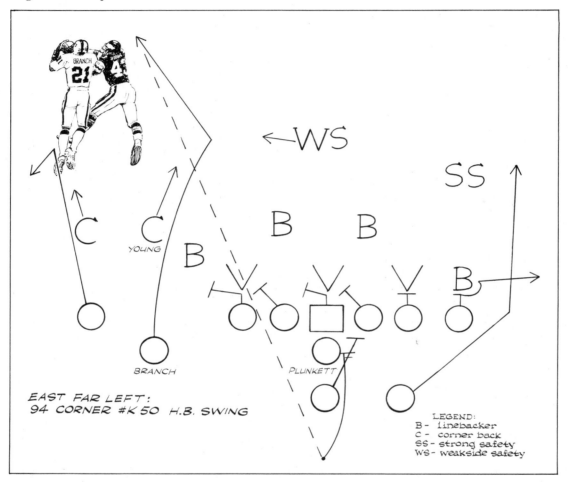

EAST FAR LEFT:
94 CORNER #K 50 H.B. SWING

LEGEND:
B - linebacker
C - corner back
SS - strong safety
WS - weakside safety

Ray Guy gets the Raiders under way by using his strong right leg on kickoffs as well as punts.

The Raider Way of Football • 2

Fear and pressure. That is the eternal essence of Oakland Raider football.

Fear. It is an offense with a five-man firing squad of receivers who back defenses against the wall while a strong-armed quarterback hollers, "Hut-ready-hut-aim-hut . . . fire."

Pressure. It is a defense with courageous cornerbacks and safeties as relentless and rough as Rocky Marciano, combined with a devious front seven which packs a surprise Sunday punch.

It was that fear, that pressure, that essence the Raiders used to surge back to the top of the pro football world in 1980–81 as world champions. It was no fluke. It was a design so old it was new to many of the players who carried it out.

There was wide receiver Cliff Branch personifying fear itself, a bullet shot deep into the heart of defenses. There was wide receiver Bob Chandler, plus tight ends Raymond Chester and Dave Casper, fullback Mark van Eeghen and halfbacks Kenny King and Arthur Whittington, who perforated whatever other vital areas defenses left unprotected.

And, of course, there was quarterback Jim Plunkett, who had been in limbo and whose strong arm rifled football's forgotten team back to the top.

On defense, cornerback Lester Hayes bumped and ran and intercepted until he finally was recognized as the best in the game. He, corner Dwayne O'Steen and safeties Burgess Owens and Mike Davis made it a long-odds gamble to pass against Oakland. Up front, veteran linebacker Ted Hendricks was literally everywhere, creating constant confusion, and often considerable pain, for opposing quarterbacks.

That was Oakland Raiders football, 1980, but it was hardly new. It began in 1963 with the arrival of a brash, 33-year-old coach named Al Davis, who has since moved on to be managing general partner. And, through no coincidence, the Raiders have since moved on from being a loser to being the most consistent winner in pro football.

But they weren't supposed to win in 1980. They had just slipped out of the playoff picture in 1978 and weren't expected back. Not yet, anyway, despite a stern warning from Davis.

"The Roman Empire fell, the New York Yankees fell, the Boston Celtics fell and none of them looked good doing it," Davis said after that 1978 season. "It won't happen here. I won't let it."

Then, even as the experts scoffed, he moved boldly ahead by reaching back. Back to those basic theories which first launched his Raiders on their winning course.

"Our philosophy of football since I came here in 1963 has been the deep pass—the bomb," he reminded. "It carried us all the way through the 1976 season when we won the Super Bowl. But in the middle of the 1977 season I started to feel that we became what I call a lateral passing team rather than a vertical, or deep, passing team. In 1979 we were totally lateral and the long ball wasn't there.

"We are going to get back into throwing the ball deep," he announced only days before the Raiders reported for their 1980 training camp in Santa Rosa. "It is exciting for the fans. It is not mad, deep throwing, but controlled, deep throwing. It's pressure football as opposed to percentage football."

The Raiders already had made most of the necessary personnel arrangements, beginning with the March 15 trade that sent medium-range, sharpshooting quarterback Ken Stabler to Houston for long-ball throwing Dan Pastorini, who, ironically, set the stage, then gave way to an injury and Plunkett.

From Buffalo came Chandler (for linebacker Phil Villapiano), whose abilities would complement the speedy Branch. From Houston came King (for safety Jack Tatum), the halfback who would give speed to the running game and even more vertical depth to the receiving corps. From Los Angeles came O'Steen, who solidified a bothersome cornerback spot, where former all-pro Monte Jackson had been a disappointment. From the New York Jets came Owens (for a No. 6 draft choice), the alert free safety who made it possible for Hayes and O'Steen to taunt receivers with

Some of the Raider brain trust on the sidelines follows the flow of action. Left to right, Willie Brown, Charlie Sumner (partly hidden), Tom Flores, Earl Leggett, Steve Ortmayer.

pesty bump-and-run coverage. From San Francisco came Cedrick Hardman, the pass-rushing defensive end who would make sweet, savage music in concert with Hendricks and young defensive end Willie Jones.

So these were the players the Raiders provided coach Tom Flores, who had seen this plan work before. After all, he was Oakland's first strong-armed quarterback. He could remember how the Raiders changed from losers to winners with this same plan and such names as Art Powell, Billy Cannon, Clem Daniels, Hewritt Dixon, Jim Otto, Danny Birdwell, Fred Williamson, Dave Grayson and Kent McCloughan.

And the system was carried on by Daryle Lamonica, Warren Wells, Fred Biletnikoff, Gene Upshaw, Harry Schuh, George Blanda, Pete Banaszak, Carleton Oats, Tom Keating, Ben Davidson, Dan Conners and Willie Brown. They carried on so well they became part of the first Raider Super Bowl season in 1967.

But by 1980 those names were gone, except Upshaw. Still, the essence of super Raider football remained—fear and pressure.

And where did this aggressive approach originate? On the baseball fields where Davis had seen the explosiveness of the New York Yankees. On the basketball courts where John Wooden coached. These are some of the people who planted the seeds which later flourished into a foundation of formidable football. Davis also admired the pugnacity of Eddie Stanky. "Stanky was a good, solid manager who stressed all the usual fundamentals," Davis recalled. "But his philosophy on the bases was different, and I liked it. Everybody else preached that a runner should take a lead but not go unless he was told to.

"Stanky's approach to base-running was to keep the pressure on the defense, keep them in fear of what was about to happen. He told his runners to go unless they were told to stay. And he rarely told them to stay. It was exciting and effective and left a big impression on me."

Later, Davis was even more impressed with Wooden's basketball teams at UCLA.

"I remember in his early years how Wooden used the zone press defense," Davis said. "It created tremendous pressure. I watched [Gail] Goodrich and [Walt] Hazzard and all those guys. Hell, they were beating teams much bigger—Cazzie Russell and that group. Those guys couldn't handle the pressure."

But before the Yankees' explosiveness would be converted to a mad bomber football offense and before Wooden's zone press principle would be translated into a bump-and-run football defense, Davis had to do some busy work.

As an assistant coach to Sid Gillman with the San Diego Chargers, it was Davis' task to gather and analyze films of every passer and receiver in pro football.

"The passers were all dropping back five, seven or nine yards and were ready to throw on a timing thing," Davis said. "That was the National Football League passing game. Timed passes. I had known that for as long as I could remember and always wondered why it was so dogmatic. I accepted it at first because I thought there must have been a reason."

But now he was a receiver coach and he had questions. The answers he got showed that quarterbacks did not watch for the receiver to get open: "Unitas said he threw on the break, so-and-so said he threw after the receiver made the break, and somebody else threw even before the receiver made his break."

Davis scrutinized the timed pass from all perspectives—quarterback, receiver, defensive back and linemen.

"It made it tough on receivers because if they slipped for a split second or if the defensive back outguessed them, they were vulnerable to an interception," Davis surmised. "That hurt the quarterback, too, but he was helped somewhat because he could throw quickly to the spot and avoid a sack.

"And because he knew where he was going to throw, the quarterback could keep the free safety from reading him. He never had to look until the last second. It was all timed. That helped the offensive linemen, too, because they knew just how long they had to keep out the pass rush. For defensive linemen, of course, those quick passes were frustrating."

Davis stored all this information in his mind, along with Stanky's baserunning and Wooden's zone press. Somehow it all seemed to fit together.

"These things were all running through my head and nobody I talked to could figure out what the hell I was talking about," Davis said. "Oh, Sid understood. He understood more about the passing game than anybody. But he was an advocate of timing passes, too. And at the time Sid was not ready to go in another direction."

So Davis kept on analyzing and thinking . . . and thinking. Finally the pieces to his puzzle began to fit together.

By the time Davis was named coach and general manager of the Oakland Raiders in 1963, the puzzle had become a clear picture. He could see it in his mind. Now all he had to do was put it on the football field. He started with the offense, obviously with the Yankees in mind.

"Al coached the home run theory—if the bomb is there, go for it," Flores said, recalling his days as a quarterback. "A lot of teams looked for the bomb but didn't go for it as frequently. Davis told us to always go for the deep six, even if what we called in the huddle was a good play. If the touchdown was there, go get it."

But Davis knew that the threat of a long pass would not be real unless there was a great wide receiver for defenses to fear.

"We have always had that guy, that one outstanding wide receiver that defenses feared," Davis said. "They would go to bed the night before a game knowing they had to double him."

So the first thing Davis did when he became Oakland's head coach was get a wide receiver who struck fear into defenses—Art Powell. And signing him was almost as difficult as covering him.

"He had played out his option with the New York Jets and already had signed with Buffalo under the table," Davis recalled. "I knew about it and flew to Toronto, where he was living. Buffalo had not submitted the contract to the league office because they were scared there would be compensation.

"I wasn't scared. I just signed him, came back, sent the contract in to the league office and announced that we had Art Powell. It was the first thing of consequence that I did with the Raiders."

"He was such a great receiver that defenses had to double him," Flores said. "So we spun everything around him. We'd send him across an area and, pfft, it was cleaned out so a back or somebody else would be wide open there. Everybody was trying to play man coverage in those days, and he made it difficult.

"If they paid too much attention to him we could always go deep to somebody else. That's mostly what we did with Bo Roberson. He was a world class sprinter, but not really a great pass catcher. But when he stretched a defense, they couldn't ignore him. Defenses found that between Powell and Roberson they were being stretched beyond the point of being able to cover."

And Davis had only begun his stretching exercises. His next innovation was the East Formation, which put Powell slotted inside of Roberson, usually on the right.

"Teams were stubborn about changing in those days, so defenses usually tried to cover Powell with a safety on that side while leaving the cornerback on the other side," Flores recalled.

"Eventually they wised up and moved a corner over to cover Art, but by then we had something else for them.

"We had a halfback, Clem Daniels, who was a great receiver. When we went in East Formation and defenses moved both cornerbacks to cover our wide receivers, then we would send Daniels out long on the other side."

Davis gleefully remembered the confusion that, and his next step, caused.

"They tried to cover Clemon with linebackers, but there was no way," Davis said. "So they started letting the safety hang and wait for Daniels and let the linebacker cover our standard tight ends, Bob Mischak or Ken Herock."

It was time for stretching exercise No. 3.

Art Powell was the first great wide receiver threat in Raider annals.

"Our next move was to switch Billy Cannon, a running back who was a great deep pass catcher, to tight end," said Davis. Thus Cannon, the Heisman Trophy-winning halfback from LSU, established Oakland's tradition for tight ends who were bomb threats, a tradition that carried right through to Chester and Casper.

"Until then, tight ends were mostly plodders, strong blockers with average speed. We were the first team to take the tight end and make him a consistent deep receiver."

Actually, the Chicago Bears with Mike Ditka and the Baltimore Colts with John Mackey were also beginning to exploit the tight end as a deep receiving threat in the NFL.

By 1964 the Raiders had stretched their attack so far this way and the other way that opposing defenses were almost helpless. That year Powell caught 76 passes for 1,361 yards (17.9 yard average) and 11 touchdowns. Roberson grabbed 44 for 624 (14.2, 1 TD). Daniels went 42 for 696 (16.6, 6 TDs). Cannon had 37 for 454 (12.3, 5 TDs). And Herock even got into the spirit of things with 23 catches for 360 yards (15.7, 1 TD).

But the Raiders had only just begun to change the accepted theories of offensive football, if not the structure of pro football itself. In 1966, Davis left the Raiders briefly to become commissioner of the American Football League. When he returned two months later, the old NFL and the young, pass-crazy AFL had been merged.

He went back to the Raiders not as a coach, a job which had been filled by John Rauch, but as managing general partner. Yet his impact on the field was still as obvious as those long, graceful passes which had become a Raider trademark.

Between 1966 and 1967, the offense was bolstered with players hand-picked to fit his design. He traded Flores to Buffalo for Lamonica, the quarterback with an even stronger arm. Looking back, the deal was an obvious forerunner to the Stabler-for-Pastorini swap. And the results were similar, deeper passes and a Super Bowl appearance.

Lamonica immediately began to earn the nickname "Mad Bomber." In 1967, he threw for 3,227 yards and 30 touchdowns. Powell, like Flores, had been traded away, so Lamonica's targets were Cannon, Biletnikoff, Daniels, Dixon and Bill Miller. There was also a new free agent wide receiver fresh from two years in the service who was destined to become one of Oakland's all-time greats—Warren Wells.

Of course, somebody had to give those statistical stars the time to perform that razzmatazz which stretched defenses to the breaking point. Without that time, the maneuvers were just so much fancy footwork and the strong arm was useless.

"Our whole passing game was, is and always will be predicated on a strong offensive line," Flores said. "Our patterns are deeper, even the curls and the outs. And our quarterbacks don't throw on timing; they wait until the receiver comes open. So without a great offensive line, our passing game would be impotent."

From the beginning—until 1975 when he retired—that formidable front wall was anchored by Hall of Fame center Jim Otto. And during the early years he had able help from players such as guard Wayne Hawkins and tackle Harry Schuh, both All-AFL stars.

But the Raiders were looking to the future. And that future was going to include seeing Buck Buchanan, Kansas City's gigantic defensive right tackle, at least a couple of times a season.

"Buchanan was about 6′ 7″, 280 pounds and if I had to play against him for the next 10 years, then we wanted to make damned sure we had somebody to line up against him," Davis said. "So in the first round of the 1967 draft we selected Eugene Upshaw from Texas A&I and made him our left guard. He was about 6′ 5″, 255 pounds.

"Everybody said we were crazy because in those days they were using short, squatty guards. I wanted big men up front to protect the quarterback."

The next year Oakland took an even bigger man—6′ 5″, 270-pound Art Shell from Maryland Eastern Shore—and put him at left tackle. And there it was, the famous left side tandem that gave the Raiders time for passing and room for running through two Super Bowl triumphs, XI and XV.

But what about defense? Other teams would soon pick up on the Raiders' passing system. Not just the scheme of vertical and lateral stretch, but

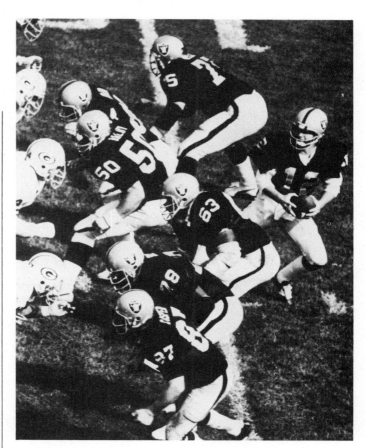

The offensive line provides a shield for retreating quarterback Ken Stabler (12). Top to bottom, John Vella, George Buehler, Dave Dalby, Gene Upshaw, Art Shell, Dave Casper offered the protection that became a Raider trademark.

those intricate little patterns which Biletnikoff utilized to disorient defensive backs. How could this be combated?

Well, combat was the word, all right. Davis realized this during his first workouts as Oakland's coach when he watched cornerback Fred Williamson clowning around in practice.

"He would get up on top of receivers and knock the crap out of them, then run with them," Davis said. "I could see, No. 1, that if the quarterback was trained to throw on timing, he couldn't. No. 2, the quarterback had to follow the receiver to find out when he got open because sometimes he got jammed one way and sometimes he got jammed another.

"When the quarterback had to follow the receiver with his eyes, now the free safety could see where the quarterback was going to throw. This gave the safety a great advantage that he never had on those timed passes."

As Davis watched Williamson, he remembered Wooden's zone press.

"So we began to teach the bump-and-run," Davis said. "It was predicated on the fact that we could always keep the free safety free and give the cornerback the security to play tight man-to-man based on a basketball concept.

"What we tried to do is have the defensive man play almost as if the basket were directly behind him and he was going to keep the offensive man from getting even or beyond him where he could drive to the basket."

But Williamson didn't stay around long enough to work Oakland's bump-and-run in games. He was long gone before Kent McCloughan became Oakland's first real bump-and-run corner-

back in 1965. Two years later, as the Raiders revved up for their first Super Bowl, Davis made a trade with Denver to get the best bump-and-run defensive back of all time.

"I'd watched Willie Brown when he was a rookie in 1963 at Denver and he was doing it, but he didn't really know what the hell he was doing," Davis said. "God, he was great. The best who ever played that. One reason was he was fearless."

Brown, now an assistant coach with Oakland, insisted he knew what he was doing even as a rookie, although he acknowledged he didn't call it bump-and-run at the time. It was just the way he played.

One-on-one. Charlie Joiner (18) labels stickum-festooned Lester Hayes the toughest bump-and-run cornerback he has ever faced.

"I wanted to stop all passes, everything," he said. "I wanted to start as close as possible without being offsides and deny everything—the out, the in, the long pass. Everything. I would hit him at the line, then mirror his every move, always staying as close as possible."

And yes, he was fearless.

"Confidence is the most important factor if you are going to play that close," Brown emphasized. "I would love for a team to put its best receiver on me and try to throw to him on third down. I knew that if they tried to throw there, the pass would have two chances—slim and none. I knew that meant we would turn the ball over to the offense. I just had all the confidence in the world in my ability to stop anybody, anytime and everytime."

Assistant coach Charles Sumner was with the Raiders when Brown and the bump-and-run burst on the scene. In 1979, he returned to see its effectiveness reborn in a latter-day Brown named Lester Hayes.

"I don't recall anybody playing up on a receiver that close until we did it consistently with McCloughan and Brown," Sumner offered. "The big thing before that was to just try and chop a receiver down at the line with a linebacker who was backed up by a defensive back. As you can see, this was a totally different thing."

While these receivers were being buffeted and badgered by Oakland's cornerbacks, a defensive back many thought was too small was having a field day at safety. It was no coincidence that in 1968 and 1969, Grayson was an all-league selection along with Brown.

In his six years with Oakland (1965–70), Grayson became the American Football League's No. 1 career interceptor with 29. In 1971, the Raiders drafted a hard-hitting sensation out of Ohio State named Jack Tatum, who started his first preseason game at free safety and owned the position until 1979.

All this jostling in the secondary gave the front seven—the defensive line and linebackers— more time to show off a few more tricks.

"The philosophy of offensive blocking in the 1960s was to use big men on big men, with linemen blocking linemen and backs blocking line-backers," Sumner reviewed. "We tried to come up with ways of mixing that up so we would get their backs blocking our linemen or just simply confusing them so badly that somebody was left unblocked."

Although the concept wasn't unusual, the way the Raiders went about causing this confusion was unique. In the early years, they lined up defensive lineman Dan Birdwell here, there and everywhere in an attempt to cause confusion. He was a lineman functioning more like a linebacker.

The Raiders had given pro football a new position, the rover. It was to become every bit as much a Raider tradition as the vertical passing game and bump-and-run coverage.

Carleton Oats served much the same purpose, a lineman who functioned as a linebacker. Then came Tony Cline, who would sometimes get down like a defensive end and other times stand up and play linebacker, changing Oakland's front from three to four men at will.

Then came big Monte Johnson, a second string tackle at Nebraska who became the starting inside linebacker in that makeshift 3–4 defense which took Oakland to a Super Bowl XI victory. He changed the trend. he was a linebacker who ruined offensive blocking schemes by playing like a lineman.

After the unsuspecting offense was set, Johnson would calmly alter Oakland's front from a 3–4 to a 4–3. He would simply plant his large 6' 5", 250-pound frame right in front of a guard and make like a defensive tackle.

This ploy was so effective in the 1976 AFC championship game against Pittsburgh that the Steelers gained only 72 yards rushing. Some blamed that small total on the fact that Rocky Bleier and Franco Harris were out with injuries. Maybe so, but the men in the pits, the Steeler linemen, knew otherwise. They were so rattled they couldn't have made decent holes for O. J. Simpson and Jim Brown that day.

"I knew they were a little confused when I got down in front of their guard, Jim Clack, and he leaned on me instead of pulling to lead a sweep," Johnson said. "As we were unpiling, another Steeler came over and asked him why he didn't pull. He said, 'Well, I didn't think I should

Linebacker Ted Hendricks (83), strong safety Mike Davis (36), with free safety Burgess Owens in the background, pose a menacing threat on defense.

because this linebacker or tackle or whatever he is was right in front of me.'"

"We always had one player like that to give our front seven the versatility it needed to cope with different formations and to just generally cause confusion," said John Madden, who contributed to that up-front trickery.

"In the '60s, the NFL was still using that old, vanilla 4-3 with few variations," Madden said. "I remember we played the 49ers in an exhibition game in 1967 and because of injury problems we used a three-man front, just as we would because of injuries in 1976 when we won our first Super Bowl.

"Anyway, the 49ers didn't know what they were looking at. And they thought the bump-and-run was illegal. Later that year we began moving Birdwell all over, using him to overload a certain area or just cause confusion. Nobody had seen a player in the pros like that before—a rover."

But they certainly would see one again. In 1980, Hendricks perfected the position. The 6′ 7″, 225-pound linebacker dominated the attention of opposing quarterbacks. He would line up here and rush. He would line up there and rush. He would line up way over there and drop back into a passing zone.

"Before you could do anything else," Philadelphia Eagles quarterback Ron Jaworski said, "you had to know where Ted Hendricks was, although that still didn't mean you knew what he was going to do."

Davis credited Sumner for the resurgence of Hendricks as a dominant force. Until 1979, Hendricks was taken out on passing downs, when the Raiders would go to four linemen and four, five or six defensive backs. When Sumner rejoined the Raiders, he made it clear that he thought Hendricks would be an important part of Oakland's defense on all downs.

"He's too talented, too experienced, too smart, too dangerous to keep on the bench, especially in key situations," Sumner said. "He studies and remembers. He is big, 6′ 7″, and even when he is blocked he can reach out and make a tackle with those long arms, or reach up and block a pass or a kick."

So Sumner spent part of each week calculating how best to bother the next opponent with Hendricks.

"Charlie knew early in his career that to beat somebody's pass protection, he had to learn how they pass protect, their combinations, everything," Davis said. "So during a game he watched for their adjustments, then made his own. He knew how to confuse them and free a rusher. The versatility of the defense in this case was our defensive coaches. But Hendricks was one of the great players who usually made it work."

"At first we used Ted mostly on the right, in combination with Cedrick Hardman, on passing downs," Sumner said. "They are both veterans with a good feel for pass rushing and it was highly successful. Then we began moving Ted around and offenses became so concerned about where he was that we were able to free other people to do the damage."

That certainly proved to be true in the Super Bowl. The Eagles concentrated so hard on staying away from Hendricks that they all but forgot about another quick linebacker, Rod Martin. He rudely reminded them of his presence with five tackles and three interceptions. Hendricks was able to add three tackles, a pass deflection and an important blocked field goal.

Fear. Pressure. There they are again. And if the Raiders weren't causing them on offense or defense, they would find another way.

Tom Flores proved himself in his first two years as head coach a capable and respected tactician, with the courage of his convictions. It's a trait that runs in the Flores family. Ever since Tom, Sr., a native of Guadalupe, Mexico, left the

home country at the age of 12 to escape the plundering of Pancho Villa's renegades.

Tom Flores, Sr., made his way to Del Rey in the San Joaquin Valley, where he met Nellie, whose parents were also from Mexico. Young Tom, Jr., their second born, became a fine athlete at Sanger, Calif., High School, starring in football, basketball and baseball. He was the quarterback for two years at College of the Pacific. Shoulder problems threatened to abort his athletic career, but after surgery he signed with the Oakland Raiders of the newly formed American Football League and became their starting quarterback, ahead of veteran Babe Parilli.

Flores remained with the Raiders for the first seven years of their existence, although he had to sit out 1962 with a siege of tuberculosis, and he still ranks third (behind Ken Stabler and Daryle Lamonica) in the team's passing records. After playing hitches with Buffalo and Kansas City, he retired in 1971, figuring football would no longer be a part of his life. He took a job in Oakland with a plastics company, but two weeks later the Bills called him back to become their quarterback coach.

In 1972, he rejoined the Raiders to stay and become a vital member of the coaching staff until he was elevated to the head job as the successor to John Madden in 1979. Tom didn't walk in timidly, feeling his way. He insisted on and instituted a computerized program to facilitate the analysis of the Raiders' football performance, and he also installed a sophisticated photographic setup to keep track of the team's progress, even in practice sessions.

Flores showed that he was a painstakingly prepared coach, cool and confident, a skilled teacher who was able to transmit his ideas to others and never flustered during the stress of a game. Madden was always at his peak in the crucial closing minutes of a game, and so was Flores.

There was definitely a change in style, since Tom—the first Hispanic-American coach in the NFL—tends to be low key, thoughtful, keeping his emotions in check. That's not to say the fires don't burn within him—he just controls them with the same meticulous care he takes with his appearance. This is a guy in charge but recogniz-

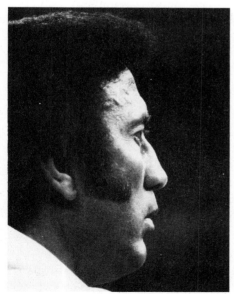

Tom Flores

Lew Erber

Ray Willsey

Sam Boghosian

ing that coaching a professional football team isn't a one-man job.

So around him, he has also gathered a capable, mature staff to whom he's not loathe to delegate authority. Lew Erber, who handled the receivers and tight ends, joined Oakland in 1976 but is approaching a quarter of a century of coaching experience, with an extensive college background and service with the San Francisco 49ers. Ironically, he has the longest tenure in Oakland next to Flores and has exhibited an intense competitive streak.

"He's personable," said Tom, "communicates well with the players and is a hard worker." In practice drills, you'll also find him throwing unerring tosses to the receivers, a legacy of his days as a single wing tailback at Montclair State in New Jersey.

Ray Willsey, in charge of the offensive backfield, made a difficult adjustment moving from defense, an area in which he had spent a major part of his 27 years as a coach, to offense. "He's very loyal, dedicated and serious," said Flores. Willsey played at the University of California under Pappy Waldorf in 1951–52, tried a year of football in Canada—he's a native of Regina, Saskatchewan— and then went into coaching. He was the head man at his alma mater for seven years and came to the Raiders in 1978 after serving five seasons as the defensive coordinator of the St. Louis Cardinals.

"What exemplifies the Raiders," said Willsey, "is that they're a very unselfish group. To compete on the professional level today, you must be a complete football player. And that means giving of yourself."

Erber and Willsey were in the press box dur-

ing games, filtering information from their perch down to Sam Boghosian, who could be seen with earphones patrolling the sideline next to Flores. Sam, who got his early coaching training at UCLA, was responsible for the offensive line. Previously, he had been offensive coordinator and line coach for the Seattle Seahawks and was also an assistant with the Houston Oilers. Squat Sam, an All-Coast guard himself on UCLA's national championship team in 1954, brought competitive drive to the Oakland staff when Flores hired him in 1979. Ever the optimist, he set a goal of molding the best offensive line in football and succeeded.

Charlie Sumner was nominally in charge of the linebackers but he was also invaluable in calling the defensive signals from the sidelines and in helping put the defensive game plan together. This was Charlie's second time around with the Raiders after joining the staff in 1979. Charlie had a distinguished career in the NFL as a defensive back with the Chicago Bears and Minnesota Vikings, then began his coaching career as an assistant with the Raiders when Davis took over the Oakland club in 1963.

"I believe in tough, hard-nosed football," said Sumner. "Know how to get the most out of the players and what it takes to win."

After six seasons, Sumner moved on to Pittsburgh and New England. He was one of the most knowledgeable defensive tacticians in the game. On the sidelines, he coordinated the moves with Chet Franklin, the defensive backfield coach who came to the Raiders in February, 1980. Franklin, a graduate of Utah, had more than two decades of coaching experience at a high college level and

*Ball aloft, Rod Martin (53) celebrates a Super Bowl
interception. Mike Davis (36) and Burgess Owens
join victory romp.*

The Philadelphia bench has a good, if dispirited view of Bobby Chandler (85) clutching a pass in mid-air, with cornerback Roynell Young of the Eagles diving after him in futile pursuit.

Facing page:
The bulk and force of the Oakland Raider offensive line is apparent as Jim Plunkett (16) takes his stance behind center and starts the snap count against the Dallas Cowboys.

Willie Brown, left, listens intently to Charlie Sumner, with headphone, while Tom Flores in middle listens to the coaching conference on defense. Tackle Joe Campbell is at right.

Facing page:
Hewritt Dixon in the 1960's set a standard for Raider fullbacks who could both run with power and catch with finesse.

Al Davis, watching his troops in a pre-game warmup drill, must like what he sees. Note the Super Bowl XI ring on his finger.

DEE-FENSE *is evident in the Superdome as a flock of Raiders gang up on fullback Leroy Harris of the Eagles and stop him cold.*

The grime of battle still marks the spattered body of fullback Mark van Eeghen after a game in the trenches.

The leg extension that makes Ray Guy the greatest punter of all time is evident in this follow-through of a long boot.

then with the Kansas City Chiefs, San Francisco 49ers and New Orleans Saints. "He relates well to the players," noted Flores, "and has a good philosophic concept of the game."

Also arriving with Franklin before the big Super Bowl year was Earl Leggett, who had been an All-American defensive tackle at Louisiana State and, physically, was as imposing as the men he coached on the Raiders' defensive line. Leggett played for 13 seasons in the National Football League, starting with the Chicago Bears for almost a decade, moving to the Los Angeles Rams and winding up his active career in New Orleans. He topped that off with nine years of coaching experience at the college and pro levels before the Raiders tapped his expertise in the sound techniques of playing in the so-called pits. "Above all," said Leggett, "I would like to think that I am relentless."

Another great player brought into the coaching orbit was Willie Brown, who starred for 12 seasons in the Raiders' silver and black before retiring at the end of 1978. Willie was regarded by many as the best cornerback ever to play the game, and Flores particularly wanted him on the staff because of his "very positive attitude." Willie's enthusiasm for secondary play was transferred to the men on the field.

"I like to think positive," said Willie, "and I want the players to be the same. It builds confidence."

Flores was also able to exploit the knowledge of two men thoroughly imbued in the Raider way of football. One was Bob Mischak, who completed his eleventh year in the organization as a combination coach and scout. A former All-American end at Army, Mischak had been part of the Davis team at the start in 1963, when he played both tight end and offensive guard. The quiet and intuitive aide helped tutor the tight ends and ran the weight and conditioning programs for the team, an increasingly important area in recent years. During games, sitting in the coaches' box on high, he provided input. And on Sunday night or Monday morning, he delivered a scouting report on the Raiders' next opponent, based on his study of films and other transmitted information. Occasionally, Joe Madro was sent ahead to scout upcoming opponents, too. Joe was one of the grand old coaching veterans of the sport, with more than 40 years of experience at all levels of the game, the last quarter of a century in professional football. Madro developed many of the great linemen of modern professional football, including Hall of Famer Ron Mix, who finished his playing career in Oakland. He also worked in the personnel area, evaluating future Raiders.

The jack-of-all-trades on the coaching staff was Steve Ortmayer, in charge of football operations (a euphemism for dealing with player problems) and special teams. That meant, in the latter instance, the vital Raider kicking game was en-

Charlie Sumner

Chet Franklin

Earl Leggett

Scouting opponents is one of Bob Mischak's duties.

Steve Ortmayer handles the Raider special team brigades.

trusted to Steve, who came to Oakland in 1978 after spending three years with the Kansas City Chiefs, where he also guided the kicking and other special team units. "Detailed preparation and being physically ready are the keys to special teams," said Steve. With the Raiders, Ortmayer carried on a tradition of careful attention to this crucial phase of the game.

"I think we have had the best special teams people in pro football," Davis said. "George Blanda was the greatest field goal kicker because he was never bothered by pressure. Some might kick longer or for a better percentage, but George would make the field goal that won the game with no time left.

"And of course there is Ray Guy, the greatest punter in the history of the game. They said we were crazy when we drafted him in the first round back in 1973. You don't hear them laughing any more, do you?" Guy's strong leg was also used to kick off.

And there seemed always to be a great return man waiting to run the ball back down the throat of a kickoff or punting team. Claude Gibson, Rodger Bird, George Atkinson, Neal Colzie, Clarence Davis, and others.

"We've had so many great players on offense, defense and special teams and so many great coaches that I believe some day the Raiders will have more players than anybody else in the Hall of Fame," Davis predicted. "You need those great players to make a sound philosophy work. And we've always managed to get those great players. But you need the sound philosophy, too.

"We've known all along what our philosophy would be. Ever since I was a kid I listened to everyone talking about playing percentage football. Even then I felt that was not my way. Let them go for the percentages. That isn't for me. Attack. Fear. Pressure. That's what we want."

And therein lies the eternal essence of Raider football, which began two decades ago.

The Borning Years • 3

In the beginning, there was only a dream.

The dream was born of young men like Lamar Hunt, who was 26 years old and wanted to own a professional football franchise. In the early part of 1959, he went looking, first to George Halas, who was on vacation in Phoenix, Ariz. When Lamar called about the possibility of an expansion franchise—since Papa Bear headed the NFL expansion committee—and offered to go to Arizona, Halas said, "Young man, you'd be wasting your time. There's not a chance. You'd also be wasting your money."

Now money was not a problem with Hunt. So he veered and explored the possibility of buying an existing franchise—namely, the Chicago Cardinals. He was offered a piece of the team, but only as a minority owner, and this didn't interest Lamar. "Of course, you realize," said Walter Wolfner, who ran the Cardinals, "big money has been after us." And he ticked off a list of cities—Minneapolis, Houston, Denver, Buffalo and so on.

"I got to thinking," recalled Hunt, "if there were that many cities interested, why not start our own league?" And thus was the American Football League germinated.

He contacted some other men of substance around the country—Bud Adams of Houston, Barron Hilton of Los Angeles, a Minnesota group, later Ralph Wilson, who wanted a team for Buffalo—and by August of 1959 the new AFL was shaping up. But the NFL, which at first had mocked and spurned the new venture, quickly struck back. First, it tried to sabotage the new league by offering Hunt and Adams a chance to get into the NFL fold with teams in Dallas and Houston—expansion was feasible "now." The two Texans remained loyal to their project. The NFL did succeed in enticing the Minnesota people away—ironically at a time when the AFL was holding its first draft of college talent, in Minneapolis. A substitute franchise was needed quickly, and on Jan. 30, the AFL reached out west to Oakland, Calif., and decided to settle a team there.

It was not a time when an organization knew it would be getting anywhere from five million dollars to ten million dollars in television money alone. The risk was enormous. And the men who grouped together to acquire the Oakland team quickly called themselves "The Foolish Club."

Yet one word more than any other described the early attitude of the American Football League and helped it through some tenuous times. The word was tenacity.

When Jim Otto arrived to join the fledgling Oakland Raiders back in 1960, he brought with him what he described as "all my clothes packed in pressed cardboard suitcases."

He recalled that Wes Fry, the first general manager the Raiders hired, told him that he had brought an unusually large amount of clothes for the occasion.

"I told him I've come to stay," Otto explained.

Apparently, Otto somehow knew something nobody else did. Not about himself, because he was a talented and dedicated athlete destined for enshrinement in the Pro Football Hall of Fame, but about the Raiders.

Few, in those now remote days, felt secure about the survival of the franchise. Probably none could have foreseen the prosperity and success which has been attained following the turning point in 1963.

After all, it was Oakland and the East Bay which had failed to support its Pacific Coast League baseball team, the Oakland Oaks, who under the generous ownership of Clarence (Brick) Laws and field leadership the likes of Casey Stengel and Charlie Dressen had dominated the league, only to have to seek sanctuary in Vancouver.

And it was the same area which had caused the national AAU basketball champion Oakland Bittners to flounder at the gate and ultimately dissolve.

For the first three years there were strong hints that the American Football League franchise might be added to the list.

It is said by somebody or other that you appreciate things more if you have to suffer first.

Fans of the Oakland Raiders—the early ones at least—will say that somebody or other is right in that appraisal.

Jim Otto, famed Double-O, was a Raider original destined for the Hall of Fame.

Long before the teams that were to become champions of first the American then the entire National Football League came teams that sputtered and sometimes seemed to come to a dead stop.

The beginning was not encouraging, admittedly, but it was at least a beginning. And even that was difficult to come by.

The first three years of their existence, the Oakland Raiders resembled only in name the organization which has since become the most successful in professional football. It was rather like building a solid foundation on the fourth floor, but in all fairness that's where it really began.

It was July of 1959 when then National Football League Commissioner Bert Bell told the press he had learned a new league was being formed, a six-team league that would include Houston, Denver and Minneapolis "definitely" and maybe Dallas, New York and Los Angeles. Bell died of a heart attack the following October and was replaced temporarily by Austin Gunsel.

Attorney Marshall Leahy was considered the front runner to become Bell's successor at the NFL meeting in January, 1960, but after a lengthy debate, the league first chose young Los Angeles Rams general manager Pete Rozelle as its new leader, then granted expansion franchises to Dallas and the Twin Cities of Minneapolis and St. Paul, the first new NFL franchises since Cleveland, Baltimore and San Francisco had been admitted in 1950 as part of the merger with the old All-America Conference.

Spokesmen for the newly born American Football League called the selection of Dallas and Minneapolis an "out and out attempt to put the AFL out of business" since franchises in the new league had been earmarked for those cities.

The Dallas Texans, under the ownership of Lamar Hunt, a founder of the AFL, remained determined to operate and challenge the Dallas Cowboys of the NFL, who would begin to compete the very same year.

In Oakland, Calif., meanwhile, Mayor Clifford Rishell declared, "There is little doubt Oakland will be awarded a franchise," a statement which proved excessively optimistic.

Two Oakland-based groups had surfaced, both with the ambition of securing either a franchise or the attendant publicity of being in the thick of it trying to get one.

East Oakland auto dealer Bill Jackson, with Ed Goldie as his major partner, headed a financial syndicate which included, among others, former Stanford football great Ernie Nevers.

Then there was another ambitious potential financial syndicate headed by Emeryville industrialist Ted Herrer, a group that appeared to have the blessing of city officials.

Rishell, admitting that there was no place in town for the team to play, if indeed there was to be a team, again was overly optimistic when he forecast that the University of California's Memorial Stadium might well be available. He added, in more realistic fashion, that San Francisco's Kezar Stadium or Candlestick Park might be viable alternatives until Oakland provided a suitable facility. He saw parking and accessibility problems at Kezar, but as it turned out these "problems" were dwarfed by other headaches at Kezar.

First off, the crowds weren't big enough when the Raiders actually did play their first season there in 1960 to create any major traffic jams or insurmountable parking problems.

What he had not noted, however, was the fog which shrouded Kezar to the extent that on not infrequent occasions a kick could vanish into the atmosphere, only to emerge from the grey stuff and descend at some unpredictable spot.

Oakland City Councilman Frank Youell, a mortician by profession and a sports enthusiast by avocation, urged a bond issue at the June 3 election towards construction of a stadium in Oakland, but despite active promotion by Councilman Dan Marovich, the proposal was ridiculed by Rishell as "too vague" and subsequently rejected.

Neighboring Hayward also was talking of a seven million dollar bond issue to construct a 50,000 seat stadium in that city. This, too, never advanced beyond the talking stages.

While attention was being focused on the Jackson-Goldie group on the one flank and the Herrer group on the other, a third unit was quietly marshaling its forces—one which was said in initial reports to include real estate developer Y. C. (Chet) Soda, Oakland Councilman and San Leandro industrialist Robert Osborne and Charles Harney, the builder of Candlestick Park.

The Jackson-Goldie group had gone so far as to post a twenty-five thousand dollar "faith" check with the AFL, but when a league meeting was held in Dallas that group was not represented.

Former Notre Dame coach Frank Leahy, who had become the general manager of the Los Angeles Chargers, flew into Oakland with the avowed intent of attempting to bring the two rival financial groups together, but when he didn't attend a scheduled conference it was assumed, correctly, that the third group now had the inside track.

While San Francisco Mayor George Christopher went on record as questioning the wisdom of having two professional football teams play in San Francisco, Herrer had in his possession a letter of commitment from the San Francisco Park and Recreation Commission. This was undoubtedly the cornerstone for the eventual use of Kezar Stadium as the Raiders' first home field.

Osborne, Soda and builder F. Wayne Valley were in Dallas to make the presentation for an Oakland franchise after the Herrer group all but dropped out.

The Oakland delegation faced another big obstacle. Houston owner K. S. (Bud) Adams was solid in his support of Atlanta for the eighth franchise.

Balloting began in Dallas amid conflicting reports. Miami and Jacksonville had been virtually abandoned as potential choices, while San Francisco, with a group of would-be owners, was quickly shrugged off.

It was down to Atlanta and Oakland. And the "odds-on" choice depended on who was talking and what the hour of the day was.

On the third ballot, Atlanta had the edge 6–1. But that was before Barron Hilton, owner of the Los Angeles franchise, went to work campaigning for Oakland because he wanted another team on the west coast as a natural rival. The fourth ballot found Oakland ahead, 5–2. The fifth was unanimous.

Oakland had its professional football franchise.

Joe Foss, the first commissioner of the AFL, cited as the reasons for the selection the west coast rivalry between Los Angeles and Oakland. Two west coast teams gave the league a better geographic balance, and the "great interest" in professional football in the Bay Area was evidenced also by civic leaders who had come to the fore in its behalf.

Now the only thing to do for the franchise was everything.

Oakland had a franchise, yes, but it didn't have a front office staff. It didn't have a coaching staff. It didn't have a place to play. Little things like that.

It also didn't have much of a roster. Oakland had been willed the Minneapolis draft choices, but while the Oakland ownership and non-existent administration pondered the situation, more experienced and skilled football minds were at work and some of the prize plums of the Minneapolis draft had been wooed away by other teams.

Abner Haynes, for example was a Minneapolis choice. He was quickly grabbed and signed by Dallas.

Another Minneapolis selection, Jim Otto, had been taken by Houston. "I guess they didn't think that much about me because they didn't pursue it," Otto reflected.

That turned out to be the first big break the Oakland franchise received, for he was to become the principal solid link between the early years and the years of respectability and success.

Among the many things the Metropolitan Oakland Area Football Club, Inc. (the original name and forerunner of The Oakland Raiders, a limited partnership) didn't have was a name for the team. Oakland, yes. But the Oakland "what?"

"Mavericks" was a much-promoted name for no apparent reason. Some nostalgic folks suggested "Oaks" in memory of the former Coast League baseball franchise which non-support had shuffled off to Vancouver. "The Gaels" was also advocated by those recalling the glory days of St. Mary's College and its "Galloping Gaels."

But there was no one with "the" name. The logical move, it was determined, was to have a contest. Let the fans become immediately involved.

Good idea. Bad result.

The winner in the contest? "The Oakland Señors." Really.

Wayne Valley, driving down the freeway to his office, heard the announcement on the radio and blanched. "Señors"? A lamp bulb figuratively lit in his skull. Chet Soda, one of the owners, habitually addressed all his friends, "Hello, señor." Someone obviously had planted the name with the Junior Chamber of Commerce, which was running the contest and would award the winner a trip for two to Hawaii.

Valley, Osborne and a couple of the other owners got together and decided to do their own judging of entries. A name which came up was "Black Raiders." They amended it, simply, to Raiders and magnanimously gave the winner a trip for two to Acapulco.

The eight original investors, nicknamed in the press "The Big Eight"—Soda, Osborne, Valley, Harney, E. W. McGah, Roger Lapham, Jr., Don Blessing and Harvey C. Binns—were gradually to disintegrate over the formative years after continual power struggles. (Binns later gave way to Wallace Marsh.) Of that group, Ed McGah emerged as the strong man and was the lone survivor by 1980, remaining a guiding force.

Wes Fry, who had been the number one assistant to Lynn O. (Pappy) Waldorf in awakening what Waldorf called the "sleeping giant of Strawberry Canyon" and revitalizing the University of California football team in nearby Berkeley, became the Raiders' first general manager, and on February 9, 1960, Soda presented Eddie Erdelatz as the Raiders' first head coach.

Erdelatz had been rumored in line for the job, but was also rumored to be offered the job at California. When the Golden Bears chose Marv Levy instead, Erdelatz was in with the Raiders.

It was a popular choice with the public. He was a San Francisco native and a former St. Mary's College star who had gained national acclaim for his successful work as coach of the U.S. Naval Academy.

The popularity diminished as the first season unfolded, starting with an August 31 pre-season 20-13 loss to Dallas before a crowd generously listed as precisely 12,000 people, which probably included the sea gulls swooping into Kezar Stadium.

His tenure ended after two league games in 1961 and Erdelatz departed with a 6-10-0 record. All of the victories came in a 6-8 opening season in which the Raiders finished third in a four-team Western Division, four games behind champion Los Angeles.

The first three years the Raiders stayed at the Palomar Hotel in Santa Cruz for their pre-season training at Santa Cruz High School. During the season—up until 1970, when the Raiders finally had their own practice field—it was a case of moving from site to site every year, and sometimes moving again within the season.

Because of Erdelatz's Navy connections, the Raiders were able to arrange for the first year to practice at Alameda Naval Air Station, which was the best arrangement of those early years. At least they were assured of security.

But things were not going all that well with the team.

On the pioneer Raider squad, Coach Ed Erdelatz drew up plays for quarterbacks Babe Parilli and Tom Flores, right.

Erdelatz, Otto recalled, was "like a college coach, lots of rah-rah, dealing with a professional football team."

He well remembered the opening game of the 1961 pre-season.

The Raiders flew to Hawaii, where they were to be soundly defeated by the AFL champion Houston team which had defeated Los Angeles in the 1960 playoff. "After the game we had an 11 p.m. curfew," recalls Otto, "and the game didn't get over until 10:30!"

He recalled something else about that trip. The flight was made in an old DC-6, as were most of the Raider trips then, "and it took us eight hours to get there, nine to come back."

After losing their first two league games of 1961 to Houston and San Diego by the convincing margins of 55-0 and 44-0, the Raiders dismissed Erdelatz and elevated Marty Feldman, one of his assistants, to assume leadership.

Feldman is remembered by Otto as a "fine person, but not cut out to be a head coach. He probably would have been a good assistant, but not a head coach."

Feldman had experience in coaching, but not in playing the game. He had been a participant in rugby in his college days, but not in football.

After the first five games of the 1962 season (and five losses), Feldman, who had compiled a 2–15–0 record, was dispatched and succeeded by "Red" Conkrite, a man better suited for personnel matters than on-field coaching.

If people thought the first two years were bad, they just hadn't seen the third, which was an exercise in futility and frustration.

By then the Raiders had found themselves a physical home which had some connection with Oakland, after having played the first year at Kezar, the second at Candlestick. Frank Youell Field, named in honor of the dedicated city councilman who had spearheaded the eventual bond issue, was a steel scaffold type of makeshift facility with 19,000 capacity, near downtown Oakland just off the Nimitz Freeway, where Laney College now stands.

The accessibility of the stadium—a temporary arrangement in anticipation of construction of a permanent home a few miles down the Nimitz in East Oakland—didn't do much for attendance, however. At Kezar, the average home attendance in 1960 was 9,875 and at Candlestick it slipped to 7,655.

In Oakland, attendance finally began a tortuous climb, but the gains were minimal. For the 1962 season average home attendance was 10,942. And some San Francisco media people were reporting rumors of the Raiders moving. Where? Just about any place that didn't have an AFL franchise.

The continued losing pattern did nothing to improve the situation, of course. Only the final game of that 1962 season provided a victory, and that was a bit tainted.

The Boston Patriots had been eliminated from the championship race when Houston had won the day before to cinch the Eastern Division crown.

"Some people say that Boston just laid down for the final game," Otto remembered. "I don't know. We played a fairly good game that day."

At any rate, Oakland won 20–0.

That lone victory in Conkrite's tenure as head coach deserved an asterisk. Conkrite was off on a scouting trip and an assistant coach had been left in charge. Red departed with a 1–8–0 record.

In three years the Raiders had gone through three coaches, as many publicity men, numerous front office staffers—and no less than nine quarterbacks.

You have doubts about the number of quarterbacks? Want names? Okay, you have them. In alphabetical order to avoid favoritism based on accomplishment—a value judgment—there were Cotton Davidson, Hunter Enis, Tom Flores, Chon Gallegos, Don Heinrich, Paul Larson, Nick Papac, Babe Parilli and M. C. Reynolds.

There were some constants, however. Otto was one.

While the Raider player nucleus in 1960 was supposedly the inherited Minneapolis draft choices, the staff brought in many of the northern California players whose names and accomplishments were more familiar to spectators and media. Actually there were so many area athletes, Otto thought maybe he had been cut at the first picture day in Santa Cruz when he was ignored while photographers were focusing both their attention and their cameras on the home grown products rather than the new guy from Miami of Florida.

One of those "home growns" was Tom Flores, a product of the College of the Pacific in Stockton, who opened the 1960 season as the first Raider quarterback, little suspecting he would eventually coach the Silver and Black to one of their two world championships.

Even Flores, "The Iceman," proved vulnerable. Spots were discovered on his lungs which required Flores to sit out all the 1962 season, a major factor in the heavy traffic at the quarterback position. Tom came back in 1963 after his siege of tuberculosis to remain on the Raider roster as a player through 1966.

Another area player was Wayne Hawkins, also from Pacific, an offensive lineman who was to remain a Raider mainstay for 10 years and gain All-AFL honors at guard. And while he remained with the team for only the first year, a popular choice of the fans was Don Manoukian, a 5' 8", 245-pound guard from Stanford who, Otto recalls, "could block anyone." And there was Charlie Hardy, a wide receiver from San Jose State, who remained for three years.

Otto, however, was the one who received the immediate attention and respect of his peers. He was the only Raider to be named to the All-League team in 1960 and he was chosen every season thereafter through 1971.

The turnaround for Raider fortunes began at the outset of the 1963 season. It was abrupt. It was visible.

By this time the Raider ownership had shaken down to two general partners, McGah and Valley, and 25 limited partners.

At a quiet press luncheon at the Leamington Hotel in Oakland, Al Davis was introduced as the new coach and general manager.

With complete authority.

Tom Flores bravely withstood pressure as Oakland's first starting quarterback.

Clemon Daniels

Dan Birdwell

Davis, who migrated from his birthplace in Brockton, Mass., to Brooklyn, where he played football, baseball and basketball at Erasmus Hall High, was already highly regarded in the football profession although hardly a household name at that time.

He had been active in sports at Syracuse University and at the age of 20 joined the football staff at Adelphi (New York) College, working with the line and also publishing technical articles in coaching magazines which earned him considerable attention and respect in the profession.

He entered the army in 1952 and assembled a football team at Fort Belvoir, Va., that defeated the national college champions from Maryland in a practice game.

When he left the service in 1954, Davis did some scouting and recruiting for Weeb Ewbank of the Baltimore Colts; then in 1955–56 he was line coach and chief recruiter at The Citadel in Charleston, S.C.

From there, Davis came west to serve as line coach at the University of Southern California from 1957 through 1959 and when the AFL began in 1960, Davis was ready for a new challenge, taking over as offensive end coach for the Los Angeles Chargers, working and learning under Sid Gillman.

His greatest challenge lay ahead in 1963. Davis was ready.

There were some players he inherited and made better. People like Clem Daniels, a hard-running back from Prairie View, who was to become the Raiders' leading rusher and scorer. And Dan Birdwell, a colorful Texan who was the mainstay of a developing defensive line.

When Davis took over, Otto remembered, "We started going first class."

One of his early moves was to relocate the Raiders' training camp in Santa Rosa, where it has remained and is now regarded by many as the best such facility in football.

In his first year, Davis also signed talented wide receiver Art Powell, who had migrated from team to team before becoming a free agent from the New York Titans at the end of 1962.

Powell has been generous and sincere in his praise of Davis.

"I don't want to butter him up, but I'll tell you this," said Art. "I used to be bored when other coaches talked offense. But this man really knows pass offense. I doubt if anyone else has as much football knowledge as Al. In addition, he has a way of handling players that makes them feel like giants.

"Some of us guys have kicked around from club to club, but Davis makes us feel wanted. He puts confidence in guys that don't have it. And they give 100 per cent of themselves."

In his first year, Davis also brought to the Raiders Dave Costa, a big, rough, tough defensive tackle from Utah, and Archie Matsos, a superb linebacker from Michigan State who was to become a fans' favorite with his free-wheeling, all-out style of play.

Daniels continued to improve and became the Raiders' premier running back in those early years. A quiet, unpretentious "team man," Daniels possessed great natural ability, with the added ingredients of dedication and willingness to work hard. Ironically, the Dallas Texans, who had signed Clemon Daniels as a free agent in 1960, since he was not drafted by any team in pro football, used him as a defensive back. When they released him, the Raiders signed him and converted him to offense. By the time Davis took over the team in 1963, Daniels was an accomplished multi-threat, one of the finest deep receivers ever to come out of the backfield in the history of football.

Dan Birdwell was the resident "character" of the early years.

Possessed with great physical strength, Birdwell was known to flip tops off soft drink bottles with his mammoth thumb.

He was also remembered for having been on the wrong airplane on one Raider road trip.

Everyone was on the charter flight except Birdwell, so a search party was dispatched to locate the colorful product of the University of Houston. He was found sitting on an airplane, sure enough, but one which was parked nearby at the Oakland Airport. He was wondering where everyone else might be.

Birdwell, after he retired from football, maintained his interest in the game, finding an outlet in assisting to coach youth teams in southern California.

He was in varied businesses but was primarily interested in development of exercise equipment designed to ward off heart malfunction. Birdwell had a post-career history of heart problems and ironically it was a heart attack which finally claimed the life of this man who was as gentle off the field as he was fierce on it.

Birdwell was possibly the most comical of the Raiders in the early years, at least visibly so.

But there were other colorful individuals like Fred (The Hammer) Williamson. He was a sometimes brilliant defensive back for the Raiders from 1961 through 1964 and was never reluctant to discuss his talents—which he may have only slightly exaggerated. He was later to go on and attain a degree of prominence as a film actor, after playing with Kansas City in Super Bowl IV.

There also was Bo Roberson, the fleet wide receiver from Cornell, who played for the Raiders from 1962–65.

The eloquent Roberson could enchant Raider Booster groups as well as he could delight them on the field. Trouble with his speaking "pitches" for the Raiders was, through no fault of his own, they were being directed to people who already were Raider loyalists.

And while he was not highly visible, except on the football field, there was Warren Powers, a defensive back from Nebraska. He went on to college coaching after his 1963–68 career with the Raiders and is now the successful head coach at the University of Missouri. He had the basic ingredients, the Raiders honed them and he went on, as so many have, to a fuller life which he can pass on to others. Claude Gibson, another defensive back, became director of athletics at Mars Hill College in North Carolina. Alan Miller, a fullback, went on to a prominent career in law.

The Raiders won their first two pre-season games of 1963 and three out of five. The AFL season began auspiciously as the Raiders won their first two, defeating Eastern Division champion Houston, 35–13, on the road, then opening at home before the biggest-ever Oakland crowd of 17,568 at Youell Field and defeating Buffalo, 35–17.

Then came frustration—four consecutive losses, the last three of them on the road, returning home with a modest 2–4 record to face the New York Jets at Youell Field and win, 49–26.

Warren Powers went on to become football coach at the University of Missouri.

Oakland didn't lose another game that season, climaxed by a wild 52–49 victory over Houston in a game which saw Powell make four touchdown receptions, a Raider single-game record which still stands. Tom Flores threw six scoring passes for the day.

The Raiders' first-ever winning season had ended 10–4–0, as contrasted with 1–13 the previous year.

And, quite properly, Al Davis was chosen AFL Coach of the Year.

In 1964, Davis acquired the brilliant Billy Cannon and also signed Big Ben Davidson, a defensive lineman of much raw ability. Davidson was molded into a formidable giant with a pass rushing talent who intimidated quarterbacks throughout the league.

Davidson, who stood 6' 8" and sported a handlebar mustache, gained considerable notoriety for an injury which he actually did not cause. Joe Namath, the Jets' quarterback, was put out of commission in a game against the Raiders, and the word was that Davidson had caused the injury. In fact, those on the inside knew that it was Ike Lassiter who made the destroying hit, but Davidson, also a very gentle and sincere man off the field, did nothing to dispel the reports.

"Good for my image," he explained.

Cannon, a Heisman Trophy winner at Louisiana State and now a dentist who specializes in orthodontics in Baton Rouge, admitted after the 1964 season, "I had been dragging for two seasons. Davis brought me out of it. I hope he knew I was driving my insides out to help him. I learned more pro-type football in a cram course than I had learned all the years before. Davis does more things right than any coach I've ever known. You have to measure up to his respect."

Cannon had been the first great star of the young American Football League, as an all-purpose running back for the Houston Oilers. But bothered by a bad back and general disenchantment with that team's management, his career had sloughed off drastically in 1963. The Raiders, however, recognized his potential as a receiver. He had the size (6' 1" and 220 pounds) to do a good blocking job, too. So when they acquired him in a trade, they immediately converted him to tight end, and he became a valued receiving threat for the next half dozen seasons. He was the first tight end with superior speed.

Another player to join the Raiders in 1964 was Dan Conners, who like Otto was a product of Miami of Florida. Conners was to remain as middle linebacker for 10 seasons, picking up All-League honors along the way.

Conners became another Raider fans' favorite. Linebackers can be very visible and those who excel are adopted by fans. Those who disappoint? That's obvious. Conners didn't disappoint.

Ben Davidson
　　　　　　　Billy Cannon
　　　　　　　Dan Conners

The team, whose 10–4 record in 1963 fell just short of the 11–3 championship mark of the Chargers, by now in San Diego, slipped in 1964 to 5–7–2, the last losing record the Raiders have had.

Hit by early season injuries, the Raiders rebounded by winning their last five games but still had to settle for a minus record.

Davis responded with a major triumph when time came for selection of college products. The 1965 draft was regarded as one of the Raiders' best.

That was indeed a vintage year for the Raiders. They made what was accurately described as a "clean sweep" of success with their top draft choices, starting with the first pick, Harry Schuh, an offensive tackle from Memphis State. Then Davis signed Fred Biletnikoff, who had been Detroit's third choice in the NFL but promptly accepted Oakland's offer as its second pick.

Bob Svihus, a 6′ 4″, 259-pound Southern California offensive tackle, bypassed a richer offer from the Dallas Cowboys, who had drafted him fourth, and came into the Raiders fold as their third selection.

The Raiders had no fifth, sixth, seventh or eighth choices, but signed their No. 9, Rich Zecher, a 6′ 2″, 250-pound lineman from Utah State and their No. 10, Bill Minor, a linebacker from Illinois.

Zecher lasted a year, Minor none, but Schuh was to be a Raider through 1970, Biletnikoff through 1978, Svihus through 1970. All three were starters.

The same year the Raiders also signed Isaac (Ike) Lassiter, the defensive end, plus defensive back Kent McCloughan, defensive tackle Carlton Oats, linebacker Gus Otto, running back Larry

Todd and another running back from Minnesota, who was an often used backup, Roger Hagberg. Hagberg remained a Raider until his tragic death in an automobile accident in 1969. The others had distinguished careers.

And in 1965, the Raiders also acquired the services of Dave Grayson, the accomplished defensive back, who was to gain All-League status that same year, along with Otto and Powell. The Raiders progressed to an 8–5–1 record, a mark they were to duplicate the next year, which would be a milestone in Raider history.

In the new Raider class of 1966 were, among others, two prime running backs, Hewritt Dixon, who was to succeed Daniels as the key ground gainer, and the durable Pete Banaszak. Also brought into the fold was the skilled and highly intelligent defensive lineman, Tom Keating.

But the draft was not the big story of 1966.

There were two other events of dramatic import to the Raiders, the first in April, the other in September.

On April 8, Davis resigned as Raiders' coach and general manager to succeed Foss as commissioner of the AFL.

In September, the Oakland-Alameda County Coliseum, with a capacity of 54,000, was opened.

Why Davis as commissioner?

His amazing success story with the Raiders was an obvious reason. But it wasn't just his record. How it came about was most significant.

The AFL had taken a drubbing from the NFL in three successive draft-signing battles, but the Raiders stood out as an exception.

Although the NFL teams were more established and frequently had more funds at their disposal, Davis was not only selecting prime pro prospects, but he was also signing them, which was the lifeblood of a successful pro football operation.

The battle for survival between the two leagues had heated up to a point where the AFL felt that its very existence was threatened unless it had an adequate battle plan to compete with the NFL for talent. And a man to implement that plan.

Joe Foss had projected a good image in the early days of the AFL as a public figure, but his forte was travel and appearances rather than the nitty gritty of administration. For a year, in their inner counsels, the owners of the AFL had been debating the possibility of a successor to the old World War II flying ace. Gen. Curtis LeMay, a cigar-chomping, dashing Air Force figure, had been mentioned. So had Bud Wilkinson, who compiled that amazing football record at the University of Oklahoma and then went into politics.

Wayne Valley, one of the Raider general partners, along with Ed McGah, felt that what was needed was a younger, aggressive man who understood football—and had energy. Sitting with Lamar Hunt, the owner of the Kansas City Chiefs, before an exhibition game in Oakland, Valley said to Lamar, "I got a candidate."

"Who's that?" asked Hunt, whose role in founding the AFL secured him a niche in the Pro Football Hall of Fame.

"Al Davis. We're in a war. Let's get the best soldier."

Through the fall of 1965, the name of Davis was planted with the other owners, and at a league meeting in Houston in early April, he was formally offered the job. This was a time of baby-sitting college prospects, luring them with all kinds of inducements. Ralph Wilson, who owned the Buffalo Bills and was the nominal president of the AFL, felt along with the other owners that

Precision and dedication were Fred Biletnikoff's traits as a wide receiver.

their league needed a concerted plan to attract playing talent, along the lines of what Davis had already developed in Oakland. They felt—actually, they knew—their NFL counterparts feared that Davis' pattern in Oakland could work for the entire AFL.

With the assurance of solid financial footing pledged by the league, Davis accepted the challenge—and succeeded.

In a little more than three months, he had the older league in a mini-panic. The method was simple. Who's the most important single man on a team in terms of esthetic and artistic success? The quarterback. So the AFL teams fanned out to sign the best established quarterbacks in the NFL. Men like Roman Gabriel of Los Angeles, John Brodie of San Francisco and Sonny Jurgensen of Washington. Also such key stars as Mike Ditka, the all-pro tight end of the Chicago Bears.

Meanwhile, behind the scenes, the NFL had become more conciliatory about working out a merger of the two leagues. Within two months there was what some interpret as a capitulation, with the eight AFL teams coming into the greater NFL orbit, a common draft and a world championship game between the league titlists until the final solution—one league, two conferences, in 1970. There was another important stipulation, from Oakland's standpoint. Pete Rozelle would remain as commissioner. The merger was announced June 8, 1966.

That meant the Raiders, who had grown to respectability under Davis, could now get him back into their organization. During his two-months' hiatus in New York, the Raiders had elevated John Rauch, an assistant, to head coach and made Scotty Stirling, who was also in the organization, the general manager. To entice Davis, the Raider partners gave him a piece of the action—10 per cent of each of their stock—and gave him operational control of the team as managing general partner.

Coincident with Davis' return was the imminent availability of a new playpen for the Raiders. The team played its entire pre-season schedule on the road and broke even in the first two league games away from home. The splintery, makeshift stands of Frank Youell Field were now just a memory, consigned to football lore. On Sept. 18, the Raiders played their first game in the new Oakland-Alameda County Coliseum before a throng of 50,746.

The fact that they lost to Kansas City, 32–10, was just incidental to the moment, because now the Oakland Raiders were truly big league in every sense of the word.

A 36 million dollar television contract had been negotiated and signed for the AFL with the National Broadcasting Company, and that helped bring solvency and security to the entire league. The Davis regime had brought to the Raiders respect, stability and continuity. It would be there for the entire nation to see as pro football entered a new era of burgeoning popularity.

The Pride and the Poise • 4

In the life of every organization, there is a transitional time which determines its future course. A bold move. An intuitive decision. A calculated gamble. And on them ride success or failure. Such a time came to the Oakland Raiders in the spring of 1967 and set up the springboard which would propel them to the "winningest" team in professional football.

First, the bold move. Tom Flores, their first string quarterback and a man who had been with the team from the beginning, and Art Powell, the all-pro wide receiver, were traded to the Buffalo Bills. Flores was coming off his most productive season as a pro, having thrown 24 touchdown passes, and he should have been approaching his peak at the age of 29. Powell had caught 53 passes, 11 for touchdowns, and averaged 19.4 yards per catch. In exchange, the Raiders acquired Daryle Lamonica, who had been a reserve quarterback with the Bills for four years and in sputtering appearances the year before had completed only 39 per cent of his passes, and Glenn

Bass, an injury-dogged wide receiver who had caught just 10 passes in 1966.

Lamonica, however, was the key. With the Bills, he had been stymied ever since coming out of Notre Dame, playing behind Jack Kemp, now the distinguished Congressman from upper New York state. Daryle had one key ability which intrigued the Raiders. He had one of the strongest throwing arms in football. And despite his limited playing time, he never lost confidence in himself. He was built like the prototypal quarterback — 6′ 3″ tall and a sturdy 218 pounds and a good athlete who spurned a possible baseball career to play football. Bass was really a throw-in. He never appeared in a regular season game for the Raiders.

Over the next six years, Lamonica would become known as the Mad Bomber and establish himself as one of the outstanding passers in the game, fitting in perfectly with the Raider concept of the long aerial threat to keep defenses on edge and open up avenues for other facets of the offense.

Daryle Lamonica (3) stood strong in the pocket to become known as "The Mad Bomber."

Willie Brown as cornerback intimidated receivers and picked off passes.

Next, the intuitive decision. The defensive scheme being put together by the Raiders called for corner backs who were fast, physical and fearless because they would be isolated with the game's swift receivers one-on-one. The way to check those receivers was the technique called bump-and-run. They already had an ideal exponent of that style on one corner in Kent Mc-Cloughan, plucked from the Houston Oilers in 1965 as a rookie, drafted on the eleventh round. They needed another corner. Al Davis had been impressed with Willie Brown, a cornerback from the Denver Broncos, and set his sights on him.

Willie had come out of Grambling in 1963 without being drafted. Houston signed him as a free agent but cut him early. He caught on with Denver and quickly developed into an outstanding defensive back, being named to the all-AFL team in 1964. But Willie had been nagged by injuries for a couple of years. A confident, competitive person, Willie also chafed at the ineptness of the Broncos, who had finished last every year he had been with them—and let it be known how he felt. Sensing that Brown was available, Davis dangled a little used tackle named Rex Mirich and a draft choice before the Broncos, and Willie also came to the Raiders in the spring of 1967.

Now the Raiders had a two-pronged weapon on the corners to intimidate receivers—the bump-and-run revolutionized pass coverage and proved to be so harassing that ultimately it was modified by NFL legislation to restrict the depredations of

defenders such as Willie Brown. With the Raiders, for whom he played through the 1978 season, completing 16 seasons of pro ball, Willie became the greatest of all cornerbacks and a cinch to be voted into the Professional Football Hall of Fame after his name would become eligible in 1983.

The Lamonica and Brown trades, both coming in the same year, were a bonanza and among the best player deals ever made. But in the destiny of the Raiders they carried no more import than a calculated gamble also made that same season of 1967. Houston wanted to unload a 40-year-old quarterback named George Blanda, who had been playing professional football since 1949 (when he debuted as a rookie quarterback with the Chicago Bears). George had been one of the early stars of the AFL and, like Willie Brown, he was also a man who spoke his mind. With Oakland, George could be an experienced backup to Lamonica since old Cotton Davidson, another AFL original, was on the verge of retirement. More important, the Raiders also knew that Blanda was one of the most reliable place-kickers in football and could relieve Mike Eischeid of that chore, letting him concentrate on punting. The gamble was that at an age when most men are starting to scour travel folders for their retirement sites, Blanda had enough strength left in his leg to kick the ball through the uprights.

The result is legend. George played until he was 48 years old, stretching his career over 26 seasons and 340 games, both of them all-time pro foot-

George Blanda (16), with Daryle Lamonica holding for a field goal, became legendary for his clutch feats.

ball records unlikely ever to be equalled. He scored more points than any man in history—2,002—and he delivered some of the most stirring thrills in the annals of the Raiders. At 48, he could still step spryly back into the pocket and throw a pass that led the receiver perfectly. In 1981, he became one of the few players elected to the Hall of Fame in Canton, Ohio, the first year he was eligible.

There were other significant newcomers to the team in 1967. A free agent named Warren Wells, who had been released by both the Detroit Lions of the NFL and the Kansas City Chiefs of the AFL, was signed right after the pre-season. He had a relatively brief, mercurial career that lasted only four years until personal problems forced him out of the game, but his career average of 23.3 yards per catch remained the best in Raider history. He was unsurpassed in catching the long bomb. He scored touchdowns on more than 25 per cent of his receptions, a total of 42 out of 156.

And finally, that pivotal season for the Raiders witnessed the debut of a man who, as much as any other, personified the Pride and Poise that Al Davis felt was the cornerstone of being a successful player. In the 1967 college draft, the Raiders reached down into a small school in the southwest, competing in the Lone Star Conference, and made a relatively unknown offensive lineman, Gene Upshaw of Texas A&I, their No. 1 choice. The 22-year-old rookie immediately brushed past some accomplished veterans and won a starting job as an offensive guard. Fourteen years later, he

was still a vital contributor in the blocking of the offensive line but also was respected as the team leader, the man around whom the Raiders rallied in adversity because of his mental toughness.

The Raiders as a team were just on the verge of greatness, with such notable stars as Fred Biletnikoff, disciplined wide receiver, defensive tackle Tom Keating and Hewritt Dixon, a staunch fullback. Dixon was another example of organizational perspicacity. An eighth round draft choice from Florida A&M by the Denver Broncos in 1963, he had been used mostly as a tight end. The Raiders traded Archie Matsos, an under-sized linebacker, for Dixon in 1966 and returned the 6' 1" 230-pounder to fullback, his college position.

The pre-season schedule featured a memorable milestone when for the first time since peace had come to professional football, AFL and NFL teams met in head-to-head competition on the playing field. On September 3, the San Francisco 49ers came across the Bay to Oakland and in an intense, hard-hitting game, the 49ers won by a close score of 13–10.

The tipoff to the strength of the Raiders, however, came the opening week of the regular season when they crushed the Denver Broncos, 51–0. The passing of Lamonica ignited their offense and sparked Oakland to a season total of 468 points, exceeded in pro football only by Houston with 513 in 1961, when defense in the AFL was as porous as a mound of sand in a flash flood.

The quality of the Raiders became apparent the third week of the season when they hosted the Kansas City Chiefs, the defending champs of the AFL, participants in Super Bowl I, and a team that habitually beat them (their series stood 9–5 in favor of Kansas City). The Raiders upset the Chiefs, 23–21, with the decisive score resulting from a 29-yard touchdown pass thrown by Lamonica to veteran tight end Billy Cannon.

The following Thursday, as the Raiders boarded a bus in downtown Oakland for their trip to the airport and a flight to New York, where Joe Willie Namath and the Jets awaited them next, a gunman climbed aboard the bus, too. The players quickly emptied out of the vehicle before the gunman was corraled. Maybe it was an omen. The Raiders lost, 27–14. It would turn out to be their only defeat in a brilliant season.

Their biggest test came when the San Diego Chargers, atop the AFL Western Division with a 4–0–1 record, came into Oakland with the Raiders in second place at 4–1. The home team bombed the Chargers, 51–10, and was on its way to the top won-and-lost mark in Oakland history. (The 13–1 record was matched by the 1976 team.)

The Raiders were colorful, with players like Ben Davidson and his handlebar mustache. They were exciting, with Lamonica throwing 30 touchdown passes. And they were efficient, with veteran Bill Miller, who hadn't caught a pass the previous two years and had been cut twice from the roster, replacing the departed Art Powell as a starting wide receiver. They also demonstrated ability to rebound from adversity. Clemon Daniels, their most dangerous back, broke an ankle in the ninth game and was lost for the season, but young Pete Banaszak, an unheralded, relatively slow ball carrier who gained a total of 18 yards as a rookie in 1966, stepped into the void and played brilliantly down the stretch.

In early December, the Raiders showed their first rout of the Chargers was no fluke by invading San Diego and trouncing them again, 41–21. A week later, they won the division title with a 19–7 triumph over Houston. The margin was four field goals kicked by that reclaimed 40-year-old darling of the geriatric set, George Blanda. On the plane home from Houston, Ben Davidson, inspired by the new topless craze that was sweeping the San Francisco Bay area, stripped to the waist and served champagne.

On December 31, in the AFL championship game, the Raiders romped over the Oilers, 40–7, after Hewritt Dixon touched off the scoring with a 69-yard run from scrimmage. Lamonica was named the most valuable player in the AFL. Johnny Rauch, in his second season, was selected AFL Coach of the Year. And the Raiders moved on to Super Bowl II in Miami, Fla., against the imposing Green Bay Packers. The Raiders were established as 10½-point underdogs.

This was at a time when the AFL was still being denigrated as "minor league" or "Mickey Mouse," and the Packers' 35–10 humiliation of the Chiefs in the first title meeting between the leagues still rankled. It was not called the Super Bowl then. It had the elongated title of AFL-NFL World Championship Game, and the first one—in the Los Angeles Coliseum—was played before 30,000 yawning seats. Lamar Hunt hadn't yet gotten the inspiration to re-name the game after watching his daughter bounce a "Super Ball" higher than the garage of his house.

Miami was more receptive to the new classic, and the Orange Bowl was virtually sold out, at $10 a seat (in Super Bowl XV, the tab would be $40). But the result for the AFL was the same. The Packers took a 13–0 lead before Lamonica hit Bill Miller with a touchdown pass to cut the margin to six. The turning point came just before halftime when the Raiders had the Packers backed up to their 16-yard line on fourth down, with fewer than 30 seconds remaining.

"We didn't use the clock right," claimed Davis. "Rodger Bird [the Raider safety] was back to receive, and our coaches wanted him to signal for a fair catch to stop the clock. What we should have done was take time out before the punt and put a return on because we were down where George Blanda could kick a field goal and cut the lead to three."

Instead the ball bounced off Bird's chest, was recovered by Green Bay, and Bart Starr completed a pass to put the Pack in range for a 43-yard field goal by Don Chandler that jumped the lead to 16–7. A breakdown in secondary cov-

John Rauch, making a point to Daryle Lamonica, succeeded Al Davis as head coach in 1966.

erage gave Green Bay an easy touchdown in the third period, and the Packers won, 33–14. It was the last game coached in Green Bay by Vince Lombardi. For the Raiders, it was a learning experience.

Nine years would pass before the learning would be applied. But they were good years as the Raiders steadily built the best winning record in football. By 1973, a line on the back of the team's annual Media Guide proclaimed, "The Last Decade . . . Pro Football's Best Record." And each succeeding year, it was updated: "Pro Football's Best Record . . . For Last 11 Years." ". . . For Last 12 Years." And the line never came off.

For a team coming off a championship year, as it did in 1967, which meant that it picked next to last in the combined NFL-AFL draft, the Raiders made some amazingly good choices which buttressed their lineup right to the present time. The 1968 crop was amazing: second round, Ken Stabler of Alabama; third round, Art Shell of Maryland State (now Maryland Eastern Shore); fourth round, Charlie Smith of Utah; seventh round, George Atkinson of Morris Brown; tenth round, Marv Hubbard of Colgate. All of them not only became starters but also stars for Oakland over the next decade.

An era did come to an end, however, with the pre-season release of Clemon Daniels, at the time most prolific ground gainer in Oakland history, the first 1,000-yard rusher (1,099 in 1963), and a brilliant pass receiver as well. No Raider has exceeded the 200 yards he gained in one game against the Jets.

In their third season under Rauch, the Raiders opened fast again in 1968, routing Buffalo, 48–6, with rookie defensive back George Atkinson racing 86 yards for a touchdown on a punt return. After winning the first four games, they were upset, 23–14, by San Diego as Lance (Bambi) Alworth, a future Hall-of-Famer recruited for the AFL by Davis when he was on the Charger staff, caught nine passes for 182 yards and one touchdown. Bump-and-run wasn't positive insurance against sheer talent.

When Daryle Lamonica was hurt against Denver a month later, George Blanda showed there was still plenty of life in a 41-year-old arm by flinging four touchdown passes. This was followed the next week by one of the most memorable games in Oakland history—memorable because the nation was deprived from seeing as dramatic a finish as the Raiders have ever staged. With 1:01 remaining and the Jets leading a see-saw battle, 32–29, on November 17, NBC-TV cut off the national telecast of the game from Oakland to put on a movie called "Heidi," in hopes of getting the nation's toddlers riveted to the screen.

Instead, they roused football viewers across the country to a passionate fury because they missed the last minute heroics of the game as follows:

With 40 seconds left on the clock, Lamonica hit young Charlie Smith coming out of the backfield with a pass that went 43 yards for a score and put the Raiders in front.

On the ensuing kickoff, Preston Ridlehuber, an obscure reserve back, put himself in Raider annals forever and into the minds of trivia buffs, by falling on a fumble in the end zone to seal the victory, 43–32.

Moral: never take the Oakland Raiders for granted.

Lesson: the fever of professional football was truly nationwide.

The Raiders finished the season with a 12–2 record, tieing for the Western Division title with Kansas City. In the showdown playoff, the Raiders won handily, 41–6. They moved on to New York for the Conference finale, fully expecting to qualify for a second straight appearance in the Super Bowl. Awaiting them were Joe Willie Namath, at the zenith of his flashy career, and the revived Jets under Coach Weeb Ewbank.

Although the Jets led 27–23 late in the fourth quarter, the Raiders prospects for being the AFL representative were bright as Lamonica led a march which reached the New York 24-yard line. At the two-minute mark, the quarterback called a play in which Charlie Smith flared wide to his right. The timing was off, and Lamonica's pass fluttered to the Shea Stadium turf behind Smith. Ralph Baker, the outside linebacker for the Jets, alertly realized the ball was live because the backward trajectory of Lamonica's throw made it a lateral. He pounced on the ball for a fumble re-

covery and sealed the Jets' victory which ultimately led to their sensational upset of the Baltimore Colts in Super Bowl III, the first triumph for the AFL.

A short time later, Rauch resigned as coach of the Raiders to take over the Buffalo Bills. On February 4, 1969, a headline in the *Oakland Tribune* proclaimed: "Madden a Mystery Man." At the age of 33, after just two years of experience in the pro game as the linebacker coach of the Raiders, John Madden became the youngest head man in the NFL and started a reign which produced more than 100 victories in 10 seasons. Madden had grown up in the Bay area, in Daly City. A college tackle at California Poly, he was signed by the Philadelphia Eagles in 1959, but a knee injury in training camp ended his playing career. He came to the Raiders after serving as defensive coordinator for Don Coryell at San Diego State. A big, beefy man, Madden exuded natural wit and

Safety George Atkinson typified the aggressiveness of the Raider secondary.

established a fine rapport with the players. Equally important from the viewpoint of the Raider brass, he impressed them with his ability to transfer his football philosophy and strategy to the blackboard so that the players could understand it.

From the day he took over, the Raider pattern of success was intact. The team won six games and tied one the first half of the 1969 season, equalling the AFL record of 15 consecutive unbeaten games before Cincinnati, a 12-point underdog, upset the Raiders, 31–17.

During the pre-season, they had lost Ken Stabler, their fine young lefthand quarterback prospect. He was stuck in a reserve role behind Lamonica and Blanda and also bothered by domestic problems, so he quit the team and went home to Alabama for a year. Blanda announced he would "retire in 1970," but he continued to make valuable contributions to the Oakland offense.

The Raiders' third home game, against Buffalo, a 50–21 runaway for the host team, drew a sellout crowd of 54,418, and they would never again play before a less-than-capacity crowd until the 1980 season began.

After the Cincinnati reversal, the Raiders closed with six straight victories, topping the Western Division with a 12–1–1 record. Kansas City was second at 11–3 but qualified for the play-offs under a new plan, the precursor of the "wild card" system.

In the opening playoff game, while the Chiefs upset the New York Jets, winners of the Eastern Division, 13–6, the Raiders rode over the Houston Oilers, 56–7, as Lamonica threw six touchdown passes, which remained on the books as an NFL playoff record. Again, the Raiders were within one step of the Super Bowl when they hosted the Chiefs, whom they had defeated twice in regular season play. The AFL finale ended on an Oakland downbeat after such a rousing season. And it came down to one helmet banging. In the third quarter, with the score tied 7–7, Lamonica hit the plastic hood of defensive end Aaron Brown as he followed through on a pass. Bruised and swollen, the hand pained him the rest of the game and severely impaired his effectiveness. After passing

John Madden was always a fiery figure on the Oakland sidelines.

successfully 12 times in 22 attempts before the injury, he dipped to four completions in his final 17 throws and had three passes intercepted. The Chiefs came on to win, 17–7, and then firmly establish parity for the AFL with a convincing 23–7 victory over Minnesota in Super Bowl IV.

Individually, though, the Raiders fared well. Lamonica won honors for the second straight year as the MVP of the AFL. Six other Raiders won all-pro attention—center Jim Otto, corner back Willie Brown, receiver Fred Biletnikoff, safety Dave Grayson, defensive tackle Tom Keating and offensive guard Gene Upshaw. Madden in his debut as head man was named Coach of the Year.

Also that fall, *Look Magazine* had come out with an article on Al Davis, the managing general partner, calling him "The Most Hated Winner in Football," but also acknowledging that he had built the most successful organization. On January 1, 1970, in a column he was writing then for *Pro Football Weekly,* Brent Musberger (who would become much better known for his oral description of sports) typed a list of the previous decade's "Best" and included the following:

George Blanda

Jack Tatum

"Commissioner of the Decade—Al Davis. Sorry, Pete, You lasted longer. But you weren't as much fun."

The Raiders then entered the Decade of the Seventies firmly entrenched as one of the winning dynasties. And they promptly won their fourth straight Western Division title (a record later surpassed by the Pittsburgh Steelers, who won six straight). For the first time, they were playing in a combined NFL, split into American and National Conferences—Baltimore, Cleveland and Pittsburgh shifted over from the old NFL alignment to become part of the AFC and balance each conference at 13 teams.

In 1970, Ken Stabler, still relegated to third string quarterback, finally made his appearance in a regular season game and threw two completions in seven attempts against the San Francisco 49ers. Raymond Chester was another significant addition, cracking the starting lineup at tight end after the Raiders drafted him No. 1. He was named to the Pro Bowl and won the Bert Bell Award given by NEA to the rookie-of-the-year.

But the real heroics of that season were performed by the 43-year-old ageless wonder. George Blanda caught the fancy of the nation with a sensational run of clutch feats starting the last Sunday in October, when he entered the Pittsburgh game with the score tied 7–7 and promptly threw three touchdown passes and kicked a field goal as Oakland won, 31–14. The next week, with three seconds left to play, he booted a 48-yard field goal to tie Kansas City at 17. That was followed by a 23–20 victory over Cleveland produced by his tieing touchdown pass with 1:34 remaining and a

52-yard field goal as time ran out. A week later, against Denver, with the Raiders trailing and 2:28 showing on the clock, he pitched a 20-yard scoring pass to produce a 24–19 victory. Then, for the fifth week in a row, he provided a miracle finish by kicking a field goal against San Diego with seven seconds to play. It was the winning margin in a 20–17 victory. And George Blanda was certified as a football immortal. The irony was that this was the year in which Blanda had announced he was going to retire. And just before the start of the season, the Raiders had put him on waivers, without another team in the NFL claiming him. Actually, the Raiders had no intention of letting him go. It was a maneuver to save a place on the roster for one of the younger players.

Blanda ran out of miracles, however, in the playoff game for the AFC title against the Baltimore Colts when he replaced Lamonica, who for the second straight year was hurt during the action when his passing arm connected with a tackler's gear. The Raiders bowed to the Colts, 27–17, the key play coming on a 68-yard touchdown bomb from John Unitas to Ray Perkins.

In 1971, the Raiders failed to make the playoffs for the first time in seven years and finished second to Kansas City, but the defensive unit added two rookies who would play vital roles the rest of the decade. Jack Tatum, a hard-hitting defensive back from Ohio State, was the top draft selection and moved into the secondary as the free safety, quickly picking up a reputation as one of the hardest hitting tacklers in the game. Phil Villapiano, a No. 2 choice from Bowling Green, won a starting job as an outside linebacker. Horace

Phil Villapiano

Otis Sistrunk

Jones, a twelfth rounder from Louisville, moved in at defensive end.

The Raiders had always pursued a policy of rebuilding while winning, never letting their talent go static, and their judgment on players who were relatively obscure had an extra-sensory quality. For instance, in the summer of 1972, Al Davis was in Los Angeles for an NFL Management Council meeting and was invited by Tommy Prothro, then coaching the Los Angeles Rams, to come out and watch a practice session. Davis was struck by the intensity and strength of a rookie defensive lineman named Otis Sistrunk. Sistrunk, at 25, was a little older than most rookies. He had never gone to college. The Rams discovered him playing semi-pro football with the Neptunes of Norfolk, Va. His chances of sticking with the Rams, who were already loaded with defensive tackles the likes of Merlin Olsen and Larry Brooks, were remote. So the Raiders struck a deal, sending a third round draft choice for the following year to Los Angeles for Sistrunk and a fourth round pick.

Sistrunk, besides being ideally built for interior line play, had one other feature that stood out. He was as bald as Daddy Warbucks. Despite his lack of big-time competition, he stepped immediately into the Raider lineup and was a mainstay for seven seasons. On a Monday night telecast, knowing that "Trunk" had never matriculated formally at any college, Alex Karras, doing the commentary with Frank Gifford and Howard Cosell, identified his school as the "University of Mars." It fitted.

Arriving in the Raiders' entourage at the same time was a world class sprinter who was little noted for football. The Raiders nursed him carefully, letting him sit most of his first two seasons but working him severely in practice, and then sprung Cliff Branch on the NFL as one of the most dangerous wide receivers of the decade.

The Raiders' leading ground-gainer in 1972 was Marv Hubbard, who came out of a pseudo-Ivy League environment at Colgate, not the usual training ground for NFL stars, failed to stick when first drafted and was farmed out to Hartford of the Atlantic Coast League. Now he emerged as one of the power backs of the NFL, gaining 1,100 yards, a Raider record at the time.

The 1972 season was concluded with the bitterest defeat in Oakland history. In the final minute of a divisional playoff game in Pittsburgh, Ken Stabler, replacing Lamonica at quarterback, had scrambled down the left sideline for 30 yards and a touchdown to put the Raiders in front, 7–6. With the clock down to 22 seconds, the Steelers were stuck in a fourth-down-and-10 situation on their own 40-yard line. Terry Bradshaw, fading back to pass, was almost sacked, managed to elude the grasp of the Raider linemen surrounding him and, with one of them still holding on, got rid of the ball desperately in the direction of Frenchy Fuqua, a Steeler back. Fuqua and Oakland safety Jack Tatum both went up for the ball. It ricocheted backward. Pittsburgh rookie fullback Franco Harris, trailing the play, managed to grasp the ball knee-high while in full stride and raced into the end zone to complete a 60-yard touchdown play. Did the ball bounce off Fuqua? If so, it was an illegal play because NFL rules at the time did not permit two offensive players to touch a

Marv Hubbard

Ken Stabler

thrown ball. Was it deflected off Tatum? That made it legal. The officials were in a quandary, none of them really being in a position to make a decision. Play was held up while they consulted with league officials in the press box. Finally, it was ruled a legal play and the touchdown was allowed, giving Pittsburgh a 13–7 victory.

Harris' catch became known as "The Immaculate Reception," but to this day it has never been definitely ascertained which player, Tatum or Fuqua, was touched by the ball.

The next fall, after the Raiders lost two of their first three games, Stabler finally moved into the regular lineup, ahead of Lamonica, and for seven seasons was the most spectacular quarterback in football. Lefthand passers were a rarity in pro ball. The only previous successful one was Frankie Albert of the 49ers right after World War II. But Stabler showed rare touch. In the short to medium range there was never a more accurate passer. He was also a natural leader, calm under fire, and showed a flair for bringing his team from behind in the closing minutes of a game.

The Raider proclivity for boldness in finding new talent asserted itself again in Ray Guy, a rookie punter, and Monte Johnson, an inside linebacker. No team in the NFL had ever made a specialist kicker the first pick in the draft. The Raiders did and were rewarded with the greatest punter in the history of football. Johnson, chosen on the second round, wasn't even a first string player in college at Nebraska. Nor was he even a linebacker. But scouting him in a post-season all-star game, the Raiders perceived that his ranginess —6′ 5″ and 240 pounds—might better be suited

for linebacker than down lineman. Requiring completely new indoctrination in technique and assignment, he became the regular middle linebacker in the 4–3 alignment by 1975 and gradually acquired a reputation as an astute diagnostician, reading and reacting to the flow of the other team's offense.

In the second game of the 1973 season, the Raiders snapped Miami's winning streak of 19 straight—the Dolphins were coming off their 17–0 sweep through Super Bowl VII. The game also drew the largest home crowd in Oakland history. Actually, it was played in neighboring Berkeley, at the University of California, drawing a crowd of 74,121, because the Oakland A's baseball team had a prior claim on the Coliseum.

Division titles kept piling up, but a playoff jinx seemed to envelop the Raiders. It was also becoming apparent that the AFC had emerged as the dominant conference in the NFL, which meant the Raiders were facing the stiffest competition in the persistent presence of teams such as Miami and Pittsburgh. There were high spots. Oakland derailed Miami from a fourth straight Super Bowl appearance and a chance for a record three straight triumphs by ousting the Dolphins in a thriller. With his team trailing, 26–21, and time running out near the Miami goal line, Stabler was apparently trapped on fourth down. But as he lurched toward the ground, he brazenly flipped the ball in the air. Halfback Clarence Davis was in the end zone surrounded by a sea of white Miami jerseys. Somehow he managed to wrench the ball away from them for the winning score. Davis, a dependable running back and a solid blocker, was supposed to have poor hands.

In 1975, Pete Banaszak, generally consigned to spot duty for his first decade as a pro runner, got his first chance to play regularly because Marv Hubbard's shoulder kept popping out, and Pete tied Art Powell's record for Raider touchdowns in one season at 16. Pete was too small to be a fullback, too slow to be a halfback. He was like Eddie Stanky as a ballplayer: he couldn't hit, he couldn't run — all he could do was play. And that got him the Gorman Award as the "Player Who Best Exemplifies the Pride and Spirit of the Oakland Raiders." If the Raiders released him, no other team in the NFL might pick him up. "We keep Pete," said owner Davis, "because he's good for three or four games a season in key spots." In this season he was good for all 14 and thrived when the going got toughest.

"Years ago," he explained, "I used to shake when I'd have to go in a game. You could put a pillow between my knees. But I learned you can't afford a mistake. So I just concentrate on my job, knowing what my assignment is, carrying it out, making the play. The rest will happen.

"And I think it's a good experience. It's really thrilling. This is something you learn in football and can apply to life. It's character, the fact of never quitting. Facing adversity. When you have nothing to fight for, you've got nothing left in the world."

If anybody else said it, it would be corny. Trite. But Pete Banaszak got by with such expressed thoughts because for him they really applied. "I don't have ability," he said candidly, "but I got a lot of heart."

Pete was an important contributor again in 1976 as the Raiders had the most successful year, artistically, in the 21-year history of the organization. Everything fell into place. Stabler was at his peak, achieving career highs in completion percentage (66.7) and touchdown passes (27). He had

For short yardage when it was needed most, Pete Banaszak (40) delivered.

Dave Casper, "The Ghost," quickly rose to all-pro status at tight end.

a brilliant new target in Dave Casper, who took over the starting role at tight end. When the Notre Dame graduate was drafted in 1974, there was some thought of switching him to offensive tackle because of his blocking prowess. But his affinity for getting open and making unbelievable catches precluded such plans. Besides pacing the Raiders as a team, he led all the tight ends in the NFL with 53 receptions and 10 touchdowns. Against the double zones which were becoming prevalent among NFL defenses, it was imperative to have a big tight end who could go deep. Few middle linebackers, whose job it was to pick him up in that defensive scheme, could keep up with him.

A 48–17 blowout at New England in the fourth game of the schedule was the only detour for the Raiders that fall. Ironically, that was the game in which Casper had the best performance in Raider history with 12 catches. He also caught two more for touchdowns which were negated by penalties. The Raiders rebounded by winning their last 10 games, avenged the New England defeat by nipping the Patriots in the opening playoff game, drubbed the Steelers for the AFC championship (Pittsburgh played without its regular running tandem of Franco Harris and Rocky Bleier) and qualified for their second visit to the Super Bowl.

This time, the Raiders were psychologically ready, not awed by all the national attention, not distracted by the hoopla, not taut, because John Madden gave them leeway as individuals to enjoy themselves as well as prepare for a game. Their headquarters in Newport Beach — the game would be played 35 miles to the north in the Pasadena Rose Bowl — looked like a resort with families and kids flowing over the place. But the preparations for the Minnesota Vikings, the NFC representative, were detailed and thorough. Strategically, the Raider coaches were convinced they could run effectively to their left against the Vikings — Alan Page and Jim Marshall on that side of the Minnesota line couldn't stand up physically to Gene Upshaw and Art Shell. The Raiders were basically a leftside power team.

Marshall, outweighed 60 pounds by Shell, was never visible to the crowd of 103,424 in the Rose Bowl, and right behind Art came Clarence Davis with the ball. The squat (5′ 10″, 195 pounds) back had his finest game as a pro in Super Bowl XI with 137 yards on 16 carries, the Raiders gained a record-breaking total of 429 yards and the final score was a decisive Oakland 32, Minnesota 14.

Yet is wasn't quite as easy as the figures indicate. At 10 minutes of the first quarter, with the score 0–0, Guy suffered the first blocked punt of his career, which left the Vikings camped on the Oakland 3-yard line. Fortunately for the Raiders, Willie Hall, playing inside linebacker in the 3–4 defense to which they converted that year, fell on a fumble by Brent McClanahan. Still, the Raiders were in a hole and couldn't move the ball on two plays. Then they turned the game around with their pet running strategy. On a play called "17 Bob-Trey-0," Davis took a handoff from Stabler and ran off left tackle. The idea was only to get a little extra room so Guy wouldn't have to punt from the end zone. Casper and Shell double-teamed the defensive end. Upshaw took the tackle. The other guard, George Buehler, pulled and led through the hole. When Viking linebacker Wally Hilgenberg jammed the gap, Davis swung wide around the end and sprinted for a 35-yard gain that changed the momentum of the contest. The Raiders moved on to the first score of the game. "After that drive," said Shell, "we felt we could move the ball and were in position to take it to them."

Halfback Clarence Davis was steadily productive if unspectacular.

Fred Biletnikoff, in his last big hurrah as a receiver (although he played two more seasons) was voted the Most Valuable Player for Super Bowl XI. The four passes he caught helped set up three Oakland scores. The man with the straggly, thinning blond hair, the man who also introduced "stickum" to pro football as a catching aid, was another example of a player who maximized modest talents through concentration. Fred was never timed for the 40-yard dash, the criterion for a player's speed. They were afraid it might show he wasn't fast enough to play pro ball. He was average in size, at 6′ 1″, 190 pounds. In his 14-year career with the Raiders, he caught 589 passes and scored 76 touchdowns, fourth among all receivers at the start of the 1981 season. He was a meticulously prepared player who ran precise routes, had great hands and had a knack for finding the open spot. He also had deceiving quickness which fooled defenders who tried to play him too close.

The receiving corps of Casper, Branch, Biletnikoff meshed brilliantly. Mark van Eeghen, another Colgate product who took over at fullback from Hubbard, emerged as a 1,000-yard rusher and teamed well with Clarence Davis in the backfield. The defense jelled in its new 3–4 alignment, with a huge front of Sistrunk, John Matuszak and Dave Rowe, and the linebacking getting a boost from veteran Ted Hendricks, signed as a free agent in 1975. The secondary had been intact since Alonzo (Skip) Thomas took over the left corner in 1973, joining Atkinson, Tatum and Brown. The Raiders in 1977 might have been the best ever from a talent standpoint. They led the NFL in scoring with 351 points.

But football can be a roll of the dice when it comes to injuries. Bruised and banged up, that 1977 team lost to Denver in the AFC championship game, but only after it had produced a super-thriller the week before. In the opening playoff game in Baltimore, Casper, who had acquired a nickname, "The Ghost," made an amazing over-the-shoulder catch to set up a field goal by Errol Mann that tied the score at 31 with 26 seconds left. The teams battled through one 15-minute overtime period without a score. John Madden, always a wily man on the sidelines despite his effu-sive, animated antics, smartly called timeout just before the expiration of the quarter, forcing the Colts to punt into a brisk wind. That gave the Raiders good field position for the second overtime, and they quickly moved to the winning touchdown on a pass to Casper. The game lasted 75 minutes and 43 seconds.

Chinks of age finally were becoming apparent in the Oakland cast. Thirteen of the players in the starting lineups (offense and defense) were past 30, and others close to that demarcation point. A couple of personnel decisions didn't pan out. They traded for defensive lineman Mike McCoy and corner back Monte Jackson, giving up first round draft choices, and neither was productive. Their own top draft choices, such as Neal Colzie and Charles Philyaw, didn't develop as expected. Stabler, operating on deteriorating knees, was finding it more difficult to elude a pass rush and the range of his throwing arm had been cut down. Although preserving their record for winning seasons, the Raiders slipped to 9–7 in 1978 and failed to make the playoffs for the first time in seven years.

The changing of the guard was signaled on January 4, 1979, when a press conference was called to announce the retirement of Madden, citing health reasons. The most successful coach of his time had been bothered with recurring ulcers. The stress of air travel unnerved him. He bowed out on top and remained with the organization to work on "Special Projects." Among them was

Monte Johnson converted well to linebacker.

the inflammatory subject of a possible move of the Raider franchise to Los Angeles. Since 1977, a schism had been developing between Raider management and the Oakland Coliseum board of directors over terms of the lease agreement. Al Davis had requested certain improvements in the stadium facilities, relating to configuration, luxury boxes, improved dressing rooms, loudspeaker system, and felt he was being ignored. The existing lease would expire after the 1979 season.

Meanwhile the Los Angeles Coliseum had lost the Rams to Anaheim, effective in 1980, and began actively to court the Raiders as a possible replacement.

The Los Angeles offer was sufficiently attractive to dispatch Madden to southern California on a fact-finding mission, and serious negotiations began for the relocation of the franchise. Ultimately the National Football League stepped in to thwart such a move, and it led to litigation, first in a suit by the Los Angeles Coliseum against the NFL, followed by an Oakland Raider suit against the NFL, plus counter-suits, which would delay any action at least through the 1980 season.

Meanwhile, there was still football to be played. On February 8, 1979, after speculation over several candidates, Tom Flores was elevated to the head coaching job. He inherited a team that was undergoing considerable change. Pete Banaszak retired. Willie Brown retired. Biletnikoff was not invited back to play. Skip Thomas, bothered by injury, was gone. Clarence Davis and Willie

Hall failed their physicals. Neal Colzie was traded. George Buehler was released. Dave Rowe was traded. Warren Bankston, a valuable leader of the special teams, retired. The Raiders struggled through another 9–7 season and missed the playoffs again, losing to nemesis Seattle in the last game.

But there were positive elements, too, in the reconstruction of the Raiders. They continued to be the darlings of the nation on Monday nights, when attention was riveted across the land to the troika of Frank Gifford, Howard Cosell and Don Meredith and its unique presentation of pro football. In 18 appearances since the phenomenon was sprung on the public in 1970, Oakland lost only one game, through 1980. That was a one-point defeat by Buffalo, 21–20, in the 1974 season opener.

Looking ahead to 1980, the cognoscenti downgraded the Raiders. *Sports Illustrated* picked them last in the Western Division of the AFC. So did *Playboy* in its annual pre-season roundup. And there were other denigrating evaluations. Still, Al Davis, when he wasn't involved in legal distractions over the move to Los Angeles — the Raiders actually sent a task force to that city in the spring of 1980 and set up a ticket office until a court injunction forced them to abandon any plans for an immediate switch — had good feelings about his team. Remember 1967 and "a bold move, an intuitive decision, a calculated gamble"?

The pattern was repeating. Stabler, one of the great quarterbacks of all time, was traded to Houston for Dan Pastorini. That was bold. Jack Tatum, long one of the great safeties of football, was also sent to Houston in exchange for Kenny King, a little used young back who seemed to have the outside speed the Raiders had long sought. That was intuitive. Matt Millen, a college tackle drafted in the second round (the No. 1 pick had been traded away), was visualized as an inside linebacker. That was a gamble.

"We're only a couple of players away from being a good team," Davis insisted. "If we get any kind of luck. . . ."

Luck, the aphorism goes, is the residue of design. And an amazing design for 1980 was in the works.

Into The Third Decade • 5

Oakland 27/Kansas City 14

The Raiders opened the 1980 season in steaming Kansas City under a cloud of self-doubt and public ridicule. According to the experts, this was to be a game that would establish a new order in the National Football League, making it evident that the Oakland Raiders had collapsed like every dynasty that had preceded it.

True, Kansas City would not challenge for a Super Bowl berth in 1980, but it was young and strong, a team on the rise. The Raiders, the experts insisted, were traveling the opposite road.

The temperature on the field at Arrowhead Stadium was 108°, just the kind of weather an aging team doesn't need. It was so hot members of several high school bands who had been practicing for a special halftime show lay scattered in the tunnel leading to the field like the wounded on the beach at Normandy as the Raiders filed past on their way to warm up.

It was an unsettling scene for a team that admitted the past was dead.

"We don't intimidate teams any more," wide receiver Cliff Branch admitted on the eve of the opener. "Teams feel when they line up with the Oakland Raiders now, they can beat them; they know they can.

"We aren't considered contenders this year. We have to go out and prove we aren't underdogs. If we do that, the playoffs will be there. In the old days, the playoffs were automatic. Now we think about them too much. Instead of just playing the 16 [games], we're always playing for the playoffs. We never used to talk about it. We just let it happen. Now it's all you hear about.

"We have to just forget it and go play the games. The playoff format is there. All we have to do is play the games."

But that was not as easy as it sounded when the Raiders opened their season. First, their new quarterback had not played well enough in pre-season to quiet critics who felt Jim Plunkett should be at the controls.

And second, they were apparently playing with a defense that had all the firmness of Jello.

All in all, even the players themselves were wondering who they were and where they were headed.

The feeling was widely held that Oakland would live and die on the strength of its offense even after an erratic pre-season. But as the world first saw in Kansas City, there was a new winning formula taking shape in Oakland, a formula in which the defense would pave the road to New Orleans.

That defense destroyed the Kansas City Chiefs, sacking quarterback Steve Fuller five times and forcing three interceptions as Oakland rolled, 27–14.

That defensive performance in no way minimized the debut of Pastorini, however. The former Oiler had his finest day in what would prove to be a disappointing season by throwing for 317 yards and two touchdowns (both to Chandler), and he would break open the game in a five-minute span of the third quarter with the aid of that defense in a blueprint for victory that would eventually become as familiar as the one-eyed pirate on Oakland's helmets.

All this destruction of dreams and predictions was accomplished in unusual fashion by Raider standards. But just as there was a new day dawning in the NFL, there was also a new defensive approach taking shape in Oakland, an approach designed primarily by Coach Flores and the defensive coaches.

As he would do all season, linebacker coach Charlie Sumner devised a defensive game plan suited to the particular idiosyncracies of the Raiders' opponent. Week after week, Sumner would do this with uncanny accuracy until the defenses reached their crowning moment in the wildcard playoff victory over Stabler and the Oilers in late December.

But Ken Stabler was not the problem in Kansas City. Steve Fuller was. He had led the Chiefs in rushing in the pre-season while also showing a marked improvement in his passing accuracy. On opening day he was unable to find the room needed to play his game.

Strong safety Mike Davis was instructed to shadow Fuller, moving in whatever direction the quarterback took. At the same time, the Raiders exhibited a newly found pass rush, one so savage that it would come to terrorize the offenses it faced.

That rush came primarily out of a four-man front and five defensive back alignment known as "the Pirate" defense, a defense so adept at causing havoc that it would eventually help scuttle 15 opponents in 20 weeks.

With that alignment came an unexpected increase in the use of the blitz from outside linebacker Ted Hendricks. All season Hendricks would rush like a hurricane, often in the most improbable situations. He would cause confusion, chaos and defeat for the opposition. And the results would cause his return to All-Pro status for the first time in four years.

It would all begin in Kansas City.

But in truth, this defensive day belonged to a man who would make no tackles, intercept no passes and recover no fumbles. It would belong, as so many others had, to punter Ray Guy.

The Chiefs took the opening kickoff and marched 70 yards through the heart of the defense to take a disquieting 7–0 lead, but Pastorini drove his team right back, moving 88 yards in 12 plays to tie the score on a 16-yard pass to Chandler. It appeared this game would indeed be a scoring battle at that stage, but from there on out the half belonged to Guy.

There were no more lengthy Chief drives, at least in part because Guy punted four times from beyond midfield and four times the ball came to rest in the Chiefs' end zone.

His first kick of the day traveled 56 yards and was followed by punts of 52, 63, and 51 yards. Not once did Kansas City return a kick in the half. Not once could it avoid starting 80 yards from Oakland's goal.

And not once was Guy terribly happy about those kicks. A case in point was the 63-yarder. He had tried desperately to drop the ball dead at the

Steve Fuller of Kansas City is about to fall in the grasp of blitzing Mike Davis (36) and Ted Hendricks.

Ray Guy

one and barely missed. Still, he left the field pounding his fists in a rage. In his mind, his mission had failed.

Such reactions were not unusual for Guy, a perfectionist of the highest order. It was the reason he was fast approaching legendary status at a most unlegendary position.

Since arriving in Oakland in 1973 as the first kicker ever taken as a No. 1 draft pick, Guy was as consistent as death and taxes. Days like the one he had in Kansas City became the rule, not the exception.

Against the Chiefs, Guy kicked seven times for a 51.8 yard average, put five kicks in the end zone, had a sixth land at the two and had only two returned. It was the type of performance that had originally convinced the Raiders to break with tradition and take a part-time player ahead of all the swift running backs and powerful linebackers that were available.

"The first day I got to Oakland Coach [John] Madden told me, 'We drafted you because we knew you could kick it,'" Guy said. "'So when we're backed up down there on first down, instead of playing it conservative and trying for five yards the first play, we might come out with the bomb. If it doesn't work, you can kick it out.'"

Guy kicked it out throughout 1980, kicking so well that he regained his spot on the AFC Pro Bowl team from Bob Grupp with a 43.6 average (35.9 net after returns, second only in the NFL to the New York Giants' Dave Jennings).

But it was not distance Guy sought against the Chiefs, just as it has never been distance which intrigued him.

"Averaging 43 to 45 yards and hanging them up is best," Guy insisted. "I don't mind one going 60 or 70 yards, but overall it's hang time that's important because if that ball is kicked on a line, you got trouble, brother." (Hang time is the number of seconds the ball is in the air after it leaves the punter's foot.)

Guy did not give the Raiders any trouble in 1980 and has really never done so. He averaged no less than 41.6 yards per punt in eight years and has kicked for well over 12 miles in total yardage (24,067 yards). What that meant to Guy was seven trips to the Pro Bowl and a rightful place as the best in the world at his job. Quite probably the best ever in football history.

What it meant to the Raiders was never more obvious than it was in Kansas City.

But just as the road to Super Bowl XV would be a rocky one for the Raiders, Guy's road to acceptance as the game's best punter has had its sour moments. Like the first one, for example.

"I shanked my first kick in training camp when I was a rookie and I remember thinking, 'Oh, my goodness, there goes my contract,'" Guy recalled. "I had broken my ankle in college my senior year and hadn't worked out much. It was strong, but mentally I was shaky.

"I heard some snickers, but I couldn't tell if they were kidding or serious. So I just looked straight ahead and the next one went 65 yards. I don't shank too many now."

He didn't shank any against the Chiefs, and it was probably a good thing since his nemesis, Grupp, was kicking the ball back at a 45-yard per kick clip himself. Although that should have made life difficult for the Raider offense, things worked out perfectly, as they would so often in 1980.

Guy and the defense steadfastly held their ground until a sudden rush of Kansas City turn-overs and a brief offensive flurry gave Oakland its first victory. It would be the way the victories would come time and again.

The punting duel dragged on into the third quarter until Oakland took over at its own 31 with 6:08 in the period. Just as suddenly as the offense had gone dead in the first half, it came alive, driving 69 yards behind Pastorini.

The first of Oakland's many big plays came on this series when Pastorini hit halfback Arthur Whittington swinging out of the backfield. Whittington took the ball over his shoulder and romped 55 yards before being dragged down from behind at the two.

Two plays later it was 14–7 with Mark van Eeghen scoring on a plunge, and not long after that Pastorini and Company were back on the field after defensive end John Matuszak tipped a Fuller pass into the arms of rookie linebacker Matt Millen.

Quickly the Raider offense did what it would become incredibly adept at — breaking the back of a weakened opponent. The picadors of the defense had done their job. Now it was time for the matadors to have their moment.

Pastorini sent Chandler down the sideline to attack millionaire cornerback Eric Harris. Chandler beat him to the outside, then slanted inside and caught a perfect 32-yard pass for a 21–7 lead. What had appeared to be a tight game had been splintered apart. The Raiders were on their way.

Such quick reversals became the Raider trademark all through the season although none in the stunned stands in Kansas City quite understood what they were seeing at the time. All they knew was that the Chiefs were beginning to unravel. The old men had failed to roll over on key.

Although the Chiefs scored once more, Guy's punting and the defense's work held them at bay, especially after Guy nailed a 58-yarder that traveled to the Chiefs' two on the next series.

"I do nothing to try and kick farther," Guy said. "If I have to kick a 32-yarder, I kick a 32-yarder. I do my best to help us win. I don't need that other stuff. I know what I can do. I don't have to prove it to anybody."

The same could not be said for the Raiders, however. One victory was not enough for that for next would come the real test in the shape of defending AFC West champions San Diego.

A new season had dawned and on the surface things appeared unchanged for the Oakland Raiders. They had won. They were on top. But not for long.

September 14, 1980   # San Diego 30/Oakland 24

Although the season was not yet two weeks old, Raymond Chester had already suffered the tortures of the damned. Only a year after his greatest season in professional football, Chester was again a bench warmer, seemingly the forgotten man of the Oakland offense.

There was, of course, no questioning his skill as a pass catcher. If there ever was, that ended the previous season when he lifted himself out of the shadow of Dave Casper with his first all-pro season since 1972, leading all tight ends with 58 re-

ceptions and pacing the Raiders with eight touchdown catches.

But that was 1979 and this was 1980. Time passes. Things change. A pair of seasoned hands lay folded in Raymond Chester's lap when the season opened.

But unlike so many of his contemporaries, Chester made no complaints. His team would not be publicly split over who could best play tight end. He would utter no word on the matter, plead no case for himself. He would merely sit and wait.

Veteran tight end Raymond Chester makes another clutch catch.

"Last year was really good for me because I'd been locked away for a long time," Chester said. "I felt a little forgotten in Baltimore (where he was traded in 1973). Doing it again at 31 was good. It was a lot of fun.

"But Casper is back now. I understand that. If I were with a team and I'd been a great starting tight end and another guy came in who was also a great player, I'd still feel it should be my job.

"Dave's given the Raiders four years of excellent play (all of them all-pro years). He should play. It's what's fair unless he falls off drastically —which he hasn't."

Such words are seldom heard in professional sports these days. But they say more about the man and what he meant to his team than all the praise he received down through the years.

Chester was the voice of reason almost his entire career, even during the bad years in Baltimore. He gave Oakland three fine seasons after being drafted on the first round in 1970 out of Morgan State. But still the Raiders saw the need to trade him before the 1973 season opened for defensive end Bubba Smith.

He admitted the trade crushed him. He was confused and unhappy. His sense of loyalty and his pride had been violated. His life had been cruelly wrenched, and he had no idea why.

He battled those feelings during his five-year hiatus with the Colts, but it was not merely coincidence that he did not again reach all-pro status until a year after Al Davis had brought him home in 1978 in exchange for Mike Siani.

Chester had his share of problems in Baltimore, as did several of his teammates, problems not of his own making. Typically, he declined to talk about them.

He spent his first year back in Oakland on the bench, catching only 18 passes, the lowest total of his career. He declined to talk about it.

He roared back in 1979 to lead the Raider receivers, yet when Casper returned four games into the season Stabler began to go to the latter more and more. Chester declined to talk about it.

Then came 1980. He was an all-pro again, but he was an all-pro with a knee that cried out to him in the night. And he was an all-pro who knew he would have to sit behind Dave Casper, an athlete who never failed to perform on Sundays but who more and more began to feel the rest of the week was his.

Raymond Chester never could understand that. But he declined to talk about it.

However, two weeks into training camp it all became too much and Chester walked out. He packed his bags, said goodbye to roommate Cliff Branch and his other friends and slipped off into the cool summer night with longtime friend MacArthur Lane.

"It came as a complete shock to me," Coach Flores said. "He said his problems had nothing to do with the tight end situation. He said he wasn't having any business problems and no problems at home. He just didn't feel like he belonged in camp.

"He didn't know if he wanted to continue to play. It was just that he didn't want to hold the younger players back and he wasn't sure he wanted to be here. It's hard to figure out. I didn't understand it."

Few did. Although Chester may have felt unsure of himself at age 32, the Raiders had no

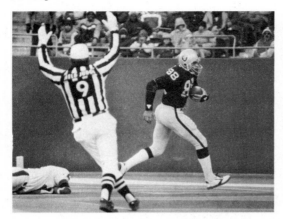

The official signals touchdown as Raymond Chester crosses the goal line, eluding a futile tackler.

There is no question about the strength of Dan Pastorini's throwing arm.

doubts. He was important to them in July and he would become more so in October when the love affair with Casper finally ended.

"Walking out like that was really out of character for him," Lane explained later. "Something was tearing him apart inside to do that."

Not surprisingly, Chester steadfastly refused to explain his actions publicly upon his return, but at least one member of the team felt he knew what the problem was.

"Raymond came and talked to me some before he left," he said. "It seemed to me he was just tired of Ghost's attitude. Dave [Casper] could be pretty selfish and Ray never could understand it. I think it finally started to bother him."

Before long it would bother the entire team. Through it all, Chester went about his job, tutoring his young teammates in the ways of the NFL and the world and talking the team philosophy that has always been as much a part of his style as his massive but pliable hands.

As he realized, his problem was simply that the Raiders had elected to junk their double tight end offense for a more conventional set in 1980. The addition of Chandler to team with Branch and the return of Casper to training camp (he sat out the first four regular season games in 1979 in a contract dispute) had made that possible.

The double tight ends had been the product of necessity. In 1979, with Morris Bradshaw out for the year early on and with Stabler repeatedly proving he could no longer strike deep with accuracy, the decision was made to team Casper and Chester, and the results were miraculous. Together they combined for 115 receptions, 1,483 yards and

11 touchdowns, and the Raiders missed the playoffs by a single game.

But that was no longer the strategy. There was no need for a desperate plan. Casper was back. He would play. Still, although he was as effective as ever on Sunday, Casper continued to wear out his welcome during the week. He was no longer happy in Oakland. He made it clear he wanted out.

Before long, catching the football was not even enough for his teammates, a most tolerant lot. After the season's sixth game Casper joined Stabler and Tatum in Houston in a deal that brought the Raiders security for the future in the form of one No. 1 draft choice and two No. 2 selections.

It was a trade that had long been rumored, but when it finally happened it left the team in shock. Casper had been such a fixture in Oakland's offense it seemed impossible to contemplate the Raiders playing without him.

How could a team that was still struggling, still searching for the formula that would allow it to win 13 of its last 15 games, trade away one of its offensive weapons?

"We feel this will in no way hurt us on the field this year," Flores said. "It's always tough to lose a guy you see develop from a rookie to an all-pro, but we felt the trade was an opportunity to help our future. And with an all-pro replacement in Raymond, we feel it won't hurt our present."

Chester had made that clear long before the deal was made. He had proven it, if it still needed proving, in the early weeks of the season when he was still on hold.

Surprisingly, this game, too, did not go according to the script. The first half turned into a defensive struggle with both teams coming away with 10 points and an assortment of bruises.

"Ghost is the starter," he would say. "I'm just here to help out. But that doesn't stop me from knowing I'm a hell of a ballplayer. Just because you don't bitch doesn't mean you aren't a competitor.

"A player has to learn to subordinate his ego and draw pleasure from the accomplishments of his teammates. You can't always lead the charge up the hill. There will come a time when they want me to play. My concern is to be ready."

On September 14, they wanted Raymond Chester to play. He was ready.

The Chargers had won the AFC West title the previous season with the most powerful passing attack in NFL history. Quarterback Dan Fouts could and would throw the ball in any situation and receiver John Jefferson would catch it with two hands, one hand or, it seemed, no hands if necessary.

Along with Jefferson came veteran Charlie Joiner and tight end Kellen Winslow, a towering brute of a man who seemed destined to supplant Casper one day as the league's premier tight end.

It was this challenge that awaited the Raiders. The experts had written off the Kansas City win as an aberration. After all, they reasoned, the Chiefs were still young and unproven. But San Diego was different.

The Chargers were everything the Chiefs were not. They were the acknowledged powerhouse in the AFC. They were a 4–3 defense that hounded a quarterback with the biggest and best front four in the game. And they were an offense that could blow out the scoreboard circuits.

Clearly, they were the team no one could beat, the team that would make AFC aficionados forget the dynasty built by the Pittsburgh Steelers during the 1970s.

For the second time in as many weeks, the Raiders took to the road to face the New Age. This time, however, the struggle would be a grim one and when it was over two things became clear — Raymond Chester could still play and the Oakland Raiders could handle the best team in the AFC.

But close observers also got another glimpse of both the Raiders' future and Chester's when Pastorini answered a Fouts-to-Jefferson touchdown with one of his own 40 seconds later.

Oakland took over at its own 18 with :42 left in the half and Pastorini quickly rifled a 23-yard completion to Chester, his first catch of the year. Pastorini then found King for 11 to the Charger 48.

With :13 left, it was time to go for broke and Pastorini cashed in his chips with a perfect 48-yard touchdown pass to a sprinting Branch to send the teams into the locker room tied at 10–10.

The game remained deadlocked until defensive end Willie Jones came sweeping in on Fouts midway through the third quarter. As Fouts was sacked, the ball popped into Jones' arm, he gathered it in at the Charger 11 and sprinted untouched into the end zone.

Oakland had what no one thought possible. It had the lead, 17–10, with 15 minutes to play. It had San Diego on the run. It had Dan Fouts' aerial circus in check. For a moment it had it all.

But on the next two series, Fouts rebounded. First, he whipped the ball upfield as he had so many times before, moving the Chargers 65 yards in six plays to tie the game on a 15-yard touchdown pass to Winslow.

That was quickly followed by a stalled Raider drive and an 80-yard San Diego scoring march in which Fouts had four completions for 44 yards. With two minutes to play, Mike Williams sprinted around right end and San Diego had the lead, 24–17.

The Raiders appeared dead. Their defense was reeling despite having intercepted four passes, forcing two fumbles and scoring one touchdown. The offense had not crossed midfield since the third quarter and had not scored since Branch's touchdown. And to make matters worse, its kicker, Chris Bahr, had already missed four field goal attempts.

Still there was time and there was Chester and that was nearly enough.

Pastorini trotted out with the ball at his 37 and with one flip of his right arm it was on the Charger 31. Then it was on the 23 after he scrambled eight yards. And then it was on the 16 after a Pastorini-to-Casper pass.

But after two incompletions, Raider prospects looked dismal. They looked even worse moments later when Pastorini was sacked by Gary Johnson. Johnson rose in exultation. Pastorini did not move.

As he was helped from the field, Pastorini was passed by Plunkett, who had come on to take his first snap in three years in a game that meant something.

With 44 seconds to play, Plunkett drew the Chargers offside, moving the ball to the 18 yard line. It was again fourth down and everyone knew what had to be done.

As Plunkett dropped back to pass, Chester ran a familiar route, heading toward the middle of the end zone and then curling back. He was running in no-man's land.

Chester sprinted hard at linebacker Woodrow Lowe, driving him toward the goal post. Suddenly, Chester whirled and Plunkett fired. The big tight end leaped at this last chance for his team and snared the ball with Lowe hanging on his back.

Touchdown. 24–24. Overtime.

"That's why they keep an old dog like me around," Chester said later. "To occasionally find a bone. Luckily, I haven't lost my knack of getting to the ball."

But that was the last time the Raiders would get to the end zone.

Insisting his knee was fine, Pastorini came back in as the overtime opened. He was limping noticeably and it showed when his first pass landed in the lap of San Diego's Glen Edwards.

But Fouts returned the favor when his pass was picked off by Millen on the next play.

The Raiders slowly began to move from the Charger 46 on five straight running plays before Pastorini badly misfired on third-and-eight with Casper apparently in the open. This brought in Bahr, who missed his fifth field goal try, this one from 50 yards.

That gave Fouts what he wanted most — one more shot at the tiring Raider defense. As expected, Fouts came out firing, completing passes of 12 and 28 yards before using his running backs to work the ball to Oakland's 24.

Now the battle was joined. With a third-and-11 situation it was logical for Fouts to send the ball in Jefferson's direction. And it was time for Lester Hayes to try and do something about it.

Hayes, who would come within one of tying the NFL's single season interception record of 14, matched Jefferson stride for stride as the two sprinted downfield. The bearded Fouts kept his eyes riveted on his receiver as Jefferson headed toward the end zone.

Just as the two sprinting men began to turn, Fouts sent the ball spinning madly in their direction, electing to take his chances with the game's greatest receiver in hand-to-hand combat with its greatest cornerback.

As they went up, Jefferson took a bead on the ball. Hayes, however, saw only a blinding California sun that was sinking behind the lip of the stadium's upper deck.

By the time Hayes' eyes cleared, Jefferson had made the catch and fallen at the two. Hayes looked frantically for his man but could not find him in the half-blind hysteria of the moment. Jefferson, however, knew exactly where he was.

He also knew he lay untouched so he began to roll toward the goal line. Without ever regaining his feet, John Jefferson scored the winning touchdown. The Chargers had "rolled," 30–24.

"When you cover a guy like that and he still catches the ball, it's baffling," Hayes said. "Dan Fouts is truly mad. He is Mr. Las Vegas. He took the chance of crapping out and he threw a seven."

Actually it was a six, but either way it would prove to be San Diego's last winning toss against the Raiders. The Chargers had escaped with a victory, but Oakland, too, had left a winner.

Although it had lost as predicted, it had escaped with the knowledge that it did indeed match up perfectly with San Diego, just as Al Davis had insisted. Before the season was out, that knowledge would be the cornerstone of Oakland's two victories over the Chargers, the first of which would return the Raiders from the land of the living dead and the second of which would propel them into Super Bowl XV.

But those days were far in the future. There were still other trials to face and they would begin a week later at the Coliseum, when the Raiders would feel the anger of their own frustrated fans for the first time.

Oakland 24/Washington 21

The Raiders were supposed to be officially dead by now. Both the Chiefs and Chargers were to have taken their measure.

Kansas City, of course, did not come close and San Diego won the game but, as it would learn later, had lost the war. But none of that was enough for captain Gene Upshaw, a man who began his career in Oakland with the Raiders' first Super Bowl appearance back in 1967. After 13 years as a starter, Upshaw knew the score.

He knew what the Raiders were and what they were not. And he knew what they were capable of if they believed neither the predictions of doom nor the recent talk of Super Bowl Sunday.

"These aren't the old Raiders," Upshaw admitted only days before the season's home opener. "We've got a lot to prove. We aren't the best team in the league, but we aren't the worst, either. That's the way it is.

Gene Upshaw, equipped for battle.

"We've got the personnel, but we have to stop talking about it and do it. We're not the team we were in the 1970s. But this is our team. This is our 45 guys."

Such talk was nothing new for Upshaw, a man who has long been the Raiders' spokesman both on and off the field. He is a man who deals with reality as he sees it. And, as his team prepared to face the Washington Redskins, he was well aware that the offense had not been overwhelming against San Diego despite scoring 24 points.

He knew too many opportunities had been missed. And worse, he knew his quarterback was having problems grasping the complicated Raider offense.

But Upshaw was the most outspoken proponent of the power of positive thinking ever to play in Oakland. Hence, even his criticisms seemed upbeat.

True, Upshaw said, the Raiders were no longer what they had been, but remember the competition was better. The other AFC's Western Division teams had awakened. They, too, had learned how to win.

So be it. For Upshaw, that did not mean his team could not win. It simply meant it would not be easy. The Raiders would learn both those lessons when the limping Redskins came to town as heavy underdogs and nearly took the bite out of Oakland's new found confidence.

Although both were 1-1, the Redskins were headed toward one of their worst seasons in recent years while the Raiders were headed to perhaps their best ever, facts that were yet to become obvious to either team.

What Redskin coach Jack Pardee did know, however, was that the Raiders had suddenly grown capable of running the football around the ends as well as through the middle. Although they were still considered an explosive passing team (and would prove it repeatedly as the season wore on), it was the running game that had Pardee thinking.

There was a new look about these Oakland Raiders, one that would force radical changes in the way teams would defense them, although it would not begin to take shape until this third game was in full swing.

Still, Pardee knew trouble when he saw it.

"King is the biggest change in their offense," Pardee admitted on the eve of Game 3. "They are still running inside, but now they can get it outside, too."

That simple fact became evident against Washington—and it became one of the major differences between the 9–7 Raiders of 1978 and 1979 and the Super Bowl victors of 1980.

Obviously, to get the ball outside one needs a running back with the speed of a Kenny King. But one also needs guards who can knock people over, guards like Gene Upshaw.

Upshaw had been a starter with the Raiders since the first day he left Texas A&I's campus as the unknown No. 1 draft choice of Al Davis in 1967. He was huge by NFL standards of the day, a giant of a man who hardly fit the mold of the pulling guard.

There was nothing stubby about his 6′ 5″ frame and certainly nothing fat about his 255 pounds. At age 35, that frame was entering its fourteenth season in a sport Gene Upshaw had thought he'd seen the last of when he left Robstown High School.

"As a kid growing up in Texas I knew they played pro football some place, but it was like in a foreign country," Upshaw admitted. "We didn't have any money to go to Houston or Dallas to watch. I wasn't all that interested in football.

"I didn't make the team until I was a senior and that was only because seniors had to play. I had always been on the B team.

"To tell you the truth, I hated football. I didn't like all that hitting. And I knew I had to be a lineman and who likes that? We all have our fascination about being a running back with swift feet, but a lineman knows right well as a kid that he can't do anything else. He's going to be a lineman all his life."

Actually for a time Upshaw figured he might be a pitcher for a good part of his life after the Pittsburgh Pirates drafted him, but his father squashed those notions with one hard glance. College was the place for his son, so college it was, although Upshaw's arrival at Texas A&I was hardly accorded the same fanfare as the arrival a decade later of Earl Campbell at Texas.

There were no long-legged coeds or alumni with oil wells waiting to greet Gene Upshaw. There were only classrooms and a football team that didn't know he existed.

"I had paid my registration fees and I walked out and saw the team practicing," Upshaw recalled. "It was my first August without football. It was out of my life. I wasn't good enough.

"But I walked over to watch and this little guy came up and asked why I wasn't playing. I told him nobody had asked me. He told me to come back in the afternoon and get a uniform."

That little guy turned out to be A&I coach Gil Steinke. In the next four years he would bend every effort to find some new uses for Upshaw's swift feet. But in the long run his young student was right. A kid knows when he is a lineman.

"I started growing that first semester," Upshaw explained. "I was 6′ 1″, 190 pounds when I arrived and I was 6′ 4″, 235 pounds when I went home in December. My parents didn't know if I was the same kid who had gone off to register in August.

"After that, every year it would be a spring project to see where to use me next. They tried me at running back, tight end, tackle, center. I even played defensive tackle for three games. Never made a tackle. Damndest thing you've ever seen.

"Finally Gil said, 'Upshaw, how can you be so close to the guy and never make a tackle? You can't play defense.' He put me back on offense and I stayed there."

Perhaps he could not tackle, but Upshaw could surely block, something Davis recognized immediately. What he also recognized was that this man would change pro football just as the forward pass and the T-formation did. His presence would be an evolutionary step for the pro game.

Upshaw was among the first successful mobile but massive guards, a man with the strength to hand-fight defensive giants and the speed to lead men like King around the end. With the presence today of John Hannah, Dennis Har-

Gene Upshaw (63), along with Mark van Eeghen, helps clear a path for ball carrier Kenny King.

rah, Joe DeLamielleure, Conrad Dobler and so many others, one tends to forget Upshaw was among the first, and perhaps he was the best of the giant guards.

But Upshaw for years meant more to the Raiders than just another overpowering lineman. He has been their spirit, the rigid backbone that has kept the flamboyant under control, the angry soothed, the disconsolate upbeat.

Al Davis used Gene Upshaw's body, it is true. But he also used his mind and his soul to keep his team ready for the weekly tests of its mettle. He would never need it more than in 1980.

"We've got a lot of young people on this team who don't know what a Raider is," Upshaw said. "We didn't win all those games just because we were a better team. We had more pride and poise and I want to instill that in the others. It's not just a motto to me.

"I have to pass that on just as it was passed on to me. [Jim] Otto made damn sure I knew what the tradition was all about. There are so many new faces now you almost have to introduce yourself. That's why it's important to me to show them that pride and poise goes a lot deeper than that jersey on your back."

Upshaw showed them in the summer exactly what he meant. Throughout the long days of double sessions in Santa Rosa, Upshaw was saddled with an aching back and weakened left leg, yet he did not miss a day when he could have easily justified a week or two of sack time.

"Whenever I come to camp, I feel I have to make the team," Upshaw said as another season approached. "That's the way I felt that first summer and that's how I feel 14 years later. I have to make the football team like everyone else.

"You're in camp to get into football shape. You can only do so much in the offseason. You can't get into football shape no matter how much running and weight lifting you do. You won't get sore in the offseason.

"In camp, the coaches push you beyond what you think you can take. It's what pays off in the fourth quarter. If there was some easy way to do it, I'd do it. But there isn't. You've got to be a doer, so I do what I can, even with a little nick."

The little nicks have seldom slowed Upshaw and never yet stopped him. He never missed a start in over 300 games, not a preseason game, regular season game or post season game. That did not change in 1980, sore back or no sore back.

But he also supplied much more than consistency and six years of all-pro performances; he produced leadership.

When calm in the face of panic was required during the dark days of 1980, he supplied it.

When stinging criticism and a shot of reality was the cure, he spooned it out.

And when praise and arrogance were in order, he handed that out as well.

It was all a part of what he saw as living the Raider motto, having the attitude it takes to dare to become a winner. Although his 1980 contribution was measured by his blocking, his biggest contribution came in the locker room several weeks after the Washington game when Oakland had lost two straight and was beginning to unravel like a pair of dimestore sweatsocks. It was then that Upshaw would lead his team around the corner.

By that time, the offense was in disarray and the defense was at the breaking point. The experts were smug. The Raiders had collapsed. Fingers began to point.

"We weren't thinking about the Super Bowl then," fullback Mark van Eeghen admitted. "We were just trying to keep the whole thing from blowing apart."

Upshaw, however, had not lost faith. He called a team meeting, loudly criticized them for their approach to the game and engaged in a verbal sparring match with Casper. The season began to turn around only six days later.

"We had the feeling we weren't putting out what it took to win," Upshaw said. "I told the team we were all under pressure and if we didn't start doing something, the staff would be gone and we'd be gone.

"We were falling down mentally. Only one guy [Casper] disagreed. Before long he was gone."

Only Upshaw could have gotten away with such a meeting because only he commanded the kind of respect from his teammates, coaches and owner required to pull it off without rancor or resentment.

He was the quintessential politician, something he hoped to parlay into a career that would land him in the governor's mansion in Sacramento or perhaps in a Congressional seat in Washington.

But thoughts of his political future were hardly on his mind despite the impending visit from some Washington dignitaries. He had Redskins to worry about on September 21.

The Washington game, like the two that preceded it, did not go as planned. Pastorini's passes wobbled and fell more often than not on barren ground or into the opposition's hands.

But although it was sorely tested all day, the defense did not break under the strain. Three times Washington intercepted Pastorini passes. Only once did the Redskins turn them into points.

Five times, that Raider defense sacked quarterback Joe Theismann. It stopped the Redskin running game cold, limiting it to 84 yards in 27 carries. And again it bought enough time for Pastorini to get both the Redskins and a stadium filled with angry fans off his back.

But most of all it allowed the Raider running game to surface.

King had his first big day as a Raider, gaining 136 yards in 25 carries. But more importantly, both King and backup Arthur Whittington made it clear that the Oakland offense now could do it all, even if only sporadically at the moment.

Although it was King who had both the big day and the big year, it was again Whittington who had the big play. His 42-yard touchdown sweep around right end midway through the third quarter broke open a surprisingly tight 10–7 contest and kept Oakland in some semblance of control.

But with Pastorini unable to get on target, full control was impossible to maintain. It also was impossible to satisfy the impatient crowd of 45,163 which made it clear it had come to bury Dante not to praise him.

In fairness, he gave them plenty to boo about, but after Washington's second touchdown he also knew enough was enough. With Plunkett warming up furiously on the sidelines, Pastorini trotted out for one last try.

As he ran toward the huddle, the boos and catcalls were deafening, but he ignored them. Two weeks later they would seem like nothing by comparison, but at the time it shocked the Raiders.

Stepping into the huddle, Pastorini noticed the ball sitting squarely on his 10-yard line. He noticed Plunkett throwing behind the bench. And, for just an instant, he heard that crowd. Then he went to work.

He completed a third-and-seven pass to Casper for 11 yards; he completed a third-and-four pass to Morris Bradshaw for 12; he sent King off right tackle for 30; on second-and-12 he drilled Whittington for 10. And finally, on third-and-goal at the five, he hit Chandler in the middle of the end zone for the game winning touchdown.

He had done the job. His team had won. But it was all small consolation.

"If your parents were in the stands and 45,000 people were booing you, how would you feel?" he asked softly after his ordeal was over. "But I'm not going to strike out at the fans. It wasn't unfair. Hell, I played like bleep. I'm just glad it's over. The defense played great. The only reason the offense was sputtering was me."

Perhaps so, but both friend and foe felt the raucous, unforgiving Raider fans had done as much damage to Pastorini as the Redskins. Part of their bitterness, of course, stemmed from the proposed move of the team to Los Angeles.

"I think the booing worked to our advantage," Washington defensive back Tony Peters said. "It was on his mind and I really think it had an effect."

It certainly did on the Raiders.

"I don't know what the fans expect," van Eeghen said. "I had never heard that around here. It upset me. It would have been one thing if he deserved it, but he didn't. Why can't they give a guy a chance?"

Only King, who had seen Pastorini evoke a similar reaction from the fans in Houston, seemed to understand.

"I don't doubt the man," King said. "I know what he's capable of doing. He'll make the big play come true. But sometimes that's not enough."

A week later there would be no big play to fall back on. And no defense.

September 28, 1980

Buffalo 24/Oakland 7

The Raiders headed for Buffalo in Week Four of what was still a most unsettled season to meet the hottest team in football and to battle an old friend, Phil Villapiano, who had become the spiritual leader of the young, undefeated Bills.

Villapiano had begun to fill the same capacity in Buffalo that Upshaw did in Oakland. Although he had been with Chuck Knox's team less than six months, the former Raider linebacker had assumed the mantle of spiritual leader, football guru to the uninitiated. He would show these rosy-cheeked Bills how games were won by Oakland.

For the most part, that was the sum total of Villapiano's contributions because his scarred knees simply protested too much for him to regain starting status. But as the game approached, they still remembered him in the locker room of the Oakland Raiders as a Pro Bowl performer whose spirit seldom flagged, regardless of the situation.

He was sorely missed in that locker room when training camp opened. The leader of an assortment of off-the-field mania, Villapiano by his presence had made more than one long, hot afternoon in Santa Rosa bearable. Now he was gone.

One of his major training camp coups in recent years was the establishment of the annual air hockey tournament that has become as much a staple of Santa Rosa summers as sweat and roster reductions.

With Villapiano now gone, center Dave Dalby stepped in to assume that responsibility just as he had quietly assumed the far more significant (although less visible) one of replacing Hall of Fame center Jim Otto in 1975.

Dalby had a most difficult task before him in the latter case. He was replacing a legend, an institution, the only man who had ever played that position in Oakland.

Ever since stepping in, Dalby had been a seldom noticed stabilizing force who sat squarely in the midst of the powerful Raider line, anchoring it without fanfare or recognition.

Dave Dalby gets a brief respite from his chores as the center of action.

In good times and bad, he had played with amazing consistency, showing up, doing his job without fail and then quietly receding into the background. Perhaps because of that, Dalby had become a stickler for continuity, something that became clear when he took over the administration of the annual air hockey extravaganza.

In the past, Villapiano usually had more than a few words to exhort the players prior to the opening faceoff and 1980 was no different after Dalby hit the button of his tape recorder. Out boomed the voice of Phil Villapiano, speaking from across the country.

Villapiano was gone, but Dave Dalby did what he could to keep tradition alive.

Dalby succeeded in that regard, but there was little he could do to change his own plight or that of his team when it arrived in Buffalo. Personally, Dalby knew that at age 29 his chance for superstar status had passed him by. His team's chances, however, still seemed bright.

Back in 1977, the same was true of the UCLA product with the massive calves and silent man-

ner. After that season, he made his first and only trip to the Pro Bowl. He had shaken off Otto's reputation after two years of trying, but it would not be so easy to shake off simple bad luck.

In 1978, in the season when he should have been establishing himself as one of the AFC's top centers, his team faltered and he was hit with a severe knee injury. It was an unfortunate turn of events on both counts since it effectively made him a forgotten man, a player so consistent even his peers failed to notice him.

That, of course, is nothing new for the faceless people who play in the offensive line. For every Gene Upshaw there are 100 Dave Dalbys, talented but unrecognized men who play the only sporting position without a single statistic by which they can be evaluated.

Fortunately, Dalby never had been the type smitten with the need for publicity. He could take it or leave it and would just as soon do the latter. As he once said, "Interviews are all bull---- anyway."

He was the epitome of the company man, an employee who gives his best effort and then goes on about the rest of his life. Were his personality somewhat different, had he hit upon a unique idea like Otto's "00" jersey, things might have been different. But then he would not really have been Dave Dalby.

"When I first played against him he came into a game as a substitute for Otto," Pittsburgh Steeler defensive tackle Joe Greene recalled. "He didn't say much. Just played. The next time we played he was the starter and I remember thinking he had improved tremendously. I thought he'd be the next all-pro center."

The next all-pro center. It was, of course, what Dalby wanted, but as he prepared to face his old friend Villapiano, he knew the moment had passed.

"It's kind of disappointing, but I feel I've got a few more good years left to make it," Dalby said. "I made the Pro Bowl once and I'd like to go back, but all you can do is play as hard as you can.

"Politics enter into it, I guess. A lot of guys have their names filled in automatically, but they're deserving of that. You do as well as you can and if it comes, fine. But you can't think about it all the time or you'd go crazy. Either way you have the satisfaction of knowing you have done it as well as you could."

Dalby did as well as he could in Buffalo, but his efforts bore no fruit. For the second straight week, the offense was sporadic and this time there was not enough defense to hold on. There was no miracle finish in Buffalo, no last second bomb to save the day. There was only a stunning 24–7 defeat that rekindled all the pre-season questions.

Under Pastorini's leadership, the offense produced nothing in the first half. Pastorini threw for a meager 24 yards as Buffalo surged to a 17–0 lead by taking the ball early in the first quarter and seldom giving it back.

For one of the few times all season, the Raider defense was helpless. Buffalo took possession early in the first period and held the ball for 8:52 as it marched 81 yards to its first touchdown. That set the tempo for a long day.

The Bills grabbed control of the line of scrimmage early, something not even San Diego could do, and refused to relinquish it. They put a stranglehold on the football that came into clear focus after the statistics were compiled and Coach Flores learned the Bills had held the ball for 41:07 to Oakland's 18:53. Such advantages are not easily overcome.

So complete was Buffalo's dominance that Oakland had only one offensive series in both the first and fourth quarters and ran off just five disastrous plays in the third.

Of course, considering what happened when they did get the ball, that was probably a blessing for the Raiders. They fumbled the ball away three times. Pastorini was intercepted twice. He was sacked four times and he was pummeled more often than Sugar Ray Leonard's speed bag.

Simply put, Oakland was never in the game.

"I never thought anyone could do that to us," Dalby said later. "If you can't control the line of scrimmage, you can't control the game. We didn't do it."

There was little the Raider offense did do, a clear factor in Buffalo's dominance of Oakland's defense. The Bills gained 325 yards, scored 24 points and had a 69 per cent success ratio in third down situations. Clearly, they had overwhelmed the Raiders, beating them at their own game.

But perhaps the clearest sign that things were falling apart came after the game when some members of the team blasted the officials for "unnecessary calls."

Not after their most disappointing defeats, not after the "Immaculate Reception" in Pittsburgh in 1972 or the 1977 AFC title game loss in Denver that involved the phantom fumble had the Raiders raised their voice in such howls of protest. Was the poise slipping away?

A week later it would appear so.

Jim Plunkett feels secure barking the signals behind Dave Dalby (50).

Art Shell could only shake his head and force one of those resigned smiles that says nothing and yet says it all. It's probably the same smile General George Custer had fixed on his face when he saw all of those Indians.

The Raiders had been stomped. Massacred. Surrounded. And slaughtered. The final score didn't even indicate the extent of it. And here was veteran offensive tackle Art Shell, in his thirteenth year of professional football at the age of 33, trying to keep one of the worst losses in Raiders' history in perspective. It was difficult. Whippings of 31-17, by the Kansas City Chiefs and before the home folks in Oakland, are always difficult for a proud team and a proud man to explain.

"Everything in the world that could have happened," said Shell, "happened to us in the first half. It was a nightmare."

In the first 30 minutes, the Raiders had five turnovers (they were destined to give up eight for the entire game), had two fumbles returned for touchdowns, were outscored 31-3 and lost their starting quarterback with a cracked tibia below the right knee. It was a half in which the Raiders played directly counter to the upbeat effort that would prevail for the rest of the season. In this half, Oakland played without emotion.

Early in the first quarter, Kansas City linebacker Gary Spani picked up a loose ball, caused when defensive end Dave Lindstrom eluded Shell and hit quarterback Dan Pastorini, and ran 16 yards into the end zone for the first score of the afternoon. This was just five minutes into the game. The stadium could have emptied then.

"I was supposed to protect the quarterback's backside," said Shell glumly but evenly, trying to keep the situation in perspective. "I set up to cut off Lindstrom, but he jumped me. Also, Dan had to hold the ball a little longer than he would have liked and he was hit from the blind side. Lindstrom didn't do anything else the rest of the game,

but then somebody else would have a breakdown. And then somebody else."

On one of those breakdowns, moments later, Pastorini crumpled under a strong tackle by nose guard Dino Mangieri of the Chiefs. He suffered a broken leg and was out for the season. His replacement, Jim Plunkett, was jittery and rusty and had played virtually no football for two years. His desperation passes under pressure reflected it.

This was hell. This was the lowest point of the season for the Raiders. In fact, this was the way pre-season skeptics had predicted the Raiders would play in 1980. They were supposed to be in a rebuilding year after consecutive 9-7 seasons. But the 31-17 rout by the Chiefs was more in the nature of a tearing down process.

The Chiefs and the Raiders had been natural rivals since the opening coin toss of the American Football League back in 1980 (the Chiefs were then the Dallas Texans). Even when Kansas City, once the power focus of the AFL in the late 1960's, came back to the flock and slumped into a losing morass in the 1970's, while the Raiders maintained a potent level of play during the same period, there were considerable fireworks whenever these teams clashed. Kansas City had beaten the Raiders twice in 1979, and 1980—rebuilding and transitional period notwithstanding—was supposed to be Oakland's turn for revenge.

The Raiders had been successful in Game One on the schedule, in Kansas City. But on this bright first Sunday in October, the Raiders' second home game of the regular season, the keynote turned out to be despair. Not only on the field but in the stands.

The crowd was far from the habitual sellout—official attendance at the Oakland-Alameda County Coliseum was pegged at 40,153—and many of them seemed in a vengeful mood. They actually cheered and clapped when Pastorini was carried off the field in the first quarter. The vet-

has been known to fluctuate upwards at times—also commanded the biggest respect among his peers in Silver and Black. Seldom did he raise his voice. His idea of a temper tantrum was clearing his throat softly and then musing, "Now why don't we try to keep this in perspective?"

There was one tipoff, though, to the fires that ran deep within the imposing bulk of Art Shell. There were those facial expressions which flitted across his mahogany face, the fierce ones at times that told the onlooker that Art Shell was not particularly enthralled with the situation at hand. Those penetrating looks surfaced only when Shell exhausted his means of compromise because basically he was a man of composure and equanimity who measured his words carefully. He said more with a few words than most say in a filibuster. When Art Shell talks, everybody definitely listens.

Such a time came, for instance, the day before the Raiders played the Chargers in San Diego for the American Football Conference championship in January, 1981. Henry Lawrence, the young tackle on the other side of the line, remembered it vividly: "Art told us about this discussion he had with Joe Greene of the Pittsburgh Steelers after the Raiders beat the Steelers in the 1976 AFC championship game. (At the time, the Raiders had assumed a bridesmaid role in NFL title play while the Steelers had become the perennial brides, with successive Super Bowl victories the previous two seasons.)

"The way Art reconstructed it, Greene came over to him while they were still on the field, congratulated him and said that the Raiders had finally found the right way to win, what it TAKES to win."

Now, relating to the upcoming test against the favored Chargers, Shell told his teammates, "You know, there have always been two teams that I always know we're going to play well against. That's San Diego and Pittsburgh." He said no more. He merely left the impression that if the guys played their own game, destiny would take care of itself. And this Oakland team was destined to win.

He had that kind of confidence both in himself and the organization. It manifested itself from the time he came out of Maryland Eastern Shore,

eran quarterback, thrown into a difficult situation as the replacement for long-time favorite Ken Stabler, was wincing in pain, but the cheering continued as the stretcher took him to the sidelines. Loudly, too. The players looked up at the arena around them in disbelief.

"If this is the way they (the fans) are going to treat us, then I'm ready to move right now," said 14-year veteran guard Gene Upshaw later in the locker room.

Shell, who has always been in Upshaw's shadow as a personality, was dressing in the next stall, mulling the disastrous afternoon, while Upshaw's baritone voice was bouncing off the walls.

In his 13 plus years with the Raiders, Art Shell led a fairly inconspicuous existence, though the record showed that he was named to the all-pro team four times, was All-Conference six straight seasons and played in the Pro Bowl eight times. His relative anonymity was deceiving. A Raider insider once said, "If you want to find out what's going on with the Raiders, ask Art Shell."

The biggest of the Raider's offense—he is listed at 6' 5" and 280 pounds, though that weight a school a little off the beaten track of major varsity football, and was the Raiders' No. 3 draft choice in the spring of 1968. Shell eventually played in 156 consecutive league games until a knee injury during the pre-season of 1979 kept him out of the first five regular season games. The damage was severe enough that some players might have had to submit to surgery, but Art diligently rehabilitated himself to return to the lineup before mid-season and start the final 11 games on the schedule.

Art was a force as an offensive tackle because of the agility that goes along with his size. As a pass protector, he was virtually impossible to run over, and it seemed like a defensive end had to run a mile simply to get around him. As a run blocker, he had unusual quickness in getting off the ball and across the line of scrimmage. He earned two letters for basketball at Maryland Eastern Shore, and he was an all-state basketball center (as well as defensive tackle) at Bonds-Wilson High School in his native North Charleston, S.C.

He was also well equipped emotionally for the highs and lows of pressure football. "I remember we were killed in the first exhibition game we played when I came to the Raiders as a rookie," he recalled with a slight chuckle. "I cried after the game, literally, and some of the older guys came over and said, 'What're you crying for? That game doesn't mean anything. It doesn't count.' You know how that first season ended up? We went to the AFC championship game."

In the calm and measured world of Art Shell, there was an awareness that worrying only begets more worrying. And gloating was an artificial reaction to the moment. He was not a slap-happy individual who led the "high fives" after victory, the pounding together of outstretched fists. He smiled, and kept his emotions contained. It was a form of keeping things in perspective.

"You have to have somebody who is not going to get too excited, somebody who is going to be calm," Shell analyzed his mellow manner. "When I came here, I had older guys who performed that role. Us younger guys were the ones who got excited. Nothing wrong with that. But now I've seen just about everything there is to see in football, and I don't get excited as I used to. Like I said, somebody has to remain calm."

Which was why, moments after that humiliating loss to Kansas City, a pivotal defeat which put the Raider record at 2 wins, 3 losses and endangered the team's entire season, Shell had remained a stoic block of calmness. With a positive feeling that things would get better.

They had to. The carnage for the afternoon showed those two fumbles leading directly to touchdowns—just before halftime Kansas City linebacker Whitney Paul wrestled the ball away from tight end Dave Casper and ran 32 yards into the end zone—and a third fumble leading to another score.

Both Raider quarterbacks, the disabled Pastorini and his successor, Plunkett, were sacked a total of six times for minus 54 yards. In desperation, Plunkett threw a club record total of 52 passes, completed 20 and was intercepted five times.

Ironically, the Chiefs' rout was not reflected statistically. The Raiders had the edge in first downs (23 to 10), net yardage offensively (332–220) and total plays (89 to 54). So maybe there was good reason for Shell's refusal to panic.

"Any time you give any team that many turnovers in the first half, you're going to lose," said Raiders' head coach Tom Flores.

There was also some solace to be gained from the fact that Plunkett (who admitted frankly, "This was the chance I was waiting for and I didn't play well at all") threw touchdown passes in the fourth quarter to wide receivers Branch and Chandler while the Raider defense shut out the Chiefs. There would be another day.

Steve Sylvester is handy man on the offensive line.

Oakland 38/San Diego 24

It was Monday, October 6, 1980. That might have been the most important day of the Raiders' whole fantastic trip to Super Bowl XV. On that day, a group of shaken, dispirited men gathered at the Raiders' training facility in Alameda to discuss The Solution.

They were one loss away from turmoil. Turmoil represented a fumble, an interception, a squandered drive, a missed tackle—miscues that had plagued them through the first five weeks of the season. Or they were one victory away from something beautiful, which meant playing up to their capabilities.

It was an especially pertinent time because coming up, back to back, were their two severest opponents—the San Diego Chargers, the favored team in the Western Division of the AFC, and the Pittsburgh Steelers, the defending Super Bowl champions.

"All we gotta do is win one game," said Gene Upshaw. "But that's the toughest thing to do after these kinds of losses [referring to the Kansas City debacle the day before]. We gotta lot of young players on this team and that means it's up to us veterans to keep them going. We can't let

up. Heck, we've only lost three games. Thirteen and three will get us into the playoffs."

Bold words that didn't really hide the self doubt. Why hadn't there been an explosive passing attack, as promised with the addition of long-throwing Dante Pastorini? Why had the Oakland quarterbacks been sacked 10 times in the past two games? Why had the Raiders lost six fumbles in the past two games? Why had Oakland quarterbacks thrown seven interceptions in the past two games? And, most importantly, why had the Raiders played so lethargically, even in victory? That lethargy was the answer to all the questions.

There were even rumors that the coaching staff was on the spot. And coming into Oakland the next Sunday were the San Diego Chargers, who had won their first meeting in overtime and were atop the AFC West with a 4–1 record and looking invincible. A loss by the Raiders would virtually confine them to also-ran for 1980. Not statistically or mathematically perhaps, but certainly mentally. They needed a big win.

So the players themselves made the first move. They called a meeting on their own initiative, without the coaches present, to try to find a

Jim Plunkett feels the force of San Diego's defensive muscle as the ball is jarred loose.

The outside speed of Kenny King adds a new dimension to the Raider attack as he turns the flank against San Diego.

solution, a reason for the floundering and a method of reversing the defeatist trend. Upshaw, nominally the team leader, spurred the idea, joined by Shell, with John Matuszak, a fearsome figure when he was riled, speaking for the defense.

The meeting triggered a rallying point for the season.

"There was a lot of pressure on all of us," Upshaw later explained, "but this was just a feeling I had about the coaching staff. I saw Tom [Flores] at our postgame party after we lost to Kansas City, and I've never seen him look so down. I never wanted to see him look like that again. That was the poorest game we've played since I've been here."

So he spoke his mind. And so did Matuszak, in pithy terms.

"It just takes one guy on defense, one guy on the special teams and one guy on offense to ____ things up," said the defensive lineman. "It was up to us to decide as players what had to be done because it wasn't the coaches' fault. We had the personnel, and we knew it."

Matuszak, a massive sight at 6' 8" and 280 pounds, spoke with fury as he addressed the players:

"Quit bleeping around. Give it your best shot. Don't party six nights a bleeping week. Party the night after the game, or the next night. But then start getting your butts ready. The damn season's only five, six months long. You got six months to goof off if you want. C'mon, you're taking money out of my mouth.

"And we don't want any special guests here. No free passes. If they don't want to bleeping play here, then they can bleeping well leave." Matuszak grabbed his gear and left the locker room.

Those last remarks were aimed specifically at a recalcitrant member of the club who had been missing team meetings and showing up late.

"I had the support of every player in that team meeting except one," said Upshaw. "I told the team that we had to ask ourselves if we were doing everything possible to be successful. He didn't see the point of it at all."

Significantly, after one more game, the Raiders traded away Dave Casper, the brilliant tight end who had been named to the Pro Bowl the four previous seasons but had been openly unhappy since holding out for three games in 1979. The trade to the Houston Oilers left the Raiders still well fixed at the tight end position because they had Raymond Chester, one of the best in the business, in the starting role, backed by Derrick Ramsey, a third-year man who had shown ability to deliver in the clutch, and Todd Christensen, another youngster who was also a leader of the special teams brigade. Furthermore, to bolster Al Davis' philosophy that you look to the future while you're taking care of the present, the Raiders secured from the Oilers first and second round draft choices in 1981 and a second round pick in 1982. That was a veritable bonanza considering that Casper, in the frame of mind he displayed in his last couple of years with the club, was expendable.

Rookie Marc Wilson makes a brief but impressive debut in a cameo role against San Diego.

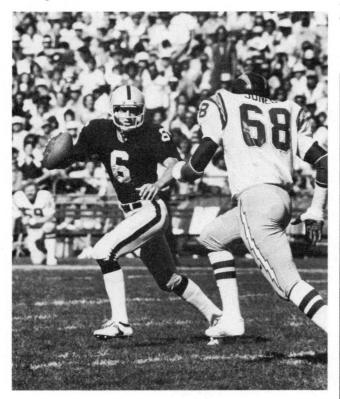

Of more import to the Raiders immediately was another player they had secured from the Oilers the previous spring. Kenny King, a 23-year-old running back out of Oklahoma, was acquired from Houston for aging defensive back Jack Tatum and a pair of seventh round draft picks.

In 1979, King, a third round draft pick by the Oilers, had ridden the bench, carrying the ball a total of three times for nine yards in his rookie season, when he played behind the incomparable Earl Campbell. But with the Raiders, he promised a new dimension to their attack. Speed. He had been a high school sprint champ in Texas.

At Oklahoma, he had played in the same backfield with Heisman Trophy winner Billy Sims and, used in the fullback slot, was noted mainly for his blocking contributions. But whenever he had been given the ball, King had shown great quickness and maneuverability. As a senior, while Sims was grabbing all the attention, King carried the ball 99 times and gained 799 yards, a scintillating 7.9 yards average. Besides his speed, at 5' 11" and 205 pounds he wasn't an easy man to knock off his feet.

There was an immediate niche carved out in the Raider backfield for a guy who had the ability

to go outside, bust through quick traps up the middle and surprisingly, considering his meager background in that phase of football, catch passes coming out of the backfield.

Later, Bum Phillips, who had him at Houston, would say that he peddled the young back because King would have been a bench performer indefinitely if he had remained with the Oilers, who could use another running foil for Earl Campbell. "His performance," said Bum, "depends on what plays you run him on. We didn't have those kinds of plays where a halfback doesn't block. Both our backs have to block."

The inference that King was deficient as a blocker was surprising, in view of his college experience and, subsequently, the way he fitted neatly into the Raider mold. The Oakland system emphasizes strong blocking by both running backs, sometimes at the expense of niftiness. Few teams in the NFL have put as much emphasis as the Raiders have on the presence of a halfback who can blow open a hole for the fullback—say the latter is a Marv Hubbard or a Mark van Eeghen.

The Raiders had been without such a man since halfback Clarence Davis retired after the 1978 season. Davis, never greatly heralded, had been a dependable all-purpose runner and an efficient blocker since 1971. And now King filled that void.

"This is the best running attack we've had in three years," said van Eeghen, who had three consecutive 1,000-yard rushing seasons when Davis was his blocker but dropped to 818 yards rushing the year after Davis left. "Kenny has made the difference."

King picked the pivotal game of the 1980 season, the sixth on the schedule, against the San Deigo Chargers, to show that difference most dramatically.

In the first quarter, he flashed the kind of outside speed the Raiders hadn't seen for years, maybe since the hey-day of Clemon Daniels, when he sprinted 31 yards around right end for the opening touchdown of the game. Jim Plunkett, making his first start in an NFL game since 1977, benefitting from a full week of practice running the Raider offense as first string quarterback, was masterful. He completed 11 of 14 passes for 164

This is the start of Kenny King's 89-yard romp, longest in Raider history, against the Chargers, with Mark van Eeghen (30) and Art Shell as his initial blockers.

yards, and in the second quarter, after the Chargers had tied the score at 10, he lofted a 43-yard touchdown toss to Cliff Branch. Dinged on a four-yard scramble in the third quarter when San Diego linebacker Woody Lowe's helmet connected with his head, Plunkett yielded momentarily to rookie Marc Wilson, who kept a drive going. Then Plunkett returned with a pass to Bob Chandler that set up a three-yard scoring dive by Mark van Eeghen and a 24–10 lead.

But the irrepressibly dangerous Chargers rebounded for two touchdowns, the second coming 34 seconds into the fourth quarter and tieing the game, 24–24. A clipping penalty on the ensuing kickoff pushed the Raiders back to their own 11-yard line. Their entire season was imperilled.

And this is where the new dimension added by Kenny King put bright hues in the Oakland picture. The play started with Plunkett handing off to King, who veered around the left end of the line in a move reminiscent of the old glory days when Gene Upshaw and Art Shell wiped out all opposition on that side. The blocking cordon worked perfectly to spring the halfback loose by the time he reached the sideline. Kenny's speed did the rest as he sprinted the entire 89 yards from the line of scrimmage, the longest running play in the history of the Oakland Raiders.

The play was called "15 Lead Odd" and was the same one which Clarence Davis ran with devastating effect against the Minnesota Vikings in

Super Bowl XI, gaining 137 yards. It was a weakside play, meaning away from the tight end, who lined up on the right side of the line. The guards, Mickey Marvin and Gene Upshaw, did not pull. King took the ball from Plunkett and followed fullback Mark van Eeghen to his left, adjusting his moves to the blocking pattern. He had the choice of darting inside between the tackle and guard or running wide, depending on how Art Shell, at left tackle, blocked the defensive end.

The Chargers' weakside linebacker felt that King was going inside and barged into the line. The weak safety also read it that way and moved up to stuff the play at the line. So King kicked out and by the time he turned the end, he had clear sailing, with only the right cornerback having any kind of shot at him. Cliff Branch, the wide receiver on the left, got a piece of the cornerback, and King shifted into high gear. At midfield, he straight-armed the last defender, and then it was simply a sprint to the end zone, and there was no one in the San Diego secondary swift enough to catch him.

It was probably the single most important play of the 1980 season.

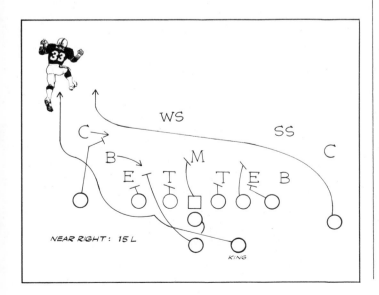

NEAR RIGHT: 15 L

On the following kickoff, the ball glanced off the hands of Chuck Muncie, standing deep for the Chargers at his own 5, he couldn't find the handle on it at the goal line and in the ensuing mad scramble in the end zone, Todd Christensen, captain of the Oakland special teams units, came up with the ball. That accounted for the final score of 38–24 and intense jubilation on the Raiders' side of the field.

Even the fans who booed the Raiders the week before for shoddy, lackluster play, were caught up in the handslapping and giddiness among the Oakland players.

"They talked about the fans all week, and somebody told us that they'd be cheering for the Chargers instead of the Raiders," said San Diego wide receiver John Jefferson of the crowd of 44,826 which spent most of the afternoon on its feet, screaming—for the Raiders. Added Todd Christensen, "The crowd can definitely make the difference in a ball game, and their cheering definitely made the difference. They rooted like crazy, right from the beginning."

Mickey Marvin, the huge guard who had cleared the way for King's first touchdown, enthused, "It was beautiful. Everybody played with emotion and everybody was into the game. It comes from within and it's up to every individual to get himself ready. You gotta have that emotion. You gotta have it." The Raiders had "it" and more. The dormant running game, led by King, was a key to the resurgence that turned the season around with this one vital victory.

Unfortunately, an ankle injury and other bumps and bruises later limited the playing time of King, causing him to miss parts of four games. But he was able to gain 761 yards for the season and earn a Pro Bowl berth. "I personally feel that Kenny could have rushed for 1,200 or 1,300 yards if he hadn't gotten hurt," said right tackle Henry Lawrence. "He improved an awful lot since the beginning of the year. He learned how to read his blocks better, and he's going to improve even more."

The Raiders were fortunate that they had a fine ball carrier in Arthur Whittington, a holdover from the previous two seasons, who became a critical factor in the Raiders' running game when King was limping or needed a breather. Whittington became the designated pass-catching halfback

As the Raiders embark on a six-game winning streak, the fans get caught up in the surge of enthusiasm.

Dan Fouts must hurry his pass as John Matuszak (72) penetrates the cordon of Charger blockers to harass the quarterback.

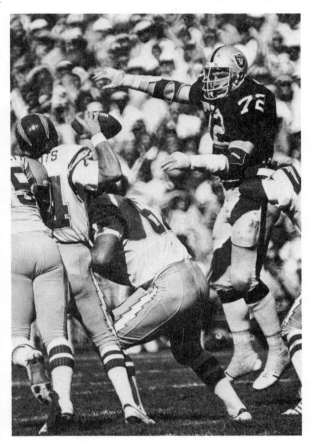

Arthur Whittington relieves Kenny King, and the Raider attack doesn't miss a step.

while King was the designated running back. Both, however, could perform the dual tasks more than adequately. Add the 299 yards Whittington gained in spot duty to the 761 picked up by King, and the position picked up more than 1,000 on the ground. Likewise, King caught 22 passes and Whittington 19 for a respectable total of 41.

Beyond mere figures, the Raiders in the aftermath of the San Diego game had a different attitude. Willie Jones, a young defensive end, stood near his cubicle looking as if he and his teammates had just accomplished a sacred mission.

"There was definitely a lot at stake," he said. "Our coaching staff was getting a lot of pressure from management, so he wanted to win this game for them more than anybody else. All the fellas know we can't play for a better bunch. Hey, they allow you to be yourself."

October 20, 1980   # Oakland 45/Pittsburgh 34

Little Cliff Branch was the catalyst of the Raiders' passing attack for most of his decade with the club. Branch in tandem with sure-handed Freddie Biletnikoff in the old days, Branch with whomever the Raiders could muster at the other wide receiver post after Freddie finally retired. Even with Ken Stabler, whose style of passing was

more a nibble than a big bite, Branch's ability to get deep, and the very threat of that ability, was a potent force for the Raiders.

Then with the added emphasis placed on the "vertical" game with the advent of the 1980 season—an emphasis buttressed by the Stabler-for-Pastorini trade and not diminished one whit when

Plunkett had to take over for injured Dante—Branch's value to the team was immeasurable. He was the man who made things happen.

This would be a crucial season for Branch, however. The wide receiver with the jitterbug steps, the steps that once gave him a professional track record in the 40-yard dash when he sprinted the distance in 4.3 seconds and even defeated the great Bob Hayes, suddenly was confronted with a barrier of skepticism in his ninth year with the club. He passed his thirty-second birthday, and there were some insinuations that his acceleration and speed were a shade diminished. Without them, he was like Dr. J, Julius Erving, unable to jump for one of his magical dunks.

Some skeptics questioned whether Branch, a Pro Bowl performer four different times, had succumbed to the dropped-ball syndrome. "During the past few years," said an anonymous Raider, "we've had a dropped ball here and a dropped ball there from these guys [Branch and the other wide receivers], and that was enough to make us lose a game here and there. That was also enough to keep us out of the playoffs the past two seasons."

The fleet little man (5′ 11″ and 170 pounds) was still catching a respectable number of passes. That was because Stabler liked those short hitch passes where all you had to do was cuddle the ball in your belly. But his average gain per catch dropped to a career low of 14.3 yards in 1979—contrast that with the 24.2 yards per catch in 1976 when he also led the NFL in touchdown receptions as the Raiders marched to Super Bowl XI.

So road-runner Cliff, and the Raider passing game in general, held the key to Oakland's improvement in 1980, and the results over the first six games were encouraging but not decisive. Cliff had broken lose for three touchdown passes, but he had also been held to one measly reception for six yards by the Buffalo Bills.

Now the Raiders were 3-and-3 for the season after their heartening triumph over the Chargers, but they were going into Pittsburgh for an important Monday night game with the defending Super Bowl champions.

"We've had guys open," said Cliff, adjusting his omnipresent Houston Astros baseball cap

The face of wide receiver Cliff Branch reflects alertness as he watches the action.

(he's a native of that Texas city). "We've had a lot of guys open. We see guys open on the films all the time. We're just having trouble getting the ball to them. Part of it is our pass protection. It's been breaking down and the quarterback has been having a little trouble reading coverages."

"We're just inches away from where we want to be," contended Coach Tom Flores. Inches away, he meant, from a Cliff Branch explosion.

On a brisk night at Three Rivers Stadium, the Steelers started out like they were going to blow the Raiders right into the confluence of the Allegheny, Monongahela and Ohio rivers. They took the opening kickoff and moved straight down the field on four Terry Bradshaw passes to a touchdown. On their next possession, recovering a Raider fumble by King, they moved to the Oakland 1-yard line and safely settled for a field goal.

But the Raiders roared back, sparked by King's 27-yard touchdown run midway through the first quarter, and by halftime Oakland had a 28–24 lead in a free-scoring game. Branch hadn't caught a pass.

The explosion came on the opening sequence of the third quarter. On second-and-10 from the Oakland 44, Plunkett staunchly ignored a Steeler blitz, which meant that the Pittsburgh secondary was left with man-to-man coverage on Branch, and hit the fleet receiver with a 56-yard scoring pass. No one covers Branch one-on-one and gets away with it over the course of a game.

When the home team edged closer again, 35–34, at the end of the third quarter, Plunkett located Branch again with a 34-yard touchdown pass that put the Steelers away for good. The Raiders won, 45–34. Branch's totals were: five catches, 123 yards, two touchdowns.

Cliff's response to interviewers after the game was surprisingly bland: "I'm healthy. We won. That's all I got to say." And he remained noncommital the rest of the season, though his performance continued at a high level.

Cliff Branch was a player of unorthodox ways at times. Before a game against the Cincinnati Bengals in early November, he missed two days of practice, one of them in which the offensive plan of the Raiders was set. He failed to contact the coaching staff to explain his absence. Branch had done the same disappearing bit a year earlier prior to a Monday night game in New Orleans and was benched for the opening kickoff. He later came into the game and was instrumental in an amazing 42–35 come-from-behind victory over the Saints. Flores fined and benched him for his mystery caper before the Bangals game, then inserted him, and Cliff responded again with three catches for a game-high total of 63 yards. Again, he repeated his litany: "I'm healthy. We won. That's all I want to say."

The following week, he joked privately about his vanishing act. "I don't know if I got fined or not," he said, grinning. "My mother gets my checks, so I don't see them. Anyway, a fine is tax deductible. I can write it off."

He missed the team's last practice before it headed to New Orleans and the Super Bowl, and his mother apparently found her son's check a bit lighter again. Yet he responded with another sparkling performance against the Eagles.

His teammates felt a special empathy for the mercurial little man who had battled the odds to reach a preeminent position as one of the game's outstanding receivers. Cliff had come into football labeled as a sprinter. That's not a bad quality if a man has other assets to tie in with the speed, as Bob Hayes did when he went from Olympic glory to a brilliant early career with the Dallas Cow-

Donnie Shell (31) of the Pittsburgh Steelers arrives too late to prevent Cliff Branch from clutching a "Monday Night" pass.

boys. Other sprinters have failed—Jimmy Hines, the world's fastest human in 1968, couldn't stick with the Miami Dolphins because he had brick hands when it came to catching a football. The same label of bad hands plagued Cliff in his fledgling period as a football player. He was a state high school sprint champ in Texas, with a 9.3 mark for 100 yards. He was more noted for track than football after he matriculated at Colorado, partly due to the fact the coaches at that school viewed the act of throwing a football with the same disdain that W. C. Fields showed for Philadelphia. But the Raiders made him their No. 4 pick in the 1972 draft because his speed intrigued them.

Within a couple of years, working diligently to concentrate on the ball, absorbing the tutelage of Biletnikoff, he had superseded Mike Siani, another wide receiver who was the top draft choice of 1972. In 1974, Cliff caught a career high total of 60 passes and scored a personal high of 13 touchdowns.

The brilliant exhibition against the Pittsburgh Steelers in the seventh game of the 1980 season showed that Branch had lost none of his swiftness or elusiveness, that he was still unmatched for getting behind the secondary for the long bomb that unnerves an opponent.

The Steelers also felt the brunt of the Raiders' force in a more physical way, from the defense. "I told the younger guys all week," said Art Shell, "that we'd have to fight, scratch, kick, whatever it took to win this game. Ain't no fooling them or finessing them when you play the Steelers. You just have to go out after them." As a result, Pittsburgh quarterback Terry Bradshaw spent a significant amount of time trying not to lose his limbs. He was sacked four times for minus 32 yards. Cedrick Hardman, one of the Raiders' designated pass rushers when they went to a four-man defensive line, sacked Bradshaw twice, including the hit that sent the tough veteran quarterback out of the game with a bruised left side.

"We were doing the same things we've been doing all year," said Hardman, "but with more intensity. We had a lot of blitzes from our linebackers and secondary, too, and they worked just fine. Mike Davis, Rod Martin, Ted Hendricks—they all did it."

And the offense played with corresponding feeling.

Plunkett, who also proved his mettle for a second straight week against the Steelers by completing 13 of 21 passes for 247 yards, showed his sensitivity to his teammate, Cliff Branch, in the aftermath of that brilliant performance. At the Pittsburgh airport, waiting to board the plane for the return trip to Oakland, Plunkett reviewed the significance of the victory—one which put the Raiders above the .500 mark—and said softly, "I was really glad for Cliff. He needed that. Cliff is a very sensitive person. This'll help him."

And, of course, it would also help the Raiders down the stretch.

October 26, 1980

Oakland 33/Seattle 14

In 1980, the Raiders picked up the perfect foil for Cliff Branch with the acquisition of Bob Chandler. He was a significant addition in a year of many vital newcomers to the Oakland cast. Not in memory has a team been able to trade for so many key players in one season—particularly a team destined to win a Super Bowl. Chandler and King on the offense, plus Dan Pastorini, who started the first five games. Safety Burgess Owens, cornerback Dwayne O'Steen, defensive end Cedrick Hardman (designated pass rusher) and defensive back Odis McKinney (fifth back in the nickel defense) all arrived in 1980 for late round draft choices, both present and future. And two other regulars, inside linebacker Bob Nelson and placekicker Chris Bahr, were picked up as free agents.

But when the Raiders announced on April 22, before the NFL draft, that veteran Phil Villapiano, one of the most inspirational players of the last decade, had been shipped to Buffalo for

Bob Chandler, isolated wide, waits for the snap of the ball to take off on a precise receiving pattern.

Chandler, reaction was practically nil. What there was might have been negative because Villapiano had been very popular in the community, while Chandler was a virtual unknown to west coast fans.

The Raiders knew all about Bob, however. Tom Flores had coached him in Buffalo during his rookie year. Chandler also had his best day as a pro against Oakland in 1977, catching nine passes. Moreover, from 1975 through 1978, he caught 220 passes, more than any other player in the NFL for that four-year period. He had not caught a pass, though, in 1979, when his time was limited to spot appearances in three games because of a shoulder injury that required surgery.

Before consummating the trade, the Raiders brought Chandler out to Oakland and worked him out. He was pronounced 100 per cent fit. Still, at 31, rounding out a decade of pro ball, he didn't figure to be more than a spare receiver. In training camp, they roomed him with Pastorini, and he came up with back spasms that limited his availability. But the Raider coaches also saw that he was faster than Fred Biletnikoff, another smart wide receiver to whom Chandler had always been compared. And he was a surprisingly effective blocker for his position.

In the season opener, he supplanted Morris Bradshaw as the starting wide receiver opposite Branch and caught five passes. He caught at least one pass in each of the Raiders' regular season games, led the team in receiving with 49 catches and scored a team high of 10 touchdowns.

Never was his effectiveness more apparent than against Seattle in the eighth game, when the Raiders stretched their win streak to three games and finally took the measure of a team that had beaten them four times the previous two seasons. In the 33–14 victory over the Seahawks at home, Chandler was the standout receiver on the field, catching five passes and scoring three touchdowns.

Chandler also fit the Raider mold as a personality. During football season, Bob did clever 15-minute sport shows on a local radio station. He showed he was witty. He was personable. He was funny. He was one of those athletes who would probably be working as a nuclear scientist

or a senator from the state of New York if he didn't enjoy catching footballs for a living. (Actually, he has completed work for a law degree.)

The long-tressed veteran with the sure hands looked like he should be carrying a surf board, as befitted a native of southern California—he was born in Long Beach and played his college football for John McKay at Southern California, where he was named the "Player of the Game" in USC's Rose Bowl triumph over Michigan in 1970. The Buffalo Bills made him their No. 7 draft pick in 1971. It was a new world back there for the slim Californian.

"I got the idea," he reminisced, "when I reported to Buffalo's rookie camp and checked into the hotel. Everyone's key fit everyone else's room, the girl at the front desk was a hooker"— he said this facetiously—"and there were rats a foot long in the halls. They made more noise than the humans. We said, 'THIS is pro football?'"

But Chandler's demeanor was eternally calm. He was as nonchalant as a stream in summer, and his favorite expression framed happiness —both on and off the field.

For a 6' 1", 180-pound wide receiver without dazzling speed, he glided past defenders with deceptive bursts of quickness. He also appreciated the change of climate from Buffalo to Oakland and the difference in ambience. "For my first five years with the Bills," he recalled, "I lived at the Buffalo South Exit 56 Motel. It was a truck stop. I bought a '53 Chevy for $100. It had no heat and the radio worked only on songs it liked."

With the Raiders, he took over a posh condominium on Russian Hill in San Francisco,

where he could savor the delights of the city. The place belonged to O. J. Simpson. O. J., who retired as an active player in 1980 to devote his time to flying through airports, was Chandler's teammate at Buffalo during most of Bob's tenure with the Bills. "O. J. was the greatest running back I ever saw," said Bob, "but he couldn't catch a cold." That last reference was to Simpson's hands. Chandler was for the last decade one of the surest handed receivers in football. With a tremendous ability to concentrate on the ball, which led inevitably to those comparisons with Biletnikoff.

"They say that Chandler is like Fred Biletnikoff," said Branch objectively. "Well, let me tell you, he's better. He's faster, quicker, smarter and tougher. The one thing he does that Fred never did is block. That makes a heckuva difference."

In the Seattle game, the Raiders held a tenuous 6–0 lead at halftime before Chandler swung into high gear. In the third quarter, Plunkett rifled a pass to him in the end zone from the five-yard line on third down. One minute into the fourth quarter, Chandler ran a flag pattern into the right corner and caught a 12-yard toss for a second touchdown.

He saved the best for last. After the Seahawks responded following the kickoff with an 80-yard scoring drive, the Raiders got good field position after an onside kick attempt and moved to the Seattle 23-yard line. On first down, Plunkett fired high toward Chandler, who again ran an "out" pattern that took him over the goal line. The receiver was double-covered by cornerback Kerry Justin and free safety Keith Simpson. "I

Bob Chandler

was trying to throw the ball away," Plunkett admitted. But Chandler went high over Justin with his left arm extended, clutched the ball with the fingers of that hand and then held on to it tenaciously as he crashed to the ground.

"Routine," deadpanned Chandler. "We practice that play all the time." More seriously, he added, "Their guy [Justin] had me covered. When the play was over, he helped me up and said, 'Great catch.' That doesn't happen very much." He meant getting such encomiums from a frustrated defender.

"I feel I've done everything the Raiders have asked me to do since I've been here," said Chandler, "and the team has started to play good football, and that's the important thing."

Chandler scored all the Oakland touchdowns against Seattle. Because of his sure hands, he also took the snap and placed the ball for Chris Bahr's four field goals.

The defense continued to sparkle, balancing the offensive fireworks over the last three games.

Jim Zorn, who habitually ripped the Raiders with his ability to move out of the pocket and find open receivers, was sacked six times for minus 44 yards (the Raiders had only gotten to him a total of five times in their previous four meetings). "That's probably the strongest rush we've felt as a team," said the Seattle southpaw. "You could see on film that they are playing more enthusiastically this season than last year." Cornerback Lester Hayes picked off two of Zorn's passes.

"We had to do something," said Hayes. "Against Pittsburgh and San Diego, we were essentially in Cover Three, which is a zone coverage, and we were dropping seven guys back. Hey, we were getting killed. We gave up over 700 yards."

Now, and for the rest of the season, they would tilt more to straight man coverage, dropping in occasional zones to keep the other teams guessing but featuring blitzes by linebackers such as Ted Hendricks to put pressure on the quarterbacks. And induce fear.

Chandler knew what that was like, having once been on the other side of the line.

"Everybody just hated the Raiders," he mused. "I think it's the color of their uniforms. They always had the reputation of being dirty and nasty players. You were put on alert right away that the Raiders were coming to town, the Raiders were coming to town.

"This is not really a dirty team, but that's an image I think we have to keep. There's something about being pictured as extra mean when you're a football player that is of benefit to you. It keeps the other teams in the league afraid of Oakland Raiders football, and I think that's good."

A smile crossed his handsome face as he said it.

Designated pass rushers Cedrick Hardman (86) and Willie Jones (90) converge on Seattle quarterback Jim Zorn for a bruising sack.

Momentum Is the Name of the Game • 7

November 2, 1980

Oakland 16/Miami 10

For years, the Oakland Raiders were a "left-handed" team, in more ways than one. Not only was the Raider quarterback Ken Stabler a southpaw, but when the team needed an important first down, it was common knowledge that the Raiders ran to the left.

There have been any number of theories to explain this tendency, including the idea that it all depended on Stabler. It was suggested that it was easier for Stabler to hand off with his left hand, and that's why he called plays to that side.

A moment's thought would have destroyed that theory. When Stabler turned around, he had his back to the line, and his left hand was on the right side of the line. To run left, Stabler had to hand off with his right hand. You can put that idea in the same bin with the one that said Stabler would never be a successful quarterback because a pass from a left-handed quarterback spirals in the opposite direction from a right-hander's pass, making it more difficult to catch.

Actually, of course, there were two big reasons for the Raiders' tendency to run left—very big. Their names were Art Shell and Gene Upshaw, and they added up to 535 pounds and eight all-pro designations, four apiece. The Raiders didn't care if everyone knew which way they were going to run. With Shell and Upshaw leading the way, their attitude was: "Let's see you stop us."

But although the rest of the NFL had little success in stopping Shell and Upshaw, a combined total of 27 years of play in the league was slowing them.

Shell suffered an injury in the 1979 season that forced him out of the first five games of the year and broke his streak of playing in 156 consecutive games.

Upshaw got through the season uninjured—with his streak of 186 consecutive games intact—but then suffered a freak, off-season injury to his back while weight lifting. Although the Raiders

maintained that Upshaw's condition was not a problem, reserve tackle Lindsey Mason was moved over to guard to help provide insurance, just in case.

Shell responded nicely following his injury, capping the 1980–81 season with his eighth Pro Bowl. Upshaw's back was not a problem, and he finished the year playing in his two-hundred-and-second consecutive league game and twenty-fourth straight post-season game.

Nevertheless, the Raider offense made a shift to the right in 1980, toward a couple of the Raider "youngsters," 28-year-old Henry Lawrence and 24-year-old guard Mickey Marvin. Shell and Upshaw had been known as "The Bull" and "Uppie," respectively, by the Raiders, but the 1980 season signaled the beginning of what may be the era of "Sparky" (Marvin) and "Killer" (Lawrence).

Marvin had arrived at the Raider camp four years before, out of Tennessee, where he had received All-American mention, and played in the East-West Game. Upshaw watched the feisty young guard in practice one day and dubbed him "Sparky" for a spunky dog Gene had when he was a kid.

Marvin was one of the biggest guards in the NFL. At 270 pounds, he was not likely to be overpowered by defensive linemen, and he was surprisingly agile. When he left the line to lead the blocking on the sweep, something Upshaw seemed to be doing less frequently, he was an awesome sight.

In the third game of the regular season, teams began to see Marvin popping up on their game films. The Raiders were having their problems with Washington at the time, holding onto a 10–7 lead in the third quarter, and their first drive of the second half had sputtered and died.

The second time the Raiders got the ball, they were 70 yards from the goal line. Three

To his fellow Raiders, guard Mickey Marvin is sometimes known as "Sparky"—so dubbed by Gene Upshaw.

Vociferous determination has earned the designation of "Killer" for offensive tackle Henry Lawrence.

straight runs got the ball to the Oakland 48, where quarterback Dan Pastorini called a sweep around the right end. Halfback Arthur Whittington was stopped for no gain, and Marvin got up and snapped his fingers. He knew he'd missed a block, but he'd learned something.

Three plays later, Whittington went around right end again. When he turned the corner, there were only two people between him and the goal line—Washington cornerback Lemar Parrish and Mickey Marvin. Parrish never touched Whittington as he scored from 42 yards out.

The play became a Raider trademark for the season. When the Raiders hosted San Diego in the sixth game of the season, Oakland scored the first time it had the ball. The fifth play of the 60-yard drive was a sweep around the right end by Kenny King, who followed Marvin into the end zone. No one touched him all 31 yards.

Marvin, a self-proclaimed country boy from Hendersonville, N.C., took it all in stride in his appealing "aw shucks" manner. The two biggest

things to happen to him, he said, were his recent marriage and his rebirth as a Christian.

"Just say I'm a Christian," he said during the season. "A lot of people say they are religious."

Marvin met his wife Lisa at tryouts for the Raiderettes, the Oakland cheerleading group. Marvin picked out his future bride as an excellent prospect. She had the same impression of him.

Henry Lawrence would be a story worth telling even if he never played professional football.

Lawrence was born 28 years before Super Bowl XV in a camp for migrant workers in Danville, Pa. His mother followed the crops north from Palmetto, Fla., and was picking potatoes just days before she gave birth to Henry, her third child.

Like his brothers and sisters, Henry went to work in the fields, spending most of the next 15 years stooped over, picking potatoes, beans, corn, cherries, peaches, apples and brussel sprouts.

Sometimes he used to see men from his hometown driving around in long Cadillacs with beautiful girls in the front seat. He wondered how they could afford such fine things.

"They're hustlers, pimps," he was told. He wondered what a pimp was. It seemed like a dream.

"There were times when we sneaked out into the potato field at night and dug them up," Lawrence said. "It was all we had. We didn't know where our next meal was coming from. I slept with a knife in my hand, and I used to practice flipping it out."

When he came back to school in Palmetto after the crops were picked, it wasn't easy to admit he was a migrant worker.

"I used to feel so embarrassed," he said. "The kids used to call me season tramp and picked at me. But I always had some change in my picket. I used to loan some of those goody-two-shoes some money. That was when I decided this ain't so bad. It's an honest living."

There was no quit in the Lawrence family. Henry's mother had six children, four boys and two girls. Each of them attended college. Henry's older sister has a master's degree and sells real estate in Los Angeles. One of his brothers graduated from Florida A&M and now runs a warehouse. One is a contractor for migrant workers. The only boy who played football was Henry; the other two received academic scholarships. Mrs. Lawrence convinced them all to believe in themselves.

"I never lacked the confidence," Henry said. "But for a while that was the only thing I had going for me."

Henry was always big, and when he was in high school he was a sensation on the football field, playing tight end, defensive end and wide receiver. As a junior, he received letters from major colleges all over the South and was all-city, all-district, all-state and listed in Who's Who in Florida High Schools.

But the integration issue closed Lincoln High School in Palmetto—which was mostly black—and Henry was bussed to Manatee High in nearby Bradenton, which was mostly white.

Neither Lawrence nor any of the black ath-letes played that year. At defensive end, Lawrence's position, the coach played a 130-pounder.

"He was a fiery dude," Lawrence said, "but he wasn't Henry Lawence."

What did the coach say when Lawrence asked why he wasn't playing?

"Never asked," Lawrence said. "I just sat there. It happens all over, you know. Not just white schools. It happens in black schools, too."

Lawrence still made honorable mention on the high school All-American team on the strength of what he'd done in his junior year, but the major colleges weren't interested any more. He planned on attending Southern University.

But that wasn't good enough for Willie Clements. Clements had been Lawrence's coach at Lincoln, and it was his dream that Henry would go to Florida A&M.

"He begged me and pleaded with me," Lawrence recalled. "Finally, he threatened me, and I decided I'd better go."

At the time, Henry Lawrence was 6′ 4″ and weighed 220 pounds. Willie Clements was 5′ 8″.

They weren't very interested in Lawrence once he arrived at A&M. He was third string through his sophomore year and thought he might quit. He called his mother, and she said that would be just fine.

"I helped you and took care of you," Mrs. Lawrence told him. "And now if you want to quit school, come on home. Just you get ready to get out in that field. The tomatoes are just getting ripe."

"Maybe I'll just stay in school," Henry told her.

In his junior year, Lawrence's third coach in three years, Jim Williams, shifted him to offensive tackle. Lawrence didn't like the position very much, and he was still third string.

On the first day of practice, he remembered something Willie Clements used to tell him—that when the play went away from your side of the line, you should get down field and knock somebody over. Lawrence decided to give that a try.

It was an unpleasant surprise for the defensive backs to get blind-sided by a run-away tackle, and they let Lawrence know just how little they appreciated it.

Henry Lawrence prefers blocking tacklers to his boyhood vocation of crop-picker.

But one of the alums, who had played a little pro ball, was at the scrimmage, and every time Lawrence would level someone, he would let out a whoop, using an old nickname of Lawrence's.

"Killer!" he'd scream. "Whooooo-eee! At-a-way-to-go!"

It was the first time anyone had complimented Lawrence since he'd arrived at A&M, and he intended to keep the compliments coming. A lot of linebackers and defensive backs went into the whirlpool after practice.

And it happened that was the day pro scouts had come to A&M, to look at the top prospects. At the conclusion of the workout, they asked, "Now where's this Killer we keep hearing about?"

The scouts timed Killer but didn't believe the time and made him run the 40 again. The scouts told Williams he had a real prospect, and the next day Lawrence was the first string tackle.

In the year of Super Bowl XV, Lawrence was playing his seventh season for the Raiders. In the off-season he still lived in Palmetto, where he had a farm. When the crops ripened, he used migrant workers to pick them. The same workers came back year after year.

At 270 pounds, Marvin and Lawrence fit the mold of the Raider linemen of the past, but they had yet to prove themselves when the 1980–81

football season began. The Raiders were still considered a left-handed team.

It is hard to say when that impression was changed, but a good example was the ninth game of the regular season, against Miami.

The Raiders went into the game with a 5-and-3 record, and were coming off that impressive throttling of Seattle, 33–14, in which quarterback Jim Plunkett threw three touchdown passes to Chandler. Plunkett had not had a sub-par game since he took over in the fifth game of the season.

In fact, over the three previous games, he had been the hottest quarterback in the NFL. But everyone wondered if he'd cool off—at least a little—and against Miami, in Oakland, he did.

The Raiders seemed to come apart all at once. Somewhere between the first half, when Oakland had taken a 16–3 lead, and the second half, the offense disappeared. Four Raider fumbles didn't help, and neither did Plunkett's three interceptions and three sacks—two of each in the second half.

But the Raiders already had the lead. The idea was to keep it, to refuse to give Miami the ball. They did it by running.

The Raiders finished the game with 192 yards rushing on 43 carries, a 4.5-yard average per carry. Oakland gained 102 of those yards in the second half, rushing 25 times.

The Raiders finished the game with 20 first downs, half by rushing. They controlled the ball for 36 minutes and 56 seconds, almost 14 minutes longer than the Dolphins. They ran 72 offensive plays—compared to Miami's 50—and gained an average of 4.5 yards on 43 runs.

The Raiders did not score a point in the second half, and although the 16–10 final score was not impressive, the totals were.

And the surprising part was that the Raiders gained 105 of those yards running to the RIGHT side, behind Messrs. Marvin and Lawrence—the other guys.

So far, no one has suggested that the Raiders are a right-handed team—or said Plunkett's the reason—but in 1980 they couldn't be called left-handed either. The offensive line had a new characteristic—balance.

The value of the "nickel" or fifth defensive back is graphic as Odis McKinney grapples with San Diego's Kellen Winslow for the football, and wins the wrestling match in front of his Raider mates.

The swiftness of Clifford Branch in the open field makes him among the most feared wide receivers in modern football history.

Kenny King lends an extra dimension of speed to the Raider running attack as he sprints wide behind his blocking escort.

John Matuszak (72) and Ted Hendricks (83) form a tall, impenetrable barrier on the left side of the Raider defense.

Gene Upshaw sets up to block, a formidable barrier for the opposing defense.

Jim Plunkett, rearing back to throw, feels safety behind the protective blocking of guard Mickey Marvin (65).

Matt Millen (55), who calls the defensive signals on the field, takes instruction from linebacker coach Charlie Sumner.

Out of the hold of Bobby Chandler, Chris Bahr (10) boots a long 46-yard field goal against the Eagles.

Oakland 28/Cincinnati 17

Maybe they weren't artistic, but the Raiders were winning. In the tenth week of the season, while the Denver Broncos were visiting San Diego and upsetting the Chargers, the new Cinderella kids of the NFL were entertaining the Cincinnati Bengals in Oakland and stretching their victory streak to five straight.

Despite a flurry of miscues, the Raiders managed to win, 28–17, and moved into sole possession of first place with a 7-and-3 record. The Raiders coughed up the ball five times, and the Bengals recovered three of those fumbles. Plunkett threw two interceptions for a total of five turnovers. Moreover, the Raiders were penalized 12 times, with Cincinnati picking up first downs on seven of those occasions. Oakland even managed to get its team doctor, Donald Fink, and the official photographer, Russ Reed, thrown off the field for questioning calls by the game officials.

Two Raider penalties nullified a pair of interceptions by cornerback Lester Hayes. If those plays had remained on the books, Lester the Molester would have broken the all-time season record in the NFL for pass interceptions.

But momentum is a strong ally in football. Although the Bengals had some success in controlling the ball in the first half with a ground attack—Charles Alexander picked up 43 yards on nine carries—the Raiders built a slim 14–10 lead by converting eight-for-eight on third down situations.

The pendulum of the game swung on the opening kickoff of the third quarter, when Arthur Whittington caught the ball on his own 10-yard line and threaded 90 yards down the field for a touchdown that gave the Raiders a comfortable 21–10 margin.

Then the defense took over. It limited Alexander to nine yards on five carries in the last two quarters and shut off the Bengal running attack with 25 yards on 11 carries. Already leading the NFL in sacks and interceptions, the Raiders tackled the Cincinnati quarterbacks, Jack Thompson and Ken Anderson, three times behind the line of scrimmage and picked off four passes. Cedrick Hardman, the reclaimed veteran end, had two of those sacks. Young Willie Jones, the other end,

also applied pressure. Odis McKinney, a New York Giant castoff, had two interceptions.

Midway through the fourth quarter, when the Bengals drew close again, the offense came alive with a scoring drive of 49 yards as Plunkett completed three passes and then carried the ball into the end zone himself the final four yards.

Basically, though, the defense was still carrying the team, in part because the training camp gamble with a Bible-reading, stocky ex-defensive tackle from Penn State was paying off. The Raiders had moved Matt Millen, a raw rookie, into a regular job at inside linebacker. Penn State is famous for linebackers, and Coach Joe Paterno had told Matt when he enrolled that he could be a professional linebacker, although he would spend most of his varsity career at tackle.

Aside from the Raider coaching staff that drafted him, no one in Oakland seemed to know much about Matt Millen when he was chosen as the Raiders' second pick in the 1980 draft.

Most of the attention went to the Raiders' first choice, Brigham Young quarterback Marc Wilson. The Raiders were so surprised to see Wilson still on the board when they had their choice that they immediately snapped him up, even though their first need was a linebacker. The Raiders had looked long and hard at North Carolina linebacker Buddy Curry and hoped that he might be available when they got their second pick. But Atlanta took Curry as the thirty-sixth player chosen, and the Raiders, picking forty-third, selected Millen from Penn State.

It was a gamble. Not only had Millen played defensive tackle for virtually his entire college career, he missed the final three games of his senior year, suffering from back spasms. But the Raiders were convinced that Millen was healthy. They also had a history of success in taking defensive linemen and "standing them up." Monte Johnson, who was expected to play alongside him as the other inside linebacker, had been a "down" lineman during his college days at Nebraska. In fact, he hadn't even been a starter for the Cornhuskers. Unfortunately, Johnson suffered an injury in the pre-season play which knocked him out of the entire 1980 Super Bowl season. When

Despite his rookie status, Matt Millen shows leadership qualities as he steps into a regular job.

Millen checked into camp, he was given number 55, the same one worn by Dan Conners, another defensive lineman in college who turned into an excellent linebacker for the Raiders and later became a team scout.

Millen was philosophical. He'd originally been recruited in college as a linebacker.

"When he was recruiting me," Millen said, "Coach Paterno told me I could play professional football as a linebacker. What he didn't tell me was that I'd have to play in the line for four years."

Certainly, Millen was one of the biggest and strongest linebackers anyone had ever seen. As a freshman in high school, Millen was a 5′ 8″, 135-pound flanker. "And then," he said, "I turned into a fanatic. There's not much to do in Hokendauqua, Pennsylvania [his home town]. People lift weights, drink beer and get into fights."

By the time he was a senior, he weighed 235-pounds and was one of the strongest men in Hokendauqua. He was also one tough customer.

When a calcium deposit formed in his arm — the result of clotheslining a ballcarrier — he found that he could not straighten his elbow. He put his arm in a vise, and when that didn't work, went to the doctor, who told him he would have to stop lifting weights. Instead, he went home and kept lifting. Eventually, the arm unlocked.

When he reached Penn State, Millen saw only one player who looked as strong — Bruce Clark, who became an All-American tackle. The two set out to test each other the first chance they got. Millen threw Clark down. On the next play, Clark took Millen down, and Millen punched him. Clark punched him back, and they began to grin at each other in mutual respect.

The two became fierce rivals and best friends, which resulted in an unofficial record when they were being tested by NFL teams just before the draft.

Clark and Millen attended the New England workout together and were told that the first order of business was to bench press 200 pounds as many times as possible.

"What's the record?" Millen wanted to know.

"Never mind about that," said the coach, "just do your best."

"What's the record?" Millen and Clark persisted.

"Well," said the coach, "no one has ever done any more than 35, but if you can't do that many don't worry."

"So we each did 45 and stopped," Millen explained later.

There was, obviously, no doubt that Millen was strong enough to play in the NFL, but there was some concern that he would not be fast enough. He reported to camp at 260 pounds, but the Raiders said they wanted him to play at 250 pounds, and he did most of the season.

The Raiders liked what they saw. Millen was bright and tough, and defensive coach Charlie Sumner made an early decision.

"They called me in during training camp and they said they were going to give me some responsibility," Millen said. "I told them that was fine, that I responded to responsibility."

Millen's job was to call the defensive signals, picking them up from Sumner on the sideline and then calling out the offensive formation once the opposition lined up. It was a mark of the confidence the Raiders had in Millen and a good psychological ploy, making Millen feel as little like a rookie as possible. For his part, Millen seemed unaffected by professional football.

"I never really followed pro football to tell you the truth," Millen admitted. "When I was in college, I followed college football, and when I was in high school that was all I cared about. I knew of some of the Raiders—like Art (Shell), Kick'em (Ted Hendricks) and Uppie (Gene Upshaw)—and I wanted to see them, but that was about it."

For their part, the Raider players were still trying to get a fix on Millen, who was beginning to look like a rookie starter in the Raider "Orange" or 3–4 defense. On one hand, there was Millen the linebacker, who had a tendency to forget that some of the practice drills were supposed to be non-contact. But after practice, there was Millen the Christian, who read the Bible with fellow rookie Marc Wilson.

Millen was called "Spike"—for the bulldog in the cartoons—by the veterans during training camp, but he quickly became "Bub," since that's what he called everyone else.

He was never seen off the field without his battered green baseball cap. When the San Francisco *Chronicle* conducted a player poll, Millen looked like a shoo-in for "worst-dressed teammate," but the award went to tackle Henry Lawrence instead. The reason, suggested guard Gene Upshaw, was that since Millen had worn nothing but shorts, sandals, a grey T-shirt and his green cap during the first weeks of training camp—"we haven't seen him dressed yet." When the veterans begin to kid the rookies like that, you can bet that they've been accepted, and Millen had been.

"They didn't hand me the starting job," Millen said, "but they sort of rolled it my way. I thought I had a good chance to play. The rover backer position was open, since they traded [Phil] Villapiano. I'm where he was."

But Millen was supposed to learn the position next to Monte Johnson, a seasoned Raider veteran, who would be starting his eighth year. That plan was ruined in the third exhibition game of the year when Johnson, playing on the kickoff

return team for the first time in years, tore ligaments in his knee and was lost for the season.

Yet the Raiders were happy enough with the play of Millen to stay in the 3–4 defense except for obvious passing downs. Bob Nelson, a free agent, filled in for Johnson, and when Nelson was injured, Randy McClanahan, another free agent, took over. The Raider defense was the surprise of the year.

"It's really an easy game," Millen shrugged. "All you do it find the ball and knock the guy down."

But the Raider defense was not finding it easy to stop the opposition, particularly on the ground, in the first seven games of the year. San Diego, Buffalo and Pittsburgh all ran for more than 100 yards against the Raiders, and Kansas City did it twice. In five of the first seven games, the Raiders surrendered more than 100 yards rushing, and lost three of them.

When the Raiders defeated Pittsburgh on Monday night football, 45–34, linebacker Randy McClanahan said after the game, "I don't think anybody stopped anybody."

Clearly, the Raiders could not depend on their offense to score 45 points in every game. The Raider defense, starting three players—Millen, McClanahan and safety Burgess Owens—who were not even on the team the year before, had to find itself.

It did, and just in time. Over the next three games, the Raider defense did not allow more than 70 yards rushing, and allowed just 13.5 points per game over the next four. The Raider offense had tailed off, but the defense was picking up the slack. Part of the reason may have been that Millen began to understand his role in the defensive scheme.

He had served notice from the beginning that he was not to be trifled with.

"Nobody, but nobody, is going to intimidate Matt Millen," said free safety Owens.

"If anybody wants to mix it up on the field," Millen said, "fine. That's what I'm there for."

Millen was finding that, like in college, he was stronger than nearly everyone on the field.

"I rely on my strength a lot," Millen said. "Maybe too much. I'm only 6′ 1½″. I'm never going to be 6′ 7″, like Ted Hendricks. All I ever cared about was getting bigger and stronger."

Teams attempted to confuse him with misdirection and "sucker" plays, trying to get him to read the blocking instead of the ball. And for a while, Millen admitted he was staying back, trying to read the play as it developed.

"At times I tried to read it," Millen said, "but the coaches don't want that. All you want to do is react—just attack. You look at their tendencies, and the down and distance, but it comes back to me—me attacking. That's what they want."

And that's what they got.

November 17, 1980

Oakland 19/Seattle 17

Three weeks earlier, in Oakland, the Raiders had totally overwhelmed the Seattle Seahawks in as crisp and effective a victory as anyone could imagine on a fall day. But the intervening games with the Dolphins and Bengals were narrow wins, and there were those who wondered aloud if the Raiders' one-game cushion over San Diego was leaving them ripe for an upset. They were very nearly right.

Fourteen seconds into the fourth quarter, Efren Herrera kicked a 37-yard field goal to cap a 62-yard, 12-play drive that gave Seattle a 17–7 lead.

Jim Plunkett's next pass was intercepted. Following a Seahawk punt, the Raiders' next drive went three plays, lost two yards and produced a punt. There were people in the Kingdome looking for their rain gear, wondering what the traffic would be like on the way home.

The Seahawks picked up six yards on their next drive and prepared to punt. As long as the clock was running, they'd settle for playing one-two-three-punt with the Raiders. At least, that's the way it seemed. After the game, Raider defensive back Lester Hayes would swear that Herman Weaver never intended to punt, that the play was a run-pass fake.

It didn't matter because it never came off. Hendricks and Hayes were in on Weaver too quickly for him to do anything except exactly what he did—kick the ball as hard as possible into the arm of Ted Hendricks.

It was, hands down, the best thing that could have possibly happened for Oakland. There were

those who complained that Hayes should have recovered the ball in the end zone after it bounced from Weaver to Hendricks.

"If I'd had a smidgen more stick'um," Hayes said, "it would have been academic."

But there was one big benefit to the punt rolling out of the back of the end zone for a safety—which is what happened. The Raiders got two important things: two points (which turned out to be the margin of victory), and the ball.

After a free kick, Oakland took the ball on its own 41, and Plunkett threw two long passes to young tight end Derrick Ramsey. The first was incomplete. The second went 58 yards, setting up a one-yard touchdown run by Mark van Eeghen. Nine points in three-and-a-half minutes. And Seattle couldn't have controlled the ball because the Seahawks never got to touch it, except when Weaver free kicked. Suddenly it was Seattle 17, Oakland 16.

Then the Raiders proceeded to wrap up the game as follows: a Lester Hayes interception at 4:20, two Plunkett scrambles for a first down, an 18-yard pass to Ramsey and a 28-yard Chris Bahr field goal. The Raiders took a 19–17 lead with nearly a minute to spare and held Seattle without a first down.

At the time it didn't seem like much, but Hendricks' block of that punt—his twentieth block and fourth safety, both NFL records—started the whole sequence that gave Oakland the lead and the game, keeping the Raiders one game ahead of the Chargers, with Philadelphia coming up—in Philadelphia.

"Colorful" and "free spirit" are used to describe Ted Hendricks but don't shroud his serious side as a linebacker.

It must have made the Raider coaches think that if Hendricks wanted to pull some crazy stunts during the week, that maybe they'd just wink at it.

Some day, Ted Hendricks would retire from professional football. In fact, after Super Bowl XV, he admitted that he had been seriously thinking about making the 1980 season his last—at least until he was named all-pro for the fifth time. Now, he said, he might just play another year or so.

The sighs of relief from Oakland Raider coaches and Bay Area sports writers could be heard all the way to Seattle. Not only was Hendricks an excellent linebacker, a proven team leader and a man who made the big play, he was as colorful as a Pacific sunset.

"A free spirit?" Hendricks asked rhetorically. "I've been called that. But I don't go out of my way to do things. They just happen spontaneously."

But somehow, they seem to happen to Hendricks more often.

Like the day former Raider coach John Madden, standing on the practice field at Santa Rosa, yelled, "All right, everybody out here right now!"

Hendricks came at a gallop.

"Just before practice I saw this guy with a horse," Hendricks said. "I talked him into bringing it over to the practice field. When Madden yelled, they opened the gate, and I rode it out to the 50 on a dead run, pulled it up, jumped off and said, 'Let's get started.'"

"Ted was one of my favorite players," Madden said. "But the thing was, if you didn't enjoy him, didn't laugh with him, he'd drive you crazy. The most amazing person in the world has to be his wife, Janet, because she has to live with that.

"I asked her once how she stood it, and she said 'I'm into bird watching.' I remember thinking maybe that's what I should do—get into birds."

Speaking of birds, it should be said that Hendricks has never been fond of his "Mad Stork" nickname, much preferring "Kick 'em," which is what the Raiders call him. But Stork has been a nickname that refused to die, despite Hendricks' best efforts to stop it, beginning at the University of Miami, where he was a three-time All-America defensive end.

With his gangly build, it's easy to see how it got started. Hendricks is a wispy 225 pounds, which isn't much on a 6' 7" frame, and when he came into the league, he was 10 pounds lighter.

But Hendricks' long arms—he wears a 37 sleeve—are a biological marvel. They are huge, appearing to have been built for a much bigger man, then grafted onto Hendricks' slender trunk. Even in the NFL, not many defenders can flatten a ballcarrier with a swipe of the arm. Hendricks can not only do it, but for him it's standard procedure.

"I'm from the old school," he said, when asked if he ever worried about hurting someone on the field. "I figure that's what you're supposed to do. If you hurt them a little the first time, they don't come back so fast the next time."

That's why Hendricks has been called "Stork," but the "mad" part can be taken more than one way.

Like the day Madden was calling out the positions on the special teams. When Madden said "left tackle," that player was supposed to yell out his name. If he forgot, it meant a fine.

"Madden was calling them out, and I was in another room," Hendricks said. "I didn't want to bust into the meeting, so I went through the switchboard and told them I had an emergency phone call for John Madden."

"You know how you are when you get an emergency phone call," Madden said. "All I could think was there was something wrong with my wife or kids."

"When he answered the phone," Hendricks grinned, "I said, 'Hendricks!'"

"What?" Madden replied.

"Hendricks!" Hendricks repeated. "Didn't you just call right end?"

With that, Hendricks hung up. Madden, who had his pride, never said a word to him about the call.

"I think," Hendricks said, "he finally reached the point where I didn't faze him."

The two parted on the best of terms. In fact, when he retired, Madden received a gift from Hendricks that was really touching—in its way.

"As soon as he heard, Ted came over to see me at home," Madden said. "On the way over, he saw a 'Yield' sign. He thought that would be a nice gift for me. So he knocked it over with his car, pulled it out of the ground and brought it over. I still have it."

But there was a method to Hendricks' madness. The Raiders, and the coaches, were quick to acknowledge the benefits of Hendricks' ability to lighten the load over the long NFL season.

For example, it took a good deal of extra effort for Hendricks to put together his "Hurricane Machine" for workouts at the Santa Rosa training camp two seasons ago.

An impressive collection of wheels and pulleys, the Hurricane Machine was for use after practice, as a supplement to weight training. Although the two large drums on either end of a steel bar looked impressive, in fact they were virtually weightless, allowing the user to run through endless lifts without getting tired.

"Sometimes," Hendricks said, "I'd do some with one hand."

Also included were devices, incorporating the maximum in appearance and the minimum in effort, for the legs, neck and stomach. There was also a holder for a can of beer.

"The point of the Hurricane Machine," Hendricks explained, "was to make you feel good. After practice, when you were exhausted, and didn't think you could do anything more, you could take a workout on the Hurricane Machine and feel strong again."

The Raider coaches, who drove the players through two-a-day practices at Santa Rosa, knew the benefits of a morale builder and let Hendricks set it up next to the weight machines. They also kept quiet when Hendricks put feathers on his practice helmet.

Hendricks' sense of humor was also helpful as the playoff pressure began to build later in the 1980 season. The Raiders' locker room became a mob scene, as reporters who had not covered a game all season jumped aboard the Raider bandwagon. Repeating the same answers to the same questions began to get on everyone's nerves. Hendricks was one of the Raiders who used humor to handle the situation.

"How can you stop a great passer like Dan Fouts?" one reporter asked before the playoff game with the Chargers.

"Well," Hendricks said, dead pan, "one year I broke his thumb, and that seemed to slow him down pretty well."

Once, as Dwayne O'Steen, a newcomer to the Raiders, was giving a television interview, Hendricks slipped behind the camera and dropped his pants. Neither the sportscaster or the camera could see Hendricks, but O'Steen got the message: don't take this too seriously.

There were times, of course, when Hendricks' antics left the coaches grinning through gritted teeth. He stepped to the beat of his own drummer, as he showed the year he reported three days late to the Raider mini-camp because he was taking his family on a long camping trip in the northwest.

And although he has always been confident of his abilities, the same can not be said of the Raiders, who sat him on the bench through most

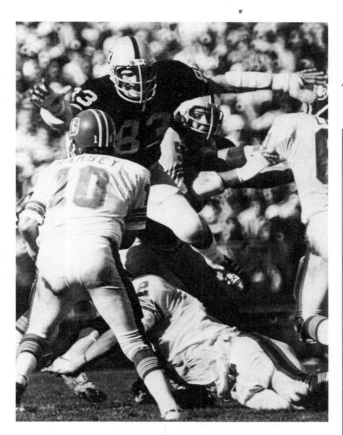

The hurtling form of Ted Hendricks has discouraged NFL quarterbacks for a dozen years.

of 1975, the year they acquired him as a free agent. A four-time all-pro at the time, Hendricks did not suffer in silence.

"I didn't come here to sit on the bench," he said. "If I had known, I probably would have gone somewhere else."

Hendricks began by going through channels. He went to head coach John Madden and asked politely to be given more playing time. Madden, just as politely, told him he was not ready to make a change.

Hendricks changed tactics.

On Monday Night Football, the ABC camera panned the bench, finishing up with Hendricks, who was sitting quietly watching the action—wearing a harlequin mask he'd purchased at the Renaissance Fair.

"To protect the innocent—and the guilty—I'll never tell how I got it on the field," Hendricks said. "The important thing is that I did it."

Actually, what was more important was that when he got his chance, Hendricks was very good.

In his first season with Oakland, he got his first real start when defensive end Tony Cline was hurt. Hendricks had three sacks and was the sensation of the game. The Raiders decided they

could put up with his pranks and traded Gerald Irons, who had been playing ahead of him.

Hendricks still had some things to teach the Raiders, but overall he was on his way. Although Ted had lost some of his speed, a necessity for the outside linebacker position, rookie linebacker Matt Millen marveled at Hendricks' sense of anticipation. And there is no telling how many postgame interviews with opposing quarterbacks began with "I had no idea he was so tall."

Hendricks used his height, and his 37 sleeve, to knock down the football with impressive regularity. When the season began, Hendricks had batted down 19 punts, field goals and extra points, an NFL record. Hendricks thought he could use the same kind of move to push the passer, but the Raiders disagreed.

They were convinced in the 1980 season, the year Hendricks was named defensive captain. It was also the year they began to leave Hendricks in the game in obvious passing situations.

Typically, he began lining up all over the field. Typically, it worked. Even Raider defensive coordinator Charlie Sumner, the mind behind the defensive scheme, admitted that the number of blitzes he called and the number Hendricks called "were about 50–50."

"If we're smart enough to rush a linebacker," Hendricks said, "they're smart enough to put someone there to block me."

And Hendricks was smart enough to go elsewhere. Sometimes, he'd start to the right, then dart into the line between the center and guard. It was a perfect ploy. Now unpredictable Ted Hendricks was driving **everyone** crazy.

By the Super Bowl, he had nine sacks, three interceptions and two blocked kicks. He was an obvious choice for all-pro, an honor he had last achieved in 1974, before he came to the Raiders. And he had become a real captain, infusing the team with his spirit, his general refusal to let the world wear him down. He refused to quit being Ted Hendricks.

Ted Hendricks just as he is was a positive factor in that defeat of Seattle in the eleventh game of the season.

Philadelphia 10/Oakland 7

The Raiders piled onto their charter on Friday afternoon, November 21, and departed for Philadelphia riding the tail of a six-game high. So far they hadn't lost a game with Jim Plunkett starting at quarterback, although the offense had stumbled at times. Their six-game victory streak had boosted them into first place in the AFC West.

There was only one team in the entire NFL that was hotter. The Philadelphia Eagles. Their record stood at 10-and-1, and they hadn't lost in seven weeks. Under Dick Vermeil, they had become an emotional, intense team—emulating their coach—which believed in itself and which had a defense that matched the Raiders in tight-wad effectiveness.

In fact, the first half was a throwback to neanderthal football. Neither team scored. The Raiders did penetrate to the Philadelphia 5-yard line early in the first quarter, but Raymond Chester fumbled after catching a pass and Jerry Robinson recovered for the Eagles. Five minutes later, Chris Bahr tried a 45-yard field goal, and the ball glanced off the right upright. Those were the only scoring threats of the first 30 minutes of play. The Eagles only got past midfield once, on their first possession of the game, when they reached the Oakland 43-yard line.

The second half started out the same way, although Tony Franklin startled the Oakland contingent by kicking a 51-yard field goal halfway through the third quarter for the first score of the game. At 3:23 (three minutes, 23 seconds) of the fourth quarter, the Raiders finally cut loose.

Plunkett had been throwing repeatedly to Bob Chandler on deep sideline patterns, with the wide receiver covered one-on-one by cornerback Roynell Young, a rookie. They had barely missed connections several times, including four straight incompletions at the end of the first half.

Plunkett had also been sacked six times (and would go down behind the line eight times during the game) and was under heavy pressure most of the day. But early in the fourth quarter, with Oakland taking over on its 14-yard line, the Raiders lined up in an East Formation, Branch and Chandler split wide to the right. At the snap, Chandler took off and cut to the middle on a post pattern, with Young again picking him up. Branch lagged slightly behind, and Eagle coverage broke down.

Cliff Branch gallops unimpeded toward the end zone to climax an 86-yard strike against the Philadelphia Eagles.

John Matuszak shows his cave man exterior, the one he also uses in a Hollywood acting career.

Cliff was all alone when he caught Plunkett's pass beyond midfield, and he raced down the right side of the field to the end zone for a 7–3 Raider lead.

With just under seven minutes remaining, the Raiders had the Eagles pinned on their 29-yard line. Quarterback Ron Jaworski, back to pass, retreated in the face of a fierce Oakland rush. Linebacker Randy McClanahan, blitzing, jumped to pounce on the Eagle quarterback. Jaworski somehow ducked and eluded his grasp, straightened up and fired a pass to Leroy Harris, a fullback noted for iron hands. The 43-yard gain spurred the Eagles to complete a 71-yard march in eight plays for the decisive touchdown.

It was Philadelphia's only sustained drive of the day because the Raiders for the most part contained the strong running attack led by Wilbert Montgomery, limiting the Eagles to 107 total yards on the ground, sacking Jaworski twice and forcing one interception.

The Oakland forward wall was impenetrable, led by big John Matuszak, who in his fifth year with the Raiders had become a Force.

John Matuszak's real name is Tooz, and he's bigger than life.

He is 6′ 8″ and 280 heavily muscled pounds and is literally the biggest, strongest person many people will ever see. In another era, he'd have been a good circus strong man. The curtains would part, Tooz would flex and spectators would gasp.

In fact, in the off-season that's more or less Tooz's off-season job. He's a circus strong man

for Hollywood. He played a wild-eyed football player (Tooz has a fierce glare) in "North Dallas Forty" and he was the biggest, strongest caveman in "Caveman."

He was, everyone agreed, a good actor.

"I can remember my lines and I can walk from one place to another," Tooz said, paraphrasing Spencer Tracy's definition of good acting. "And I've got a lot of emotion."

But it's not all acting. Sometimes, Tooz said, when he is watching a sad movie, he gets choked up. And sometimes he gets mad. Tooz has had a series of misadventures with his temper, and they were not all in good fun.

When he started college at Missouri, he went to a fraternity party and caught someone fondling his date.

"I hit him twice," Tooz said. "At 18 you don't expect to hurt anybody with a couple of smacks, but I did. He was hurt real bad. Every bone in his face was broken."

Tooz finished his college career at the University of Tampa.

Even today, those experiences clearly pained Tooz—probably because they reminded him of how they spoiled the wonderful time he was having. There is a surprisingly light heart in that heavy body.

"Could you give me your autograph, sir?" asked a small boy at the Raiders' Santa Rosa training camp.

Tooz didn't hesitate a second. He leaned down suddenly, contorting his face. "Arrrgggg," he growled at the little boy, who jumped.

At that point, Tooz stuck out his hand and shook hands. They both giggled, and the autograph book was signed with a flourish.

Tooz tells all the stories, even the crazy ones, well. He has a natural sense of timing—and lots of material. No one can remember all the Tooz stories. Even Tooz gets a kick out of some of the most outrageous ones.

Like the time he jumped from Houston to the World Football League, even though he still had a valid Houston contract. Tooz was served with a summons on the sideline during his first WFL game—between plays. He held the summons overhead and waved it to the spectators, who roared. Now THAT was something they didn't see every day. He was taken away by the sheriff.

"I only played seven plays in the WFL," Tooz said. "I wasn't doing too bad. I had two sacks and three or four unassisted tackles."

Or what about the Kansas City training camp? The Chiefs really knew they had an original when he reported. Between the morning and afternoon practices, a blonde visited Tooz's room every day, bringing white wine and cheese and staying until the afternoon practice began.

"They put two and two together," Tooz said of the Chief coaches.

It was not the last time someone used that formula and came up with the same answer. Tooz meets a lot of women.

"Like any high-visibility job, you meet all kinds," Tooz said. "And that's the problem. You don't want all kinds."

Not that he hasn't given the entire crop a careful look.

"When I was in Kansas City," Tooz said, "My ex-old lady chased me all around the camp with the car, trying to run me over. She chased me right up the stairs. That's not the best thing for your image."

Tooz began building his image when he was 11 years old in Oak Creek, Wis., when he got a set of weights promoted by Packer fullback Jim Taylor.

"Before that I was so skinny I had to run around in the shower to get wet," Tooz said.

"I got the set of weights and a history book the same day. That and a history book. I love

history. I didn't miss a workout—every other day—for the next 10 years."

As a high school freshman, Tooz was 6′ 3″ and 170 pounds. By the time he was a senior, he was 6′ 6″ and 235 pounds. He was All-State in football, All-League in basketball and the state shot put and discus champion.

Since then Tooz has had his ups and downs, but there is more to him than meets the eye. He made a point, for example, to get his degree from Tampa, in an era when fewer than half of all NFL players graduate.

"I'll probably always play the big, strong jock," he said. "But I love to read. Edgar Allen Poe, Thoreau, Shakespeare, mysteries. What they're saying is so deep, and they have to say it in such a weird way that you have to think your ass off. I love that."

Tooz is fascinated by the movies. He said he wrote most of the scenes he played in "North Dallas Forty," a movie he called "80 per cent accurate."

Among his hopes for the future were: "Another Super Bowl or two, becoming all-pro [an honor he has never received] and becoming a great actor—a great actor."

But, he admitted, the screen image of Tooz—the ultimate circus strong man—is sometimes hard to live with. When he was America's favorite tough guy, Humphrey Bogart was constantly challenged at bars by fans who wondered how tough he really was.

Sometimes that happens to Tooz, too. And sometimes it gets out of hand, "and then they want to know why a great big guy like me is picking on a little fellow."

The image finally became a real problem, one that Tooz is wrestling with to this day.

"It was like stepping on stage," Tooz said. "I'm not really like that. It became difficult to shut off the stage Tooz and be the real Tooz, who is an easy-going person who likes to talk to people. I want to give people the impression they can look up to me, not just in size, but in other ways too."

It has been a struggle for Tooz to earn respect on the football field. For starters, in his first three years in the league he wore the uniforms of five

An impassioned Tooz (John Matuszak) exhorts the crowd in the homecoming parade in Oakland after the Super Bowl.

teams, although some of the stints lasted little longer than his time in the WFL. He played 14 games for Houston, the team that drafted him, the very first pick of all collegians, in 1973; then he jumped leagues to the WFL for a game.

The Oilers traded him to Kansas City in 1974, and he played for the Chiefs for two years before being sent to Washington in August of 1976. By September, the Redskins had released him, and the Raiders picked him up as a free agent.

In Oakland, Tooz found a home and began to live up to the promise he showed when he was named to several all-rookie teams for the Chiefs. Before the 1979 season, he had played in 43 consecutive games for the Raiders, 37 as a starter. And his play became consistently excellent.

But in the 1979 season he suffered the first serious injury of his career in the exhibition season. Tooz put his arm up to fight off a block and "it felt like I was shot."

He couldn't lift his arm above his head but played the rest of the game. Afterwards, doctors told him he had torn muscles in his shoulder. He was given two options for repair.

"I didn't know if I would be able to play or not," he recalled. "They said they could cut all the muscles around my shoulder and sew it back, or I could try to rehabilitate it."

He chose the latter, undergoing a minor surgical procedure to help the process. But most of the work was up to Tooz.

While working on the set of "Caveman," he stipulated that a set of weights had to be provided in his room on every location. Using them, Tooz worked himself back into condition.

Tooz's rehabilitation was a large part of the resurgence of the Raider defensive line in 1980. With Tooz healthy, the Raiders could play both a 3-4 and a 4-3 alignment, using the former most of the time and switching to the latter on obvious passing downs.

By the time the Raiders traveled to Philadelphia to play the Eagles, in the twelfth game of the season, the three and four-man defensive fronts—combined with the strategies of defensive coach Charlie Sumner—were working perfectly for the Raiders.

But against Philadelphia, the Raiders' ability to get just enough points to win failed them.

Not that the Raider defense let down. The Raider defenders had another fine game, holding the Eagles to just 10 points.

Statistically, it was probably the game of the year for Tooz. He finished with seven unassisted tackles, two assists and sacked Eagle quarterback Ron Jaworski for a nine-yard loss. He couldn't have played better if he'd been following a script.

In fact, Tooz seemed to be getting better scripts in life. As he said, he realized that he is really only playing himself in the movies, and he learned to refine his characterization. "Caveman" was an example.

"It is almost like real life," Tooz said. "I got to be mean, nice, kind, caring and stupid. And just like in real life, you just try to eliminate the mean and stupid parts."

The Run Down the Stretch • 8

December 1, 1980

Oakland 9/Denver 3

The Raiders were tied for first place in the competitive American Conference-West with San Diego. They had been a game up on the Chargers before slipping to 8–4 with the 10–7 loss at Philadelphia four days after San Diego had outlasted the Dolphins 27–24 in overtime on a Thursday night in Miami.

Oakland was now faced with playing Denver and Dallas at home and finishing on the road against Denver and the New York Giants. There were eight teams in the AFC with records of 7–5 or better, so the Raiders knew they would almost certainly have to win at least three of their last four games to qualify for their first post-season appearance since 1977.

Denver was 7–5, and the Broncos knew their only chance to remain alive in the race would be to beat the Raiders in Oakland. The Broncos were hot—they had won their last six out of eight games, including consecutive triumphs over San Diego, the New York Jets and Seattle.

Unfortunately for the Broncos, they would be playing Oakland on Monday night. The Raiders are deadlier on Monday nights than Dracula under a full moon and Howard Cosell in front of a microphone.

Heading into the season, the Raiders were 13–1–1 on the weeknight television special since ABC gave this nation Cosell on Monday Night Football in 1970. Oakland's only Monday night loss was at Buffalo, 21–20, on the opening weekend of the 1974 season when Joe Ferguson twice brought the Bills from behind with a pair of touchdown passes to Ahmad Rashad in the final two minutes. The tie was at Denver, 23–23, in 1972 when the Raiders' George Blanda and Broncos' Jim Turner exchanged field goals in the final 36 seconds.

The Raiders' chances of improving their Monday night mark in 1980 appeared remote at best. They were scheduled for the maximum three

appearances: at defending Super Bowl champion and bitter-rival Pittsburgh and at nemesis Seattle before returning home against the Broncos.

Oakland stunned a TV audience of millions, not to mention the Steelers, by winning at Three Rivers Stadium, 45–34, the most points scored on the Steelers since a 52–14 loss at Minnesota in 1969 and the highest total ever by a Steeler foe in Three Rivers.

The Raiders played again on Monday night four weeks later and rallied past the Seahawks, 19–17, for their first-ever victory in the Kingdome.

"I don't know what it is about Monday nights," said a beaming Tom Flores after the Raiders overcame a 14–0 third-quarter deficit to beat Seattle. "Maybe we can arrange to have all of our games played on Mondays."

Flores was quick to find out the magic of the Raiders on Mondays in his first season as head coach in 1979. Oakland trailed New Orleans 35–14 with fewer than 19 minutes left in an early December Monday nighter at the Superdome before erupting for four touchdowns and a 42–35 triumph.

Oakland's game against Denver rivaled a night out in Topeka for excitement. In a duel of defenses, the Raiders prevailed, 9–3, before their first home sellout crowd of the season.

This was the night several thousand of the 51,583 fans in attendance boycotted the opening five minutes of the game to protest the Raiders' court-delayed attempt to move to Los Angeles. More than 40,000 "Save Our Raiders" placards were handed out outside the stadium and the signs were raised by the fans during the two-minute warnings before halftime and the end of the game.

"I know what the fans are trying to do and I sympathize with them," said Raider center Dave Dalby during the week of the game, "but we're trying to win a division championship and we will only be concentrating on what is going on on the

99

Al Davis, Managing General Partner of the Raiders, stalks the sidelines reviewing the Raiders on their trek to the Superbowl.

football field. If there isn't anybody in the stands when the game starts, there is nothing we, as players, can do about it. We'll still go ahead and play."

The demonstration was orderly and peaceful. The stadium was only about half full when the game started, partly because of the protesters and the late arrivers who were in a traffic jam en route to the 6 o'clock game. But all appeared to be in their seats by the end of the first quarter.

The fans who orchestrated the boycott felt it was successful, the Raider organization praised the spectators for making the demonstration incident-free, and the Raiders won the football game. Everyone, except the Broncos, their handful of followers and possibly a few fans who would have preferred more than 12 points, left the Coliseum happy.

Neither the Raiders nor the Broncos could muster much offense. Oakland amassed only 215 yards, Denver 216. The Raiders converted two of 14 third-down plays into firsts, while the Broncos were successful on a mere four of 13.

Plunkett completed nine of 19 passes for 78 yards, and he was sacked thrice for 27 yards, giving the Raiders a paltry 51 net yards passing. Bronco quarterback Craig Morton, who usually gave the Raiders fits, completed 19 of 35 passes, but most were of the short variety.

Oakland actually should have won the game going away. Its defense intercepted three passes and recovered as many fumbles, but the offense couldn't convert one of the turnovers into points. Raider placekicker Chris Bahr had a big part in that—he missed four of five field goal attempts from 31, 47, 26 and 43 yards, and he also misfired on his only extra-point try. He did make a 44-yard field goal early in the fourth quarter.

"Everything was going wide," lamented Bahr. "I couldn't figure it out. It's like trying to correct your golf swing in the middle of 18 holes. You might say the Raiders won this one without a placekicker."

Ex-Raider Fred Steinfort connected on a 41-yard, first-quarter field goal in his only attempt of the evening. Denver carried the 3–0 lead into halftime. It marked the third consecutive game Oakland had been shut out in the opening half.

The Raiders, with a big assist from the Broncos, took the second half kickoff and marched 77 yards in seven plays for the game's only touchdown, Plunkett scoring on a surprising bootleg right. The possession was kept alive when, on a third-and-one from the Oakland 32, Plunkett faked a handoff and threw long for Cliff Branch. Bronco right corner Aaron Kyle made obvious contact with Branch while the ball was air-borne, however, and the Raiders had themselves a 38-yard pass interference penalty and a first down on the Denver 30.

Plunkett executed his bootleg five downs later on a first-and-goal at the eight. "The play was specifically designed for this game," said the quarterback. "It was a play-action fake with me rolling out and trying to throw to Raymond Chester. I got outside the linebacker [Tom Jackson, who was suckered inside by the fake] and I'm not fleet of foot, so that must have had something to do with it."

Bahr followed by blasting his conversion attempt against the left upright, leaving the score at 6–3.

Denver, which crossed midfield only twice in the first half, could only get as far as its own 44 in the final two periods. From the 44, with 1:10 left in the game, Morton threw for halfback Rob Lytle and the ball bounced off fifth defensive back Odis McKinney and into the eager arms of cornerback Dwayne O'Steen for an interception. It was a fitting end to an outstanding effort by the Raider defense, which had yielded only two first downs and 52 yards in the last half.

The win was the Raiders' twelfth straight on Monday night and it raised their mark to 16-1-1 on the weeknight game. The incredibility of that achievement can only be measured by the success — or lack of it — of several of the NFL's other top teams of the 1970's. Among teams that made 11 or more Monday night appearances, Miami had the second-best record (13-6), followed by Washington (12-6), Baltimore (8-4), Pittsburgh (10-7)

and Minnesota (7-6). Dallas was 8-9, Los Angeles 8-10, Denver 3-7-1 and New England 2-9. Only nine of the league's 28 teams showed winning records on Mondays.

One reason for Morton's problems in the 9–3 loss at Oakland was the pass rush applied by both Oakland's three- and four-man fronts. Morton was sacked twice and pressured on several other occasions, including the three plays when he was intercepted. Morton didn't get much support from his running game, which netted only 95 yards.

Oakland finished the regular season with 54 sacks, limiting opponents to an average of 107.8 yards rushing. Much of the credit for these accomplishments belonged to two of the club's unheralded linemen, nose guard Reggie Kinlaw and Dave Browning, who doubled as a tackle and end. They didn't receive the media exposure during the season of a Lester Hayes, Ted Hendricks or John Matuszak, but they were every bit as vital to an 11-man unit that worked with the precision of a Swiss watch.

Kinlaw was a prize find for the Raiders in 1979. He wasn't drafted until the twelfth round and he may not have been taken at all had it not been for Ron Wolf, the Raiders' director of personnel operations, who had a keen eye for talent. Wolf liked what he saw of the fireplug 6' 1½", 235-pound middle guard at Oklahoma.

Chris Bahr demonstrates side-winding style in pre-game warmup, with Bob Chandler spotting the ball for him.

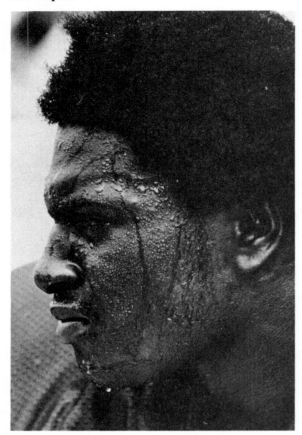

Reggie Kinlaw is an unexpected jewel you'll sometimes find in the 12th round of the NFL player draft.

"Reggie was not drafted earlier because he wasn't the kingsized player most teams were looking at in a nose guard, he had never played linebacker and he had knee problems in college," explained Raider executive assistant Al LoCasale. "Plus a number of Oklahoma kids who lack the physical size end up going to Canada, whether they're drafted in the NFL or not.

"Ron liked him for his quickness, aggressiveness and strength for a man his size. We drafted him as a nose guard, but we would have looked at him as a linebacker, too, if that would have been necessary. And, don't forget, he played for a school that went 41–6 his four years there. He already understood what it took to play in a winning tradition."

The fact that the Raiders were going for the smaller, quicker Kinlaw-types at nose guard also showed a change in their defensive philosophy from their Super Bowl championship team of 1976, when they alternated a couple of mountainous linemen, Dave Rowe and Mike McCoy, at the position. Dave Pear, 6' 2", 250 pounds, obtained by Oakland in a 1979 trade from Tampa, and Kinlaw relied more on their mobility to work with the linebackers to create a multitude of problems in the middle.

Another factor Wolf noticed about Kinlaw was that he could—and would—play with pain. He partially tore ligaments in his right knee in Oklahoma's opening game in 1977, and surgery appeared iminent. Kinlaw, who missed part of his sophomore year because of surgery on the same knee, said he didn't want another operation, explaining, "Coming back from surgery is no fun. I don't want to go through that again." Although the knee still hurt, he was back in the lineup two weeks later against Ohio State.

Kinlaw spent most of his rookie season of 1979 with Oakland on special teams and as a backup to Pear.

"Reggie was one of our best special teams players as a rookie," said Steve Ortmayer, the unit's coach. "The interesting thing is that he is a defensive player, yet he was probably the best blocker we had on our kickoff and return teams. He would knock your helmet off. He hardly played any special teams in 1980 because he was starting in the line."

Kinlaw proved to a national television audience that he indeed was suited to play in the NFL when, on a Monday night in October, 1979, he made life miserable for Bob Griese as he sacked the Miami quarterback three times during a 13–3 Raider win. It didn't take much to get Kinlaw fired up that evening—he was born and raised in Miami.

Kinlaw, who raised his pro playing weight to 245 pounds, took over the starting nose guard job his sophomore season. He wasn't even challenged by Pear, who was plagued by a variety of aches and pains during the season that began in training camp. Kinlaw came out of the lineup when the Raiders went to a four-man front and he missed two games and parts of two others with a foot injury, yet he still ended up leading Raider linemen in solo tackles during the league season with 51.

"Reggie is one of the most unique linemen I've ever been associated with," said Raider defensive line coach Earl Leggett. "He's not very tall, but he has outstanding leverage and quickness to shed a blocker. He also is very coachable.

Quickness and leverage make Reggie Kinlaw an asset as the nose guard in the Raiders' three-man front.

Versatility qualifies Dave Browning to play both end and tackle in the Raiders' shifting defensive alignments.

When you tell him something, he listens. He rarely repeats a mistake."

Kinlaw was credited with only one and a half sacks during league play, but his performance in the middle allowed the linebackers to find lanes to the quarterback.

"Offensive lines had problems getting forward progress up the middle against our three-man line because of Reggie," said Browning. "He has such strong legs and leverage that he would constantly stand the center straight up, making it almost impossible for another blocker to get a shot at him. He's a very smart player."

Leggett noted Kinlaw also could have played tackle or end; but, because the Raiders' depth at nose guard was thin, they didn't want to chance risking an injury to Kinlaw in the four-man line. "We may have spotted Reggie elsewhere had it not been for Pear's predicament," said Leggett. "We did work Reggie some as an end in training camp."

Without a healthy Pear and veteran linebacker Monte Johnson, who sustained a season-ending knee injury in an exhibition game against Washington, the Raiders were more green than silver and black up the middle of their 3–4 defense.

"Reggie had only started one game as a rookie," noted LoCasale, "and we had four inside linebackers who between them had fewer than a dozen NFL starts. Matt Millen was a rookie, Mario Celotto had no starts, Bob Nelson had one and Randy McClanahan had 10 starts with Buffalo. And Randy didn't even play football in 1979."

Browning, 6′ 5″ and 245 pounds, was "Mr. Right Side" of Oakland's Super Bowl line. He was the starting right end in the three-man front, and he moved to right tackle in the front four when designated pass rusher Cedrick Hardman would come in at end. Dave was second to Kinlaw in solo tackles with 45, and he contributed seven and a half sacks, fourth highest on the team.

"Dave is another one of those unique individuals," said Leggett. "He has the leverage and strength as an end to get into the tackle and prevent him from releasing to block on either our inside or outside linebacker and, as a tackle, he has the quickness and finesse to create problems inside. He and Matuszak worked real well inside together.

"We were a little concerned at first about how Dave would hold up at end against the 280-to 300-pound tackles, but he did it with leverage and aggressiveness. There isn't a more intense player in the league."

"Playing two positions was," said Browning, "really not that difficult. Heck, there was one game my second year here when I started at left end and ended up playing every [line] position across the board that day. It wasn't bad, but I did feel like a pingpong ball at times.

"It can be a little hectic going from one position to another. You have different blocking techniques to contend with, so there is some thinking involved. Recognizing what they're trying to do to you is the important thing.

"I had a lot of fun playing our multiple defenses. We would start out in the three-man line and go to four linemen on second and third and long. We would go to the four-man line right away in the fourth quarter and sometimes earlier when we had the lead and the other team was filling the air with passes. We stunted quite a bit in the line and we had several combinations of blitzes, mostly with our linebackers, of course, but also with our defensive backs. Our coaches did a heckuva job preparing us each week."

Although he felt he had "a good season at both tackle and end," Browning admitted it was a struggle at first: "I had some nagging injuries in training camp, like a pulled groin muscle and bruised back. That prevented me from playing as much in the pre-season as I would have hoped.

"Then we got off to the slow start. It was after we were 2-and-3 we decided to stop worrying about the season as a whole and start concentrating on one game at a time. I think that approach helped us turn it around.

"The defense just kept getting better and better. We had two new defensive coaches—Earl [Leggett] and Chet [secondary coach Chet Franklin]—and it was a matter of them getting to know us, and us, as players, getting familiar with each other in the number of defenses we were using.

"The real key to our defense, I believe, was everyone doing his job and not having to worry about what the guy next to him was doing. Ours is a defense that if everyone takes care of his own responsibility, it will work."

Most of Browning's publicity in 1980 came in May after he arrived a day late at a weekend Raider mini-camp because of the volcanic eruption of Mount St. Helens north of Portland, Ore. He was only about 80 miles east of the mountain when it blew its top. The ash from the volcano covered most of Washington and brought the state to a virtual standstill.

"It took me five days, but I finally got out of Washington to Oakland," said Browning, revealing his characteristic boyish grin at the thought. "There was ash and mud all over the place. It was almost impossible to drive your car—the dust would get into the carburetor. You couldn't get a flight because the airports were closed. It was hell up there. I was happy to be back in California."

"I've heard all kinds of excuses from players for either missing or being late for camp," Coach Tom Flores said, "But a volcano? It has to be legitimate—nobody could make up an excuse like that." Not since Mount Vesuvius, anyway.

Browning was another one of those undersized, Kinlaw-types the Raiders gambled would turn into a solid pro lineman. They made the then 235-pound University of Washington product their first choice in the 1978 draft. He was actually

Brian Sipe of the Cleveland Browns, poised to pass, feels the brunt of Dave Browning's pass rush in the AFC divisional playoffs.

taken in the second round, since the Raiders didn't have a first that year. One drafting service had him rated twentieth among available defensive ends, and another didn't mention him at all.

But the Raiders pay no attention to other scouts' opinions. They independently search for talent that is going to fit THEIR needs; they are the only NFL team that does not belong to one of the league's three scouting combines (a combine is a group of four or more teams that pools information on players eligible for the draft).

The Raiders aren't afraid to take chances with the draft. Sometimes they lose, like in 1976 when their first two picks were defensive end Charles Philyaw and quarterback Jeb Blount. Blount didn't even make the team, and Philyaw was finally cut during 1980 training camp.

A player taken in the early rounds by the Raiders is usually viewed as a possible starter in two-to-four years, and later round picks are players who could help the team immediately on special teams and, like in Kinlaw's case, some day become a starter.

Browning, however, was Oakland's first rookie starter since linebacker Phil Villapiano and free safety Jack Tatum in 1971.

"We weren't concerned about Dave's weight. He had the height and we knew he could fill out bigger," said LoCasale. "And he came from a good program. Washington's coach, Don James, does an excellent job with his players. Dave played very well in Washington's Rose Bowl win over Michigan, and we also looked at him as a leader—he was a co-captain on that Rose Bowl team."

John Madden, the Raiders' coach when Browning was drafted, wasn't surprised the baby-faced ex-Husky cracked the starting lineup by Oakland's third game of the season at Green Bay.

"Dave's biggest strength is that he doesn't have a specific weakness or strength," said Madden. "He can stunt, play straight, rush the passer and play the run."

Browning, who had his biggest rookie games during a 21–17 win over Houston when he was in on 19 tackles, missed most of the last half of his first season with an ankle injury that required surgery. He rebounded and didn't miss a start in 1979 or 1980. He wasn't about to be stopped—even Mount St. Helens tried, and failed.

December 7, 1980

Dallas 19/Oakland 13

Not all was well for the Raiders coming out of the Denver win. Starting halfback Kenny King sustained a badly sprained ankle in the game, and his backup, Arthur Whittington, bruised a knee.

That wasn't good news considering the Raiders' next opponent was going to be the always dangerous Dallas Cowboys, who were engaged in a tight division race of their own with Philadelphia in the NFC East. The Cowboys, 10–3 and a game behind the Eagles, were riding a three-game winning streak, including a 51–7 romp over Seattle in their most recent outing.

The Cowboys had a decided advantage on Oakland. They had not played since Thanksgiving Day, meaning they had enjoyed 11 precious days of rest and recuperation. The Raiders, on the other hand, were still licking their wounds from their hard-hitting match six days earlier with Denver.

Oddly, this game was going to be only the second in league play between Oakland and Dallas since the AFL-NFL merger in 1970. The two franchises were born in 1960, Oakland in the first year of the AFL and Dallas in the established NFL. Going into the 1980 season, the Raiders had the winningest record in pro football since 1963 with 168 wins, 63 losses and 11 ties, while the Cowboys were second at 163–76–3.

Oakland won the previous league meeting between the teams, 27–23, on the final weekend of the 1974 season. The outcome had no bearing on the races—the Raiders had already claimed their division and the Cowboys had been eliminated from playoff competition for the first time in five seasons. The teams also had met in six pre-season games, Oakland winning five and Dallas one.

The game was a hot item. It was sold out three weeks in advance. It was a natural: the

The Raiders contain the Dallas offense on a shoestring tackle by Odis McKinney, the "nickel" back in their defense.

Raiders, the guys in the black hats and members of Professional Football's Dynamic Organization, versus the Cowboys, America's Team, the guys in the white hats with the clean-cut, Roger Staubach image. It also was going to be the Raiders' league home finale.

With King and Whittington doubtful for duty, the Raiders practiced most of the week with fullbacks Mark van Eeghen and Derrick Jensen operating in the same backfield. They also worked versatile kick returner, wide receiver and running back Ira Matthews at halfback.

While everyone else around the country was wondering who shot J. R. in the popular "Dallas" TV series, Flores was pondering how he was going to outwit T. L. (Cowboy coach Tom Landry) with a lame backfield.

King played sparingly in the game but, except for one play, was not effective on the sore ankle. He had a 19-yard run in the second quarter that led to a Bahr field goal. His other six carries resulted in only 19 additional yards. Whittington did not play.

Linebacker Bob Nelson returned to the Raiders' starting lineup in place of Randy McClanahan for the first time since dislocating a shoulder in the fifth league game against Kansas City.

For the second straight game, Raider fans were going to witness a defensive titanic, especially in the second half when both teams would produce only a field goal apiece. This time the Raider defense had to settle for second best, Dallas' "Doomsday II Defense" prevailing, 19–13.

Oakland took advantage of good field position on its first possession of the afternoon to drive 33 yards in seven plays for a 7–0 lead. Tight end Raymond Chester caught a six-yard Plunkett pass on a crossing pattern in the end zone for the score.

The Cowboys saddled up and scored on their next three possessions, Tony Dorsett on a 20-yard dash, Rafael Septien on a 52-yard field goal, the longest in his career, and Ron Springs on a two-yard run. Dallas 16, Oakland 7.

After pulling to within 16–10 on a 22-yard field goal, the Raiders gained possession on their 25 with 3:14 left in the half and maneuvered their way to the Dallas 31 with 25 seconds remaining. Plunkett was sacked at that point, however, and Oakland came up empty as Bahr closed the half by barely missing wide right on a 41-yard field goal attempt.

Three plays into the second half, Plunkett fumbled when sacked by defensive end Harvey Martin and Ed (Too Tall) Jones recovered on the Oakland 20. Septien converted the turnover into a 34-yard field goal and 19–10 Cowboy cushion.

Oakland got a break later in the quarter when Kinlaw planted a fumble-forcing lick on fullback Robert Newhouse and corner Dwayne O'Steen recovered on the Dallas 16. The Raiders worked the ball to the 10 in two plays, but Plunkett was sacked for a 10-yard loss on third down by John Dutton. On came Bahr for a 39-yard field goal that capped the day's scoring with 18:20 left to play.

The never-say-die Raiders gave it one final fling after taking over on their own 25 with 2:11 remaining. Plunkett found Chester for a 13-yard completion on the right sideline, then went to Bob Chandler with a beautifully placed pass over the middle on a deep crossing pattern toward the left sideline for 32 yards and a first down on the Cowboys' 30 with 1:58 left. On the next play, the Cowboys defense charged like the U.S. Cavalry. Plunkett, realizing he had Cliff Branch in single coverage, arched a pass intended for the speedy wide receiver in the right corner of the end zone just as blitzing free safety Dennis Thurmond was slam-

Dwayne O'Steen proves to be a valuable pickup from the Los Angeles Rams, taking over as a regular cornerback.

ming into the quarterback. The ball fell short of its mark, and cornerback Aaron Mitchell made a one-handed diving interception in the end zone.

"I didn't have much time and I threw it up for Cliff knowing he only had one man to beat," said Plunkett, not apologizing for his attempt. "Having your wide receiver in single coverage is a good situation. I just didn't have a chance to get enough on the ball to reach Cliff."

"It's hard to understand when you see other teams beating Dallas with deep stuff and we couldn't get deep," said Branch. "I can't believe we lost to them in the Coliseum."

The Raiders lost because their offense continued to play like it was mired in quicksand. They made only 104 yards and five first downs in the second half. With a lame King and no Whittington, their rushing game produced only 83 yards and two first downs all day. The Raiders also had four turnovers on two fumbles and two interceptions that indirectly led to 10 Dallas points.

"We're just out of synch," offered Raymond Chester after the game. "I know our defense is frustrated because we aren't contributing more. But we will." Dallas would be the Raiders' final setback of the season.

Playing another one of his steady games for the Raiders was Dwayne O'Steen, who was picked up from the Los Angeles Rams for a middle-round draft choice the week of the Raiders' opening league game at Kansas City.

"I wanted this kid when he came out of San Jose State," said Al Davis. "But we had a number of good defensive backs and it's not our policy to bring in too many people at one position. If you have too many players, you spread yourself too thin and don't have sufficient time to work with all of them."

O'Steen, who started 13 games for the Rams' Super Bowl team in 1979, moved in and gradually took away the Raiders' starting right corner job from another ex-Ram, Monte Jackson, who had knee problems. The position was his by the twelfth league game.

"I wanted to get out of L.A. because we just weren't hitting it off," said O'Steen, who had three interceptions during the 1980 season.

"What happened from there is a little hard to believe. First I'm traded to a team I always dreamed of playing for—the Oakland Raiders. Then I become a starter and end up on a Super Bowl champion."

O'Steen might have started earlier in the season had he not joined the club so late.

"Dwayne did a tremendous job catching on as quickly as he did," said secondary coach Chet Franklin. "He did not have the benefit of training camp with us and he was coming into a totally different concept of defense than what he had been used to with the Rams.

"Yet he adjusted well. It didn't take him long to understand what we were doing and why we were doing it. That together with his speed, aggressiveness and ability to play man-to-man coverage helped him get the starting job. He can cover and he's not afraid to hit.

"He made some key plays for us during the season, especially in our two games against Denver. He intercepted Morton's last pass in both games when Denver still had a chance to win."

O'Steen signed as a free agent with the Rams in 1978. He played in 13 games for them that season, mostly on special teams, before suffering a season-ending knee injury in early December.

Injury problems to key secondary personnel led to O'Steen starting most of the 1979 season for Los Angeles, first for Rod Perry at right corner, then for Pat Thomas at left corner. All was well until he was returned to the bench after starting in Los Angeles' victory over Dallas in the opening playoff game.

"They put Thomas back in because, they told me, he had more experience than I did," said O'Steen. "I was told 40 minutes before the championship game against Tampa Bay that I wouldn't be starting. Bitter? You bet I was. And that's when I really began setting my mind on getting out of L.A."

O'Steen also was unhappy about the reputation he said "the L.A. press" had given him as both a trouble-maker and brawler.

"I can't recall fights as such," he said. "I was young and a hard-worker at their training camp and some of the mellow and secure veterans don't care for someone who goes all out in practice. I only know one speed—all out. And when I'm No. 2, I'm going to work my rear end off to improve my status. So there would be altercations with some of the Ram veterans who didn't appreciate my all-out efforts in practice. That's not my fault. I am what I am.

"Besides, I never had that kind of problem my first season with the Raiders. They go about their business much more professionally than the Rams organization, from the front office right down to the ballboy."

December 14, 1980   # Oakland 24/Denver 21

The next hurdle for the Raiders would be the loose, nothing-to-lose Broncos on Sunday, December 14, at Mile High Stadium. San Diego had already applied some pressure on Oakland, having defeated Seattle, 21–14, the day before.

The Raiders were in a similar position to the previous two seasons when they finished out of the playoffs with identical 9–7 records. They still had a chance to make the playoffs with two games remaining in 1978 before they were eliminated by Miami, 23–6. In 1979 all they needed was a win at home over Seattle on the final Sunday of the season coupled with a Denver loss at San Diego to qualify as a wild card. Denver, as expected, lost to the Chargers, but it did the Raiders no good because they had already been upset, 29–34, by the Seahawks. The wild-card berth instead went to the Broncos.

For a mid-December in Denver, the Raiders couldn't have ordered a more gorgeous day. It was 65 degrees and sunny, much to the delight of the players and the sea of 73,974 orange-clad customers.

Denver took the opening kickoff, and Morton directed the Broncos from their own 11 to the Raider 36 in 11 plays, where the drive stalled and

This interception return for a touchdown by Burgess Owens touches off a vital victory over the Denver Broncos.

Fred Steinfort was brought on for an apparent 53-yard field goal attempt. He could kick one that far, but the Raiders weren't too sure that was what crafty Bronco coach Red Miller had in mind.

Flashback: October 17, 1977, Oakland Coliseum, Oakland vs. Denver. Late in the first half, with the score 14–7 Broncos, Jim Turner lined up for a 32-yard field goal attempt for Denver. Holder and quarterback Norris Weese took the snap and immediately jumped up and threw a pass down field to a wide open Turner for a 25-yard touchdown. The Broncos went on to a 30-7 victory.

Sure enough, Miller had the same thing in mind, but this time the placekicker would not be the intended receiver, or so the coach said after the game.

The holder was backup quarterback Matt Robinson, whom the Broncos obtained in an off-season trade from the New York Jets. Robinson straightened up after taking the snap as Steinfort headed up field. The quarterback looked at tight end Riley Odoms, who had stepped back off the line of scrimmate to set up for a screen.

Free safety Burgess Owens saw what was developing and, just as Robinson unloaded to Odoms, he jumped in front of the intended receiver for an interception and raced 58 yards for

A brilliant move by Bob Chandler leaves him all alone as he steps into the end zone against the Broncos.

the game's opening score. The play had to rate as one of the biggest of the regular season for Oakland.

"Riley was my responsibility and, when I saw him take a couple of steps back, I had an idea what they were trying," said Owens. "Matt never saw me. I purposely laid back and I was hidden by a couple of Denver's linemen who were setting up to block for the screen. When he started to throw, I broke for Odoms—I knew that if I didn't get the interception I would at least knock the ball down.

"I had mixed emotions about that play, though. While it turned out to be very important for us, I hated to make it against Matt. We are good friends from our days together with the Jets. Both of us went through a lot of hell there."

Said Miller, "That's either a brilliant call or not a brilliant call, depending on whether it works." The play does create excitement. Both times Miller tried it against Oakland it scored a touchdown—one for the Broncos and one for the Raiders.

Denver tied the score at 7–7 on a two-yard Dave Preston run four seconds into the second quarter, but the Raiders took a 17–7 lead into halftime on a 44-yard Bahr field goal and 11-yard pass from Plunkett to Chandler, who improvised his pattern and made a nifty fake on all-pro corner Louis Wright to make the reception in the end zone.

Robinson quarterbacked the second quarter for Denver and his bad luck continued. He threw an interception that led to Bahr's field goal, and he received a concussion while trying to tackle Mike Davis after the strong safety picked up a Preston fumble late in the half.

Morton got hot late in the third quarter when, after Denver took over on its 34, the quarterback completed successive passes of 22, 33 and 11 yards, the latter to Odoms for a touchdown to pull the Broncos up to 17-14.

Oakland came back to score on a 37-yard Plunkett-to-Chandler pass, but the Morton-led Broncos countered three minutes later with a nine-yard Preston scoring run.

Morton got the ball back with 5:44 left in the game and moved the Broncos from their own 20 to the Oakland 15 in nine plays. On a second-and-eight from that point, he was sacked for a seven-yard loss by blitzing rookie linebacker Matt Millen and he fumbled the snap from center for another seven-yard loss on the ensuing play. Steinfort came on to try a 47-yard field goal and missed with a low kick that barely cleared the line.

Denver got one more crack at overtaking Oakland after regaining possession on its 32 with 44 seconds remaining. After an incomplete pass, Morton hit Odoms with a 25-yard pass. The tight end remained on the ground after the play with an apparent eye injury. The officials stopped the clock with 18 seconds left and, since the Broncos had already used up their three times out, they would be penalized 10 seconds before the next play. It was worth it to the Broncos. Had it not been for Odoms' injury, time would have expired before Denver could have started another play.

Confusion reigned while the Broncos stood at the line of scrimmage while the 10 seconds were being taken off the clock. The time dropped below eight seconds the first time while the referee stood over the ball, so the clock had to be reset to 18 seconds and the whole process restarted. The spectators, most of them ignorant of the rarely-enforced 10-second penalty, were in a frenzy as the Broncos stood and the clock moved.

The ball was finally centered and Morton's desperation sideline pass was picked off by O'Steen to end the game.

"We were fortunate to get out of there with that one," said Owens. "That was probably our worst performance on defense in our last 12 or 13 games of the season, including the playoffs. But give Morton some of the credit. He is one helluva competitor. The guy never gives up. It's a good thing the Plunkett-to-Chandler combination was clicking and Ray Guy was kicking the way he was. Ray is really a game-saver."

Guy punted five times for an average of 50 yards. His longest soared 64 yards through Denver's thin air into the end zone.

The Broncos had 507 total yards, including 448 passing. But they also committed four costly turnovers.

"We moved the ball very well, but the turnovers really hurt," said Miller, who surprisingly would be fired as the Broncos' head coach three months later. "We could have won; we should have won."

If it hadn't been for Owens, the Broncos might have won. Not only did he score with the interception, but he also knocked down a pass and was in on nine tackles, six of them solos.

Owens, who had 17 career interceptions over seven seasons with the Jets, became the victim of a youth movement in New York and was shipped off to the Raiders in 1980 for practically nothing, a sixth-round draft choice to be exact. He intercepted three passes in regular season and had another crucial interception in Oakland's AFC title game win over San Diego. He also led the team with 94 solo tackles in league play.

"I guess it hurt my pride a little that the Jets couldn't get more for me in a trade," said Owens with a grin. "But, hey, I'm naturally delighted with what happened to me. After the '79 season I'm seriously considering quitting football, and one year later I'm playing on a Super Bowl winning team. All of this surpassed my wildest expectations."

Owens became the starting free safety after Raider legend Jack Tatum was traded to Houston and Charles Phillips failed to respond favorably to off-season knee surgery.

"I never thought of it as me coming in here to make everyone forget Jack," said Owens. "It was a case of me having to prove myself all over again in my eighth season in the league. I wanted my new teammates to have the confidence in me that I could do the job.

"I have never been a backup in my football career and I didn't know if that is what I was destined for when I first came to the Raiders, but I really didn't care. I was just happy to be with a winning organization after what I had gone through in New York. I came to Oakland with the attitude I would give it my best and let the chips fall where they might."

Chet Franklin called Owens "the most conscientious guy" he has ever coached.

"He wants to make sure everything is covered," said the secondary coach with a laugh. "I mean there were times during the season when he would get on your nerves. He would keep asking questions about a certain coverage. He didn't want to chance leaving one stone unturned.

"Burgess is a very intelligent player—heck, the guy is a stockbroker. He has good acceleration to the ball, he's extremely tough and a sure tackler, and he has a great feel for the game. He's also very cool under fire. He is a stabilizing force out there for our people.

"You don't know how happy I am we got Burgess. It wouldn't have been as easy without him. All of this might not have happened without him, in fact."

December 21, 1980   # Oakland 33/New York Giants 17

The Giants remained the final obstacle for the Raiders in their run for the playoffs. A win in plush Giants Stadium in the smokestack-dotted Meadowlands of New Jersey would assure the Raiders of at least being the host team in the wild-card playoff game.

What the Raiders would do against the Giants would have no bearing on the AFC West race. The only way the Raiders could win the division would be for San Diego to lose to Pittsburgh.

Oakland and San Diego, having split their two divisional meetings, were tied with 10–5 records and had completed division play with 6–2 records, but the Raiders had a better conference mark, 9–3 to the Chargers' 8–3; best conference records were the fourth step in the NFL's complicated tie-breaking system.

Wins by both teams would make them 11–5 overall and 9–3 in the conference, so the Chargers would win the division by virtue of having scored more net points in the AFC West than Oakland (the fifth tie-breaker).

Still, beating the Giants was imperative because a loss coupled with a San Diego win could knock the Raiders out of the playoffs altogether.

The Raiders entered the game a seven-point favorite. The Giants had been devastated by injuries during the season, but they weren't to be taken lightly. They had lost by only a field goal to Washington the week before, and they had split their last six games, with wins over Seattle, Green Bay and Dallas.

This was going to be only the second meeting ever between the teams. The Raiders hammered the Giants, 42–0, in 1973 in Oakland. They had never met in pre-season.

It was cold in the Meadowlands. The sky was clear, the temperature 23 degrees at game time, and the wind blowing 12 miles an hour with gusts to 23. It was like a balmy day in the Bahamas compared to what was waiting for the Raiders two Sundays later in frosty Cleveland.

Oakland had been involved in some bizarre games during the season, but none more so than this one. After several laughs, most of them provided by the bumbling Giants, the Raiders had frolicked to a 33–17 win. New York committed five turnovers, four on fumbles. Ted Hendricks also blocked a Dave Jennings punt that gave Oakland the ball on the Giants' 11 and led to a touchdown and first-quarter 10–0 lead.

John Matuszak provided the 61,278 hardy souls on hand (there were 15,447 no-shows) with a chuckle late in the first period when the 6' 8", 280-pound defensive end pulled a fumble out of the air and lumbered 35 yards before seemingly

Ted Hendricks pressures young Giant quarterback Scott Brunner into one of the five turnovers that ensure a Raider breeze.

being wrestled down by the entire 45-man Giants' squad seven yards short of the end zone. The play was nullified by a face-mask penalty against a furious Browning.

Other entertaining moments included one of Giants' rookie quarterback Scott Brunner's attempted passes flying backward while his arm was going forward, resulting in a fumble and six-yard loss; a high, short Jennings punt hitting one of his teammates on top of the helmet; Jennings being tackled for a 13-yard loss when he couldn't decide whether to punt or pass; and Raider punter Ray Guy uncharacteristically dropping a snap and, after trying to run, being dropped for a one-yard loss. It was football follies at its worst.

The most unusual sequence of the afternoon —if not the season—happened in the game's waning seconds. After the Giants were assessed two straight five-yard penalties for touching onside kick attempts before they traveled the required 10 yards, Joe Danelo's third onside try from his own 25 was quickly grabbed by Derrick Jensen on the hop and the Raider fullback raced untouched through a wave of charging Giants for a 33-yard touchdown. There is nothing in the NFL record book denoting the shortest kickoff return for a score, but it would be almost impossible for anyone to have ever returned one for fewer yards than Jensen did.

Lester Hayes needed two interceptions in the game to tie Dick (Night Train) Lane's record of 14

In the season finale, Lester Hayes comes within one of the NFL record for pass interceptions.

Old and young compare notes as Hall-of-Famer George Blanda, left, talks over placekicking with current Raider Chris Bahr.

in a season, set in 1952 when Lane was with the Los Angeles Rams. Hayes ended up with one, and he dropped three others. He actually did get No. 14 late in the game, but it was nullified when he was called for bumping intended receiver Earnest Gray while going for the ball.

Plunkett, completing 12 of 22 passes for 164 yards, threw scoring passes of 31 and 37 yards to Cliff Branch and Raymond Chester, respectively. The one to Chester gave Oakland a 27–10 lead late in the third quarter to put the game away.

Chris Bahr warmed up for the playoffs by kicking field goals from 41 and 38 yards. His one miss hit the crossbar from 52 yards.

Bahr turned out to be a blessing for the Raiders. He finished the season with 25 field goals in 44 attempts, including an impressive six-for-seven during the playoffs. He made 11 of 15 in the wake of his one-for-five Monday night performance against Denver.

There also was his infamous one-for-six day in the Raiders' 30–24 overtime loss in the second game of the season at San Diego. He missed from 51, connected from 35 and missed from 30, 46, 53 and 50 yards.

"I would rather miss in bunches than be inconsistent by missing one here and one there," Bahr said. "If you take out those two games I had against San Diego and Denver, I'm 23 for 33, and that isn't bad.

"I started kicking better after the Dallas game, when I began stroking the ball instead of exploding into it. I was still getting the good pop, but I also was getting better control. I had always been a home-run hitter, and I guess that's why I tended to have games like San Diego and Denver. Home-run hitters have a tendency to strike out from time to time."

Chris, the older brother of Pittsburgh placekicker Matt Bahr, was a second-round draft choice by Cincinnati in 1976 out of Penn State, where he was both an outstanding placekicker and soccer player.

Bahr was criticized for being erratic by the Cincinnati press while making 62 of 130 field goal attempts during his four years with the Bengals. Cincinnati dropped him in 1980 to keep Ian Sunter. Sunter didn't stick and, ironically, former Raider Jim Breech was the Bengals' placekicker the last four games of the season.

Other than the playoffs and, of course, the Super Bowl in particular, one of Bahr's memorable moments from the 1980 season was the day after the Monday nighter against Denver.

"This guy was out in the street in front of our training camp kicking a ball off a tee," said Bahr, grinning. "It was so windy the ball kept falling off the tee, so he picked the ball up and punted it. It went over the fence and into the golf course next door. I don't think our coaches were that impressed."

Special teams coach Steve Ortmayer will also never forget the week after the Monday night before. "I got calls from all over the country from mechanics, wallpaper hangers, you name it, who had watched the game on television and said they could kick better than Chris," recalled Ortmayer. "All these guys wanted a tryout. I told Chris if this ever happened again, he could answer the phone."

San Diego whipped Pittsburgh, 26–17, on the final Monday night of the season, which meant Oakland would be the home team in the wild card game the following Sunday against Kenny Stabler, Jack Tatum, Dave Casper and the rest of the Houston Oilers at the Coliseum.

It also meant Oakland would not only have to beat Houston, but also win three games on the road to be a Super Bowl champion. No other wild card team had done it.

Oakland 27/Houston 7
December 28, 1980

On Monday, three days before Christmas, providence came to Charlie Sumner. Charlie is the greying linebacker coach of the Raiders who has a cross between a harried and a bemused look on his face most of the time. Take him out of coach's clothes and put him in a three-piece suit, and he'd look like an account executive for an advertising agency. On this day, Charlie was studying game films of the Houston Oilers.

As the motor of the projector whirred the film backward and forward, sending images up on the screen at the Alameda practice playground of the Raiders, Charlie was searching. He was looking to find some flaw in the versatile Houston offense that he could exploit and incorporate into the defensive game plan for the First Round Playoffs of the NFL.

The Oilers and the Raiders had qualified as the AFC wild card teams. Mathematically, they had tied for the leads of their respective divisions with identical records of 11 games won, 5 lost. But Cleveland and San Diego were declared the division winners through the cumbersome accounting system that sometimes takes a computer expert to decipher. Now in the meeting of the wild card entries, Oakland was the home team on the basis of a better record for games played within the conference. Oakland was 9-and-3; Houston was 7-and-5.

On a more emotional level, the game also signified a homecoming for three men who had a special niche in the history of the Raiders. Ken Stabler, Dave Casper and Jack Tatum, who until 1980 had spent all their pro careers wearing the black and silver of Oakland, were now invading the Oakland-Alameda County Coliseum adorned in the powder blue and white (with scarlet striping) of Houston.

Certainly those three would belong on an all-time Raider team. At least, they'd merit serious consideration, if not be conceded the positions outright. But this was a time to ignore the dramatic aspects of their return and concentrate on the threat they posed to the Raiders. Tatum had played only sporadically during the season, as the nickel back on passing downs. Stabler and Casper, however, were an integral part of the Texas team's offense. It was important for the Raiders to stop Earl Campbell, the premier running back in football. But it was equally important to negate the Stabler-to-Casper passing combination which had once contributed so notably to Oakland's winning tradition.

The way to attack a passing danger is to break down the protection—in this instance, to put pressure on the lefthanded Stabler, who no longer moved around as spryly as he used to. And this is what Sumner concentrated on. That Monday, he discovered the crack in the Houston armor plate.

"We saw," said Sumner after viewing Oiler films closely, "a weakness in the pass protection on their right side."

The Oilers used a two-tight-end offense, just as the Raiders had done a year before when they had Casper and Raymond Chester in the lineup at the same time. For Houston, Casper now lined up on the left side of the formation, with Mike Barber on the right side, and wide receiver Mike Renfro split out either right or left. It was Barber's side that intrigued Sumner. For some reason, when a man from the secondary moved up close to the line of scrimmage, Barber never picked him up.

The Raider "think tank" surmised that when Renfro was split to the left, Lester Hayes, the cornerback on the other side of the field, could move up to the line of scrimmage, just to the outside of linebacker Ted Hendricks. On passing plays, Barber blocked down on Hendricks if he didn't go out into a receiving pattern. The right tackle, Morris Towns, concentrated on the defensive end, John Matuszak. The guard, Ed Fisher, pulled

*The confrontation—Ken Stabler (12) receives a
strong stare from old teammate John Matuszak (72)
in the wild-card playoff game.*

into a short protection zone to help with Hendricks if necessary. The men in the backfield—Rod Carpenter or Tim Wilson at fullback, Earl Campbell deep in the "I" formation, flowed to the left. No one bothered to pick up Hayes (*see diagram*).

That became the crux of the Raider defensive strategy: on obvious passing downs, and Stabler also showed a proclivity for passing on first down, they would blitz with Hayes, the cornerback.

When the Oilers split Renfro to the right, Hayes had to drop back to his normal position in the secondary to cover the wide receiver, but strong safety Mike Davis was free to move up to the line of scrimmage in a blitzing position. And that, too, would be important in the Oakland defensive scheme (*see diagram*).

"Later," noted Sumner, "they sometimes slid the fullback over to cover Davis, but Mike still managed to get by him."

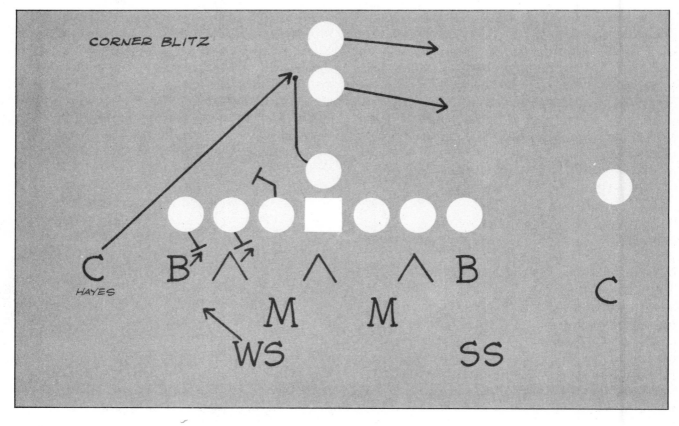

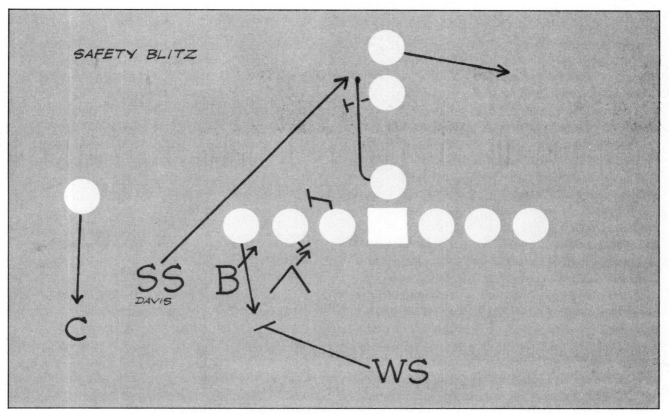

SAFETY BLITZ

SS
DAVIS

B

C

WS

The unorthodox Raider blitzing dominated the defensive action of the game. Hayes or Davis were also coming from southpaw quarterback Stabler's blind side as he dropped back to pass. It turned out to be one of the roughest days the veteran passer experienced physically in his 12 years as a pro. He was sacked seven times for a total of 65 yards and had two passes intercepted. Hayes and Davis, penetrating from the secondary, each had two significant sacks.

Yet, despite the final lop-sided score of 27–7, it wasn't all that easy.

The Raiders held Campbell to under 100 yards rushing, no mean feat—he averaged 121 yards per game for the season. And they did it just by playing the Oilers tough up front, man to man. There was nothing fancy about the Oiler running attack. They never ran a double team (using two blockers against one defender). They simply came at the Raider defense one-on-one and depended on Campbell's brute strength and elusiveness as a runner to do the rest. The great Oiler back broke through the swarming Raider tacklers on just one major drive.

After the Raiders had taken a 3–0 lead on a 47-yard field goal by Bahr, the Oilers started from their own 45 with 4 minutes and 40 seconds remaining in the first quarter. Campbell carried for six yards, and Stabler passed to Ronnie Coleman, lined up in the left slot, for 23. Then Campbell took over, carrying the ball six straight times until he plunged into the end zone from the one-yard line to give the Oilers a 7–3 lead when the first quarter ended.

Halfway through the second quarter, the Raiders moved ahead, the big play coming on a pass from Jim Plunkett to Kenny King, the ex-Oiler playing against his old teammates for the first time. It gained 37 yards to the Houston 2. On third down at the 1, with the Oilers bunched in their goal line defense, Plunkett crossed them by faking play action and flipping the ball to Todd Christensen, the third string tight end who was ostensibly in the game for extra blocking. Christensen's reception was his first in three NFL seasons. He was more noted for his aggressiveness as a leader of the Oakland special teams.

On the first play from scrimmage after the

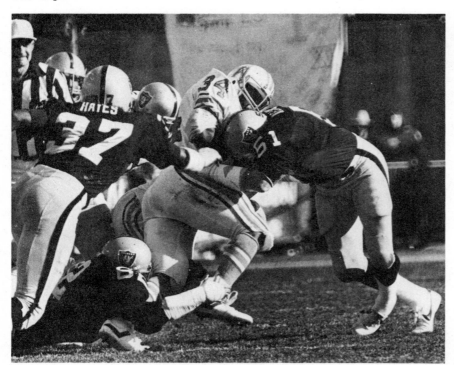

The ability of the Raiders to contain Earl Campbell (in white) through head-on tackles by Bob Nelson (51) and mates holds the Oilers in check.

kickoff, as Stabler faded to pass, there came Lester Hayes into the Houston backfield, without a hand laid on him. The all-pro cornerback tackled Stabler for a 10-yard loss and set in motion the Raiders' domination for the rest of the afternoon.

"We were outplayed and outcoached," said Bum Phillips, the head man of the Oilers. "The Raiders played as good as any team I've seen play in the 12 years I've been in pro ball. Sack after sack built their momentum, and the harder they came."

Hayes personally relished the physical part he played in keeping the Oilers at bay. "The biggest change I had to make coming into pro ball," he once said, "was controlling my aggression. I was always trying to hit somebody. Pounding on receivers always turned me on." Moreover, he was a native of Houston, born and raised there, going through Wheatley High School, where he won eight varsity letters in football and track.

Lester was born for his job—in 1980 he picked up the sobriquet of "Lester the Molester" and didn't consider it the least big derogatory—and it irked him that acceptance of his talents was such a long time in coming. Humility was not his forte. When asked to name the best cornerback in all the world, he would respond immediately, "The one you're talking to." Then upon reflection, he'd add, "Oh, there might be one in New Zealand, too."

Hayes had that bizarre outlook on life that's necessary to maintain equilibrium in a job where a man stands naked (figuratively) for all the world to see when he goofs. A mistake can easily mean six points in a game where touchdowns are measured carefully. A cornerback must have sensational athletic ability, a confidence bordering on arrogance and intense dedication and concentration. Lester had all those qualities, which is why he had a fantastic—his favorite word—1980 season for the Oakland Raiders and was the winner of the fifteenth annual George Halas Trophy, given by NEA, as the outstanding defensive player in the NFL.

The magical statistic that caught everybody's attention was his season total of 13 interceptions, just one off the all-time NFL record set by Hall-of-Fame defensive back Dick (Night Train) Lane. Lester actually would have broken the record, but four other interceptions during the season, one a 96-yard touchdown return against Miami, were negated by penalties.

In his fourth season, he became one of the most intimidating performers in the game, harassing wide receivers or runners who ventured into his area and delivering his sacks in memorable style when he blasted through against Stabler in the opening playoff game.

His teammates called him "The Judge" because he presided at left cornerback like a man with a gavel in his hand. The puzzle of Lester's life was why he was overlooked by all 28 NFL teams until the fifth round of the 1977 draft, when Oakland tabbed him. Hayes had a fine varsity career at Texas A&M, where he was one of the outstanding safeties in the country, playing in the same secondary with Pat Thomas, who became an all-pro cornerback with the Los Angeles Rams. Compactly put together at 6′ and 195 pounds, he was also a Texas state high school sprint champion at 220 yards. The Aggies had used him as a linebacker before switching him to strong safety as a junior. In high school, he played tackle.

So the memories of May 3, 1977, rankled. That was the date the teams in the NFL sat down to draft the graduating seniors. "I think about May 3 often," said Lester. "I want to make 27 teams wish they could go back to that day. There were 14 defensive backs taken before me. I want to make them pay for that. All the scouting reports said I was the No. 1 safety in the draft and I'd go on the first or second round. The phone didn't ring until 6:45 in the evening. It was the Raiders saying they'd taken me on the fifth round. I was heartbroken."

You see, Lester also stammered, and the NFL scouts decided in their resolute wisdom that this reflected on his intelligence. "Some guys picked ahead of me," shrugged Lester, "couldn't even pronounce their names."

By the end of his rookie year, on a team coming off a Super Bowl triumph, Lester had stepped into a regular job as a cornerback, a position he never had played before. The opening was created when George Atkinson was sidelined with a broken ankle and Skip Thomas was moved from left corner to safety. The early rap on Lester was that he gambled too much in his coverage, frequently straying from his primary responsibility to make a play elsewhere. But this reflected only his supreme belief in his athletic ability and an intuitive quest for the football that coaching can't teach.

Lester also picked up a trick that became his identity badge. He was the man with the "stickum." Stickum by its real name was Kwik Grip Hold Tight Paste, an amber-colored concoction of natural wood resin, isopropyl myristate, emcol,

balsom of fir, beeswax, lanolin, turpentine, petrolatum and wax victory amber #155. It was real messy. Wide receiver great Fred Biletnikoff first popularized it among the pros, slapping huge globs of it on the inside of his socks at the ankle, reaching down to daub it liberally on his fingers. He felt it helped him hang on to the football.

In Lester's first year, 1977, in a game against Houston, he was covering wide receiver Ken Burrough. The ball came spiralling his way, Hayes reached up to intercept, and it trickled off his fingers. Lester came to the sidelines, where "Fred had this jar of stickum and he gave it me." Hayes was turned on to the goo. Probably, it was more psychological than pragmatic. And it sure created a hell of a mess for equipment manager Dick Romanski and his son, Bob, who had to clean the sticky stuff off helmets, pads, shoes, etc. But progressively Lester became a demon pass interceptor. He picked off one in 1977, four in 1978, seven in 1979 and his magical 13 in 1980.

Lester Hayes comes geared for battle with huge globs of stickum and supreme confidence in his ability.

At the same time, he became one of the hardest working players in football, taking films home for incessant study of the players he faced. That study paid off in the calculated risks he took to position himself where the ball was. Lester's jumping ability helped, too. As a 5' 10" high school player on a team that won the state championship, Lester jumped center. The Raiders once held a jumping contest in their locker room, one of those tension-easing capers they like to indulge in. Only Derrick Ramsey, a 6' 4" tight end and a former basketball player at Kentucky, and Hayes were able to touch a metal air duct that ran through the room, suspended more than 12 feet from the floor.

"He's the best cornerback I've ever faced," said John Jefferson, the superb wide receiver of the San Diego Chargers. "You have to really prepare, and concentrate on each play, or he can shut you down for the day."

"He gambles an awful lot," said Stabler, "but he makes his gambles pay off."

In the third quarter of the First Round Playoffs, still trailing by only three points, the Oilers moved across midfield down to the Oakland 11-yard line. On second-and-eight, Stabler tried to drill a pass to Renfro in the end zone. Lester the Interceptor jumped in front of the wide receiver for his first interception of the day and turned the game around.

On the last play of the quarter, Plunkett connected with Cliff Branch for 33 yards to get the ball past midfield. On the first play of the fourth quarter, Plunkett hit running back Arthur Whittington with a 44-yard touchdown pass. With 5 minutes 29 seconds remaining after Oakland had scored again on a Bahr field goal, Lester Hayes delivered the coup de grace. He intercepted a Stabler pass on the left sideline and sprinted 20 yards into the end zone for the final score of the 27–7 triumph.

The Raiders had surmounted their first hurdle toward the Super Bowl.

Oakland 14/Cleveland 12
January 4, 1981

The Raiders traveled to Cleveland for the AFC Divisional Playoffs in unaccustomed style. Because of the short travel notice—no one could anticipate they'd still be alive at this stage of the season—the only charter plane available to them was a Boeing 747 owned by Transamerica Airlines. It was due to go to far-off Thailand but could be re-routed through Cleveland. Normally, it carried 484 passengers. Since the Raider travel party numbered one-fourth that figure, the card players on the team felt discriminated against. They had to sit next to each other. Virtually everyone else had his own row of seats.

The weather reports from Cleveland were discomforting. There was snow on the ground, the temperatures were sub-zero and expected to stay that way for the game. There was a school of thought in the NFL that insisted you treat the weather by ignoring it. For instance, Bud Grant

up in Minnesota where the countryside turns to tundra by December wouldn't let his Vikings use hand-heaters or any other heat-inducing paraphernalia. The Raiders decided that pragmatism was the better part of valor. In the last week of the regular season, playing on a very cold day in New Jersey, they noticed that the Giants provided "hot benches" on the sidelines to keep players of both teams warm between stints on the field. They were heated seats with receptacles to keep the feet and hands from going numb. When inquiries were made, it was discovered that the Philadelphia Eagles, due to host Minnesota in an NFC playoff game on Saturday, had first call on the "hot benches." But through the company in Pleasantville, N.J., that manufactured them, the Raiders also learned that the benches could be trucked in overnight from Philadelphia to Cleveland in time for the game on Sunday. This was arranged at a cost of $3,800.

Otherwise, the Raiders disdained the elements. The day before the game, they were bussed to a practice field at Baldwin-Wallace College for a brief workout and playfully threw snowballs at each other. They didn't take the home team Browns lightly, however.

Cleveland, with an 11–5 record, was coming off its best season in eight years. Winners of the Central Division, the Browns also had an extra week of rest while the wild card teams were slugging it out to reach the second round of the playoffs. In Brian Sipe, they had the most electrifying quarterback in pro football, named by the wire services as the most valuable player in the NFL. League statistics showed him to be the top passer in the game with a rating of 91.9. He had the most completions, 340, and 30 of them went for touchdowns. He also had the best percentage against interceptions. Sipe excelled in the clutch situations, pulling the Browns from behind so often in the final two minutes of a game that they were called the "Kardiac Kids." He was abetted by a fine corps of receivers and a versatile fullback in Mike Pruitt, a 1,000-yard ground-gainer. If the Browns were vulnerable, it was in their pass defense. They had given up more yards through the air (241.5 per game) than any team in the NFL.

And now the weather seemed to preclude attacking that weakness. At game time, the temperature was one degree below zero, with a 16 miles per hour wind whipping into the open end of Cleveland Stadium, off Lake Erie, which produced a chill factor of –36 degrees. Only one game in NFL history was ever played under colder conditions—the 1967 title game in Green Bay between the Packers and the Dallas Cowboys. Yet for the pre-game exercises, center Dave Dalby cavorted out on the field in a short-sleeved shirt as if to tell the bundled Browns that it was going to take more than cold to whip him.

Truly, it was not a day for football, which was designed to be played on crisp autumn afternoons. The snow had been swept off the field, but the turf was as hard as ice, and in some parts of the field the slick surface was suitable for hockey, completely iced over. Compounding the problem of footing and traction was the wintry blast of wind which made gripping the ball difficult,

played tricks with kicked balls and made passes flutter uncontrollably.

The open end of the stadium was particularly treacherous and would be a big factor in the outcome of the game. The Raiders won the toss of the coin and elected to receive, with Cleveland choosing to have the east, or open, end of the stadium at its back. It quickly became apparent that the condition of the field made normal football impossible. Neither team could sustain effective run blocking on offense because the linemen were sliding all over the place. And on defense, it was virtually impossible to get a pass rush because the men up front couldn't dig in on the frozen turf. There were seven punts in the first quarter alone, and the Raiders, moving against the wind, were unable to pick up a first down.

For Cleveland, Reggie Rucker, guarded by Dwayne O'Steen, dropped a pass in the end zone on the last play of the quarter. Then within the first three minutes of the second quarter, Don Cockcroft, the field goal specialist of the Browns, missed a long field goal attempt of 47 yards (the wind was against him now) and a chip shot of 30 yards. Five minutes later, however, the Cleveland defense stung the Raiders when Plunkett tried to hit Chandler on an "out" pattern to the right sideline. Cornerback Ron Bolton timed the play perfectly, stepped in front of Chandler and had open sailing to the end zone 42 yards away. Cockcroft was still having trouble with his placement kicks at that end of the field. Hendricks blocked his extra point attempt.

The Raiders finally got untracked after the kickoff and consumed six minutes on a 14-play drive, picking up five first downs as Plunkett smartly mixed passing and running, the big gain resulting from a Plunkett-to-Chester toss that went 26 yards to the Cleveland 2. On third down, with 18 seconds remaining in the half, van Eeghen plunged over right guard from the one-yard line for a touchdown. Bahr's conversion put Oakland in front, 7–6.

The key Oakland decision of the game was made when the teams, thawed out by the intermission, returned to the field for the third quarter. Cleveland now had the option of kicking off or receiving and naturally took the latter. Tom Flores chose to defend the west goal, with the wind in the Raiders' faces, during the third quarter, although neither team had been able to move the ball consistently from that position. "I figured," explained Tom, "that it would be a close game in the fourth quarter and we wanted the wind at our backs then." Smart.

Cleveland dominated the third quarter with the wind in its favor but had to settle for a pair of Cockroft field goals from short range which gave them a 12–7 lead. The minute the teams changed sides for the final quarter, the Raiders, mired on their own 19-yard line, got untracked and in the next six minutes smartly moved to their second touchdown, with Plunkett completing four passes, and van Eeghen again bucking over the middle from the one-yard line for the score. Bahr's kick made it 14–12, and for the last nine minutes of the game it became a matter of hanging on to that tenuous lead.

With a little over four minutes to play, the

Mike Davis holds on to the ball that he intercepted to clinch the 14–12 playoff victory over the Cleveland Browns.

Raiders seemed to be in control when Odis McKinney, their nickel back, fell on a Sipe fumble deep in Cleveland territory. Two plays later, they were on the Cleveland 15, third and one. But van Eeghen was stopped cold on two shots into the line, and the Browns took over with 2:22 left on the clock, the goal line 85 yards away, a perfect opportunity for the Kardiac Kids to do their familiar closing routine, wind or no wind. And Sipe was masterful in that situation.

A holding call against O'Steen on a third down pass incompletion kept the drive alive. A surprise third down sweep by Mike Pruitt around left end gained 14 yards to the Oakland 14. Cleveland took time out with 56 seconds remaining. The Browns were in field goal range, and three points would win the game and advance them to the Conference finals. All they had to do was play it safe.

But Coach Sam Rutigliano, standing on the Cleveland sideline, was nagged by doubts. He saw the goal posts and beyond them the fence which was a meager barrier to the mini-gale off Lake Erie. Cockroft had already missed two field goals in that direction. He had blown an extra point. And a third field goal try was muffed because holder Paul McDonald couldn't get the snap placed. For Sam, a field goal was no cinch. He had time to make up his mind. Pruitt probed the center of the Raider line and was held to one yard. Forty-nine seconds left as Cleveland called time again.

Then came the play Rutigliano will have to live with the rest of his career. On second down, he decided to go for the touchdown and told Sipe to aim for wide receiver Dave Logan in the end zone. "If nobody's open," cautioned Sam, "throw the ball into Lake Erie." The Browns could always run another play into the line and then try the clinching field goal.

On the Raider side, when the teams lined up, Mike Davis was startled. "We figured the Browns would run the ball up the middle," he said, "then kick it. What they did, though, was baffling." The Browns came out in a formation that alerted Davis to the threat of a pass. Ozzie Newsome, the tight end who was Mike's primary responsibility, split from the left tackle to give himself some maneuvering room. On a run, he'd be bunched in tight with the rest of the line. The Raiders had a blitz on to pressure Sipe.

As the quarterback retreated to his protective pocket, he tried to find Logan, but the receiver was covered. Through some instinctive quirk—in the heat of competition, it isn't easy to analyze responses—Sipe turned to his left and thought he saw Newsome open curling left into the end zone. His eyes deceived him. Davis was with him, and so was Burgess Owens, playing "centerfield" as the free safety. Sipe threw, and the ball, fluttering against the head wind, got by Owens, but Davis lunged forward and grasped it securely for the interception that sealed the Oakland victory.

It was the single most important defensive play in the Raiders' quest for the Super Bowl. Rutigliano was criticized severely for gambling in that spot, but the Browns had advanced that far with the pass, and they went down with the pass. "It was the right decision," said Raider assistant coach Sam Boghosian reflectively. "He told the quarterback if Logan wasn't open to throw the ball into the lake. Instead, Sipe, who was under no real pressure from us and might have waited to let Logan get open, chose to go to Newsome, who was covered."

For the Raiders, it was the best kind of luck.

"Luck," said Boghosian, "is when preparation meets opportunity." And at that very moment of his young life, when the opportunity to make the big play arrived, Mike Davis was prepared.

"He's dropped some interceptions," noted Flores of his strong safety, "but he made the one that counted. Mike is a tough competitor, wild and aggressive. And he's just starting to come into his own."

Mike Davis was drafted by Oakland on the second round in 1977. The native of Los Angeles had gone to the University of Colorado after two years of junior college at East Los Agneles, where he was a high hurdler on the track team. At 6′ 3″ and 203 pounds, he had the size for the physical style the Raiders preach for their defensive backs, and his 4.5 speed in the 40-yard dash rounded out impressive credentials.

"He was a linebacker when he came to us," said Bill Mallory, his coach at Colorado, "but we recruited him to play defensive back. I remember that he had an excellent attitude and that he kept improving game after game."

To those who knew him closely, starting with his mother in southern California, Mike Davis was a dichotomy or, if you want to dip into a fictional analogy, a Dr. Jekyll and Mr. Hyde. There was the personality of Mike Davis the football player—brutally aggressive, even intimidating, a hitter. And his words reflected those qualities:

"I think you have to be an intimidating player out there. You have to have the will to kick ass every time you step out on the field. Your reputation is at stake every time you're out there. I don't want to give a coach, a player or a fan the idea they can isolate on me and do what they want to do to beat our team.

"I have the strength and the weight to be an enforcer like a linebacker. As in any position, you must have the agility. But the main thing is being aggressive. it becomes a part of you. You don't want to let yourself or your teammates down. It becomes just the will to get the job done.

"There's a No. 1 rule around here, and that is not to take any crap from anybody. Whenever I quit playing aggressively, it will be time to quit football."

There was the other Mike Davis, out of uniform, with a beaming smile fixed on his face, a concern for people, a soft, friendly demeanor, an easy manner of communication.

"My mother calls me 'schizo' sometimes," said Mike. "She sees me playing and can't believe it's me."

As a person, he was held in such high esteem by his teammates that they named him their team representative in the NFL Players Association, a rare tribute for a 24-year-old who had played only one full season as a starter in the defensive secondary.

With a major in communications at Colorado, Mike hoped some day to have a career in television and radio. But there were years of football ahead. He spent his rookie year of 1977 on injured reserve because of a broken bone in his wrist. He was used mostly on special teams in 1978 and started out the next year again as a substitute. After the fourth game, he replaced Charles Phillips at strong safety, and the job was his for good. And for the future good of the Raiders.

Oakland 34/San Diego 27
January 11, 1981

The rollicking Raiders were being swarmed by the national press as they invaded San Diego for the final step to the Super Bowl. Newspapers in New York and Washington and other major cities sent their leading columnists west to detail the improbable journey of the mavericks from the East Bay.

No doubt some of the attraction was Al Davis himself and his one-man insurrection against the NFL establishment. Rival owner Gene Klein of the San Diego ignited a controversy during the week with an unusual blast against Los Angeles columnist Mel Durslag (*Herald-Examiner*), accusing him of being in the proverbial pocket of the Raiders' owner, charging that Durslag's criticism of NFL officiating in the Cleveland game was an "insidious plot" to intimidate the crew for the AFC Championship finale. There were even ridiculous references to Hitler, Goebbels, the Big Lie, etc. Durslag retorted, "The National Football League is not above reproach. Nor is Mr. Klein. All are fully capable, if not inclined, to punch below the pelvic region. . . ." Klein was a visible, vocal opponent of the Raider franchise's projected move to southern California.

The Friday night before the game, at the Stardust Hotel where the Raiders were quartered, Davis held a press conference for the national media, but the talk was all about football. "I admire the way the Chargers of today play football because they play to win and they're not afraid to lose. In our society, that's against the cultural pattern. Our philosophy in Oakland is to run the ball but look for the big play. You don't necessarily win with percentage throwing.

"The toughest thing in professional football is to resist change. George Weiss and Branch Rickey, when I was growing up in New York, they taught you a lesson."

Asked about his quarterback, who was completing maybe the comeback of all time, he said, "I think environment is so important in the success of a player. Quarterbacks and head coaches live in a private world, and it's a tough life. I think Plunkett's a great player. He really hasn't played the last few years. We didn't know him that well when he came to us. I've always thought he was a winner."

Nature conspired against the home team, which liked a fast track. Quarterback Dan Fouts had thrown 30 touchdown passes. In wide receiver John Jefferson and tight end Kellen Winslow, he had all-pro targets. Charlie Joiner, the other wide receiver, had also gained more than 1,000 yards. A light rain on Saturday night softened the turf, which would make it difficult for the receivers to run their routes.

The rain stopped the morning of the game, but the day remained gray and dull—unlike the electric atmosphere in Jack Murphy Stadium, newly named for the late sports editor of the San Diego *Union*. The arena was sold out, with 52,675 tickets distributed. The almost deafening loudspeakers blared a disco refrain, "San Diego Super Chargers," that was to continue all through the game so that there were no dead spots during which one could think about the drama down on the field.

It took only a minute and 35 seconds for the Raiders to receive an omen appropriate for a team of destiny. On the third play after the opening kickoff, Plunkett aimed a pass at King circling out of the backfield and down the middle. The ball skidded off the running back's fingers and landed in the cradled arms of tight end Raymond Chester, who had run a deeper pattern downfield. There was no one between Raymond and the goal line, and the Raiders had seven of the easiest points a team can pick up in so crucial a game.

A couple of sequences later, the Chargers tied the score on a 48-yard bomb from Fouts to Joiner. But then the Raiders took command with three touchdowns scored within a 13-minute time span. First, Plunkett capped a 76-yard march by scrambling five yards into the end zone. Then he threw 21 yards to King for a score. After Ray Guy pinned the Chargers deep into their territory with a 71-yard punt and Ted Hendricks pounced on a fumble, van Eeghen ended a short drive with a three-yard scoring burst.

The Raiders were playing error-free football. They had no turnovers for the game. San Diego had three (two interceptions and one fumble). Yet even with a 28–7 lead, the Raiders couldn't relax against the explosive Charger offense.

"You know," said assistant coach Charlie Sumner, "they're going to pass every down. Most of the time we used four linemen, five defensive backs and two linebackers. It was the exact opposite of the Cleveland game when we stayed in a three-man front more than normal because of the cold day."

The Chargers kept chipping away at the Raider lead. Another touchdown pass from Fouts to Joiner brought the score to 28–14 at halftime. The first two times San Diego had possession in the third quarter resulted in a field goal and a touchdown, and now the gap was only 28–24, and a feeling of desperation gripped some of the Raiders. "I must admit there was some terror in my heart at that point," said Hendricks. "Just before our offense went on the field, I grabbed Gene Upshaw and said, 'Hey, make some first downs, will you? Give us some rest.'" In his ears dinned the blast of "San Diego Super Chargers!"

At a moment like this, the character of a team is revealed. Plunkett was in the midst of a brilliant performance, one of the greatest of his long career—his final statistics showed 14 completions in 18 attempts for 261 yards and two touchdowns—but the burden was on the Raiders to return to an old-fashioned script, controlling the ball by simply grinding out yardage the hard way, going right at the opposition with basic running, throwing just enough to keep the defense wary.

Oakland responded to the challenge with a beautiful display of possession football that determined the course of the game. First, the Raiders got a little breathing room by moving 68 yards in nine plays, settling for a 27-yard field goal by Bahr. The defense, with a chance to rest, stopped the Chargers cold as the third quarter ran out. Then the Raiders used 10 plays to position themselves for another Bahr field goal. The Chargers retrieved those three points by moving 72 yards into range for a 27-yard field goal by Rolf Benirschke, which put them again within a touchdown of Oakland but also took eight minutes off the clock. When Arthur Whittington took the ensuing kickoff on his 1-yard line and was stopped

on the 25, the clock showed 6:43 remaining as the Raiders' offensive unit perched for the snap.

The importance of using up time was paramount, so Sam Boghosian, the offensive line coach, changed the blocking instructions for the men up front: "We split our line [i.e., there were greater gaps between the linemen as they took their stances]. The theory behind taking the larger splits is to create daylight before you have to block anybody. You can't do it earlier in the game because you went to keep them guessing run or pass [i.e., large spaces between the linemen would invite a pass rusher to burst through]. Mainly, the idea was to isolate their middle linebacker, to let our center, Dave Dalby, get at Bob Horn [of the Chargers]. Even on plays that weren't going at the middle linebacker, Dalby was able to push Horn right out of the middle, and van Eeghen would cut back and take advantage of the void."

Obviously, the Raiders were committed to running the ball. And the Chargers knew it. On the sidelines, tight end Kellen Winslow of the Chargers said to himself, "God, you owe us one." Later, he explained, "They hadn't laid the ball on the ground for us in a long, long time. I was looking for something, anything—a fumble, a penalty, an interception—anything to get us the ball. But it never happened. They were perfect."

Paul Zimmerman wrote in *Sports Illustrated:*

"The Raiders held the ball for the entire 6:43. When one examines those three crucial drives, one sees a proud offensive football team at its best. Oakland ran 33 plays; there were no offensive penalties, no offsides, no missed snap counts. . . . Twenty-five running plays picked up 95 yards, 62 by the dependable van Eeghen."

Dependable van Eeghen. That phrase had been synonymous with Oakland Raider football for seven years. The last five of them he had functioned as their regular fullback. He led the Raiders in rushing those five years. He gained over 1,000 yards, the magical figure for a running back, three straight seasons. He set a Raider single-season rushing record of 1,273 yards in 1977. He held the Raider career ground-gaining mark of 5,757 yards and was within 81 of breaking into the Top 20 in all of football history. He made himself into an accomplished receiver coming out of the backfield, catching 51 passes in 1979. He was a staunch blocker, either leading his halfback through the hole or protecting the quarterback. He never blew an assignment. He almost never coughed up the ball.

Also, he never made an all-pro team, or even an all-conference team. He was selected once for the Pro Bowl. He was the invisible man in one of the glamor positions of football, and Tom Flores mused, "Maybe it's because he is so steady, but I don't think he gets enough credit."

The lack of recognition never fazed the durable Dutchman from Cranston, R.I. It was enough for him to be earning a living by playing a boy's game. In fact, it was remarkable. He never intended to make football his vocation. A degree in economics from Colgate, a little intellectual school in upper New York state, isn't the usual platform for a pro career. Colgate is pseudo-Ivy League—on the academic level of that hallowed circuit of learning but not part of it. Pro football scouts gave it only cursory attention.

Yet the Raiders had been lucky in that area, for one of the toughest, roughest fullbacks in their history was a product of Colgate. Marv Hubbard immediately preceded van Eeghen, and in fact their careers overlapped in Oakland.

"I had no goal of playing pro football," said van Eeghen. "Colgate isn't exactly a football factory. I was a wishbone halfback there, and if you know anything about the wishbone, you know it isn't the best training for the pros."

He had, however, broken all of Hubbard's running records at Colgate, and he was selected to play in the East-West game in San Francisco. Annually, Al Davis spends a day watching the practice sessions of those college breds on the peninsula south of the city. It's an easy ride from Oakland. On the day he chose in January, 1974, it was raining. So the East players went indoors and merely ran around the gym floor, wearing shorts. Davis looked them over curiously, for size, movement and demeanor. And when he got back to Oakland, he announced to the Raider staff, "I've just seen our next fullback." It was van Eeghen, picked up in the third round of a draft a few months later.

Dependable Mark van Eeghen keeps adding to his total as the leading ground-gainer in Oakland Raider history.

The curly-haired rookie with the choirboy face (at least then) made the team. In his second year, with Hubbard's career fading because of injuries, Mark shared time at fullback with Pete Banaszak. In his third year, he took over as the regular and was a force in the drive to Super Bowl XI. In 1977, only Walter Payton of the Chicago Bears surpassed him in ground-gaining. "For what we do," said John Madden, then his coach, "Mark is one of the top fullbacks in the league. We require a lot from our backs. They have to be able to run, get open for passes and catch the ball and block for the run and pass, and do all these things well. Mark is proficient in all of them."

Proficient but not spectacular, and that's why a cloak of obscurity already began to envelop the 6' 2", 225-pound plugger. The longest run he ever made, 68 yards against the New York Jets, was in a 1976 pre-season game and didn't count. In the 1,436 times he took a handoff from the quarterback and headed into the line, the farthest he ever traveled past the line of scrimmage was 34 yards.

But he was consistently productive, and never was that more apparent than in the final drive of

Not even tacklers hanging all over his back keeps van Eeghen from moving irresistably forward.

the AFC title game against the Chargers, when he gained 31 yards in seven vital carries.

"We started that drive," reviewed van Eeghen, "just wanting to get a couple of first downs, keep the ball a few minutes and then punt them into a hole. But after we started going and picking up a little yardage [*from the Raider play-by-play: van Eeghen up middle for 5, van Eeghen at left tackle for 10, van Eeghen at right guard for 4*], all once we felt we could run the clock out. It was a very exciting thing to be on the field, knowing we could win the game by keeping the ball, even if it was in a very unspectacular way.

"Basically, I was just doing my job as a ball-control fullback. I don't break too many runs. I go for five, six or seven yards—maybe 10 or 12. What I have to do is use my eyes well, go where they ain't."

"He'll find the hole if there's one to be found," said Plunkett. "That's why we just knew the plays we were calling in the drive against San Diego were going to work."

For the game, the Raiders ran the ball 42 times from scrimmage, put the ball in the air just 18 times. Van Eeghen picked up 85 yards in 20 carries. The Raiders' time of possession was 35 minutes 3 seconds. And they ended with Plunkett falling on the ball safely the last two plays of the afternoon as the clock ran down to zero. The offensive line had done its part superbly with aggressive blocking.

The jubilant Raiders were already looking ahead to New Orleans as offensive captain Gene Upshaw handed the game ball to his owner and said, "I want to show the NFL and Gene Klein that Al Davis knows how to run a ball club."

Oakland 27/Philadelphia 10
January 25, 1981

Rod Martin, the effusive right linebacker of the Raiders, knew early in the week that the fates were stacked in his favor. Martin and a pair of other linebackers, Ted Hendricks and Jeff Barnes, were regulars in a card game called "crazy eights." The road trip for a Super Bowl was a lot longer than the normal quick overnight (or at most two nights) jump to another city. So, when they weren't at practice or at a team meeting or making a hasty foray into the French Quarter of New Orleans, the players had plenty of time on their hands. Which meant card games. Twice Martin won three games in a row from his mates.

"We call that the Triple Crown," said Rod, "in honor of John Matuszak's favorite drink." The "three" signified an omen of greater import. In Super Bowl XV, Rod Martin would intercept three passes by Ron Jaworski to emerge as the defensive hero of the game and a magazine cover boy as his effusive gestures in raising his hands skyward, an exultant smile on his face, flaunted the ultimate accomplishment of the Raiders.

Rod Martin latches on to an interception, one of a record-setting three for the Super Bowl. Three was his magic number.

On a defensive unit with such colorful figures as The Tooz (Matuszak), The Stork (Hendricks), The Molester (Hayes), Martin was an unlikely record-setter—the three intercepts in one game were a new Super Bowl record. Or, on reflection, maybe it was logical that he would get the opportunity.

Teams tended to pick on the right side of the Raiders' defense. The end was Dave Browning, a baby-faced 24-year-old who didn't seem to exude strength. The corner back was Dwayne O'Steen, cast off by the Los Angeles Rams. The right inside linebacker, Bob Nelson, was a free agent who had spent a good part of the season on the injured list. And there was Martin, undersized by pro standards at 6' 2" and 210 pounds, and also culled once from the ranks of the unemployed.

In a sense, he symbolized the team's luck with players ignored by other teams. Because of his assumed physical limitations, Rod wasn't drafted until the twelfth (and last) round in 1977 after a fairly good varsity career at the University of Southern California. Give the Raiders credit for seeing something in him then. But it was tough to make the roster of a team just coming off a world championship, the Raiders were loaded with linebackers, and on August 30, 1977, after the fourth exhibition game, he was shipped across the Bay to San Francisco for a future draft choice. The 49ers looked at him for just two weeks, then gave him

his outright release, and Rod went home to Los Angeles.

In early November, the Raiders, decimated by injuries, located Martin playing basketball in a gymnasium in Santa Monica and invited him to rejoin the club. Other teams in the NFL had contacted him, but he was waiting for the Raider summons. "I happen to look good in silver and black," he said glibly.

By the middle of the 1978 season, he was seeing regular service as a linebacker. At the time, Rod filled in for all four positions in the 3–4 defense. But the right, or weakside, spot seemed to be his niche, and for a couple of years he waged a spirited duel with Jeff Barnes for the starting job. A knee injury to Martin early in the 1980 training camp put Barnes ahead for a while. Then Jeff hurt his knee, and Martin took over the lead role and never relinquished it. "He just kept working and working," said Flores.

And he was ready for the Eagles, omens and all. Studying films before the Super Bowl, while some of his mates were still discovering Bourbon Street, he noted that when the Eagles lined up in their two-tight-end offense, with Harold Carmichael split wide to the left, the tendency was to throw to the tight end on Rod's side.

Flores, as the head coach, was doing the same kind of intensive job of preparing his team for the game. In the first week after the Raiders beat the Chargers to qualify for the championship playoff, Tom had them take care of the extraneous details so they wouldn't be diverted from concentrating on the Eagles. The players were measured for Super Bowl rings and for special coats and slacks given to them for the game. Their ticket allocations were made.

"We held some short workouts that first week without boring them," reviewed Tom. "We kept their spirits up. The idea was that when we got to New Orleans, it was time to prepare for the game rather than worry. We got them cars so they wouldn't feel stranded and we gave them per diem for meals that weren't required as a team."

Rumors escalated about the Raiders rousting about town, but in reality, Flores revealed, Matuszak drew the only heavy fine for his well-publicized adventure on Bourbon Street. He was the only player who missed curfew. A total of six were late for team meetings. One missed a team meal. The Raiders were levied nowhere near the $15,000 reported. Gene Upshaw flippantly tossed out that figure in an exuberant mood after the game.

On a strategy level, Flores said, "We had to worry about the fact that in our first game with them [won 10–7 by Philadelphia in November], the Eagles had eight sacks. If we could protect our passer, I felt we could throw against them. They were basically a zone team, so it was hard to go deep against them. And we had to throw on first down and complete the pass to keep us from getting in a hole."

In the November game, the Eagles were able to deploy 30 times in their nickel defense because the Raiders couldn't pick up yardage on first down and got into obvious passing situations. In the Super Bowl, however, the Raiders were able to gain four yards or more on first down 15 times out of their 24 possessions. As a result, the Eagles couldn't juggle their personnel as much, leaving their defenses fairly predictable. Plunkett was sacked only once, in the third quarter when the Raiders were comfortably ahead, and it didn't even interrupt a drive to a field goal.

The Raider defense had cased the Eagles well, too. On the third play of the game, Martin's analysis of their pass tendencies proved out. The Eagles lined up with two tight ends. John Spagnola, on the left side, hooked behind Martin, but Rod dropped back quickly with him. The pass from Jaworski wobbled into the linebacker's hands, and he raced 17 yards to the Eagle 30. The Raiders moved in for the touchdown, on a two-yard pass from Plunkett to Branch. First blood for the Raiders.

Cliff Branch clutches a pass from Jim Plunkett in the end zone to open the scoring against the Eagles, with defenders surrounding him.

They got a break later in the quarter when a 40-yard pass from Jaworski to Rodney Parker in the end zone, which would have tied the game, was wiped out because of illegal motion by Carmichael, the other wide receiver. Here, too, the Raiders forced the Eagles to press. During the regular season, the 6′ 8″ Carmichael seldom went in motion before the snap. But because of the Raiders' bump-and-run coverage, Eagle Coach Dick Vermeil installed some motion plays to free the big receiver. On this play, with his timing rusty, Carmichael turned upfield illegally and negated the score.

On the last play from scrimmage in the first quarter, the Raiders stunned the Eagles with the longest touchdown in Super Bowl history. In the Raider playbook, it was listed as "94 Out, Z-Cross." Plunkett called it on third down at the Oakland 20. Chandler, flanked right, ran a crossing pattern to the other side, intersecting Branch, who ran a deep post. Halfback Kenny King

drifted to the left flat, behind the linebacker. The best laid plans of man often need a twist. Faced with a strong pass rush by the Eagles, Plunkett was unable to find Chandler, his primary receiver, and had to scramble to his left. King, seeing this, also moved to his left and down the sideline into the zone of cornerback Herman Edwards.

"We have a rule," said Flores, "that any time the quarterback scrambles, the receivers scramble in the same direction."

Edwards also spotted Chandler coming across and started to move in his direction. Plunkett threw over the cornerback to King, who made a brilliant, turn-around catch and took off down the sidelines in a foot race to the end zone. Chandler was his escort. "I always tell Kenny," Chandler later kidded, "that if he ever gets out in the open to please cruise so I can look fast keeping up with him."

In interviews during the week, those orchestrated sessions in which the team's players gath-

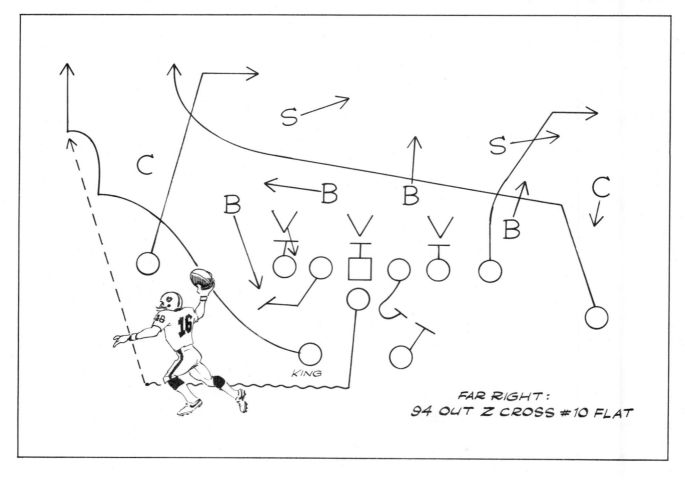

FAR RIGHT:
94 OUT Z CROSS #10 FLAT

The longest play in Super Bowl history finds Kenny King (33) escorted down the sideline by Bob Chandler (85). It goes for 80 yards.

ered in the ballroom of the New Orleans Fairmont, each with his own table, surrounded by writers, King had been asked about his development as a receiver. "Let's put it this way," he answered. "On a scale of one to 10, when I first came to the Raiders, I was a two. Now I'm Bo Derek."

"They come up with a broken play," said the Eagles' Vermeil wryly in his post-mortem reflections, "for an 80-yard touchdown. And they tackled Carl Hairston [the Eagles' defensive end] by his face mask."

The Eagles, to their credit, responded with a 61-yard march to set up a field goal by Tony

Franklin. Late in the second quarter, they were on the move again, 62 yards in 11 plays, to the Oakland 11. But Jaworski missed on three passes. Still, as they lined up for another field goal attempt, a score would have buoyed them at the halftime intermission. But Hendricks, a master at penetrating on kicks and an awesome barrier with his height, deflected Franklin's boot.

"There were two key factors in the Super Bowl in my mind," reviewed Flores. "One was blocking the field goal before the half. The other was when we came out in the second half and drove the field. That broke their backs. When we built our lead [14–3], I told our quarterback in the

Part of the ritual of Super Bowl week is the press conference. Here Kenny King does his bit for the nation's assembled writers. The table, 33, carries his number.

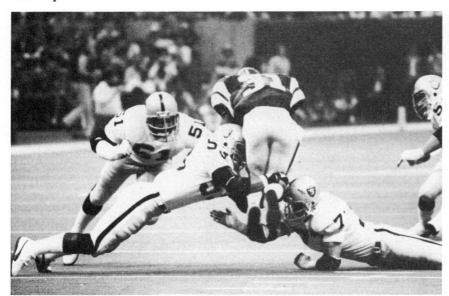

The concerted Raider defense against Philadelphia finds Rod Martin (53) and John Matuszak, on turf, right, putting a pincer movement on hurtling Wilbert Montgomery, with Bob Nelson (51) moving in to help.

locker room, 'Now don't get conservative, Jim.' An important play was when we were deep in our territory, and Plunkett hit King with a short pass. Kenny split their defenders and went just far enough for a first down to get us out of the hole.''

The Raiders had been set back for holding on the first play of the second half. King's burst brought them out to the 35-yard line. Plunkett passed again to Chandler for 32 yards. Van Eeghen ran for four. From the Eagle 29, Plunkett dropped back with good protection. Branch, lined up left, made a move to the inside, then cut back to the left flag. Rookie cornerback Roynell Young of the Eagles was right with him as they neared the goal line. Plunkett's pass fluttered and was short. Branch turned back, leaped and wrestled the ball

away from Young, twisting and falling into the end zone as he descended.

On the next Eagle possession, Rod Martin thwarted a drive into Raider territory by stepping in front of Spagnola again for his second vital interception, and that in effect wrapped up the victory although a quarter and a half remained to play. The Raiders swiftly moved to the Eagle end of the field, with Plunkett throwing passes of 16 and 17 yards, and Bahr booted a 46-yard field goal.

Philadelphia finally settled down with an 88-yard drive that lapped over into the fourth quarter and resulted in its only touchdown of the day, on an eight-yard pass from Jaworski to tight end Keith Krepfle. But Plunkett was masterful as

Cliff Branch reposes in the end zone for his second touchdown against the Eagles, with Roynell Young, left, a vain pursuer.

Jim Plunkett (16) does an adroit job of analyzing the Eagle formations and checking off with the proper plays at the line of scrimmage.

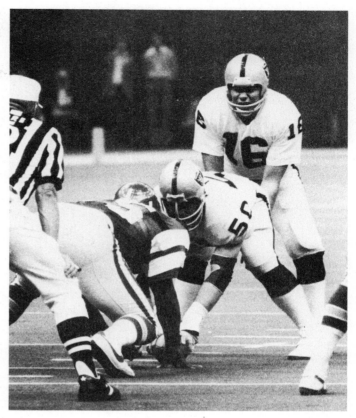

he chewed up five and a half minutes, mixing his plays adroitly, throwing sharply (three completions in his first four attempts) and setting up another Bahr field goal that closed out the scoring. The Raiders were decisive victors.

"The protection was so good," said Flores later, "that when I look at the videotape of the game, there are some shots of Plunkett throwing where you don't even see a defensive lineman in the picture."

"Plunkett came up with a great game," said Vermeil, who had been his first quarterback coach in college. "We had good heat on Jimmy, and he stepped up real good. He may never play that well again."

For his performance, the reclaimed veteran quarterback was named most valuable player of Super Bowl XV and received an automobile from *Sport Magazine.* He also dominated the postgame activities.

Beads of water, the legacy of a quick shower, glistened on the ringlets of his black hair in the interview room. With the crush of at least 100 writers squeezing in on him and television floods playing a spotlight on his gleaming face, the water soon mingled with sweat. But none of this mattered to Jim Plunkett. Or affected his composure.

He had reached one of those peaks of accomplishment few achieve in a lifetime.

He stood there on a small white pedestal, in a simple white shirt, the top three buttons open, the tail hanging loose over his rumpled tan gabardines, which covered his cowboy boots. Behind him, Rod Martin animatedly described his three interceptions, the last with three minutes to play. In front of him, Cliff Branch detailed his two touchdown catches. To his right, Tom Flores quietly expressed his elation to some writers.

But the real focus was on Plunkett, who said glowingly, "I can't even express my joy right now."

"Jim Plunkett, it's good to have you back," said Harmon Wages, a former pro back working for an Atlanta television station.

Was there, someone asked, something to be learned from all this?

"Perseverance is a good lesson," Jim answered patiently, "because there were times I wanted to throw the towel in."

Two and a half years before, Plunkett could have been claimed by any one of 27 teams in the NFL for the waiver price of $100. None did. On August 28, 1978, the San Francisco 49ers released him outright. He thought seriously then of never

An intent Jim Plunkett absorbs instruction from press box spotters.

playing football again. Yet football had been his life, the means for hoisting himself out of the barrio of San Jose, a sprawling city carved out of land that was once prune ranches. Both his parents, of Mexican descent, were blind and on welfare. He sold newspapers, pumped gas, anything to make a buck.

And the psychological scars of that upbringing never completely vanished. When he was acquired by the 49ers from the New England Patriots, his first pro team, he bought a house in the posh suburb of Atherton, though he was a bachelor. "When I was a kid," he explained, "we always used to have to move when the rents went up. So I always wanted to own my own home."

He isolated himself there when the 49ers let him go, his most depressed period ever. Two weeks later, Al Davis called Wayne Hooper, Jim's lawyer, and invited the quarterback to Oakland for a tryout.

On the face of it, Plunkett was damaged goods. He had undergone three knee operations and two shoulder operations since breaking in with the Patriots in 1971. Yet more serious was the damage to his psyche. In a profession where

ego correlates with performance, he had begun to question himself.

Like an aging film star screen-testing for a bit part, Plunkett threw passes for a critical Raider jury (which included Tom Flores, then a backfield coach) on the Alameda practice grounds. "It was ego-deflating for me," admitted Jim. "It was tough to go through. I had been a starter my whole life." At Stanford, he was an All-American, led that school to a Rose Bowl triumph and was voted the Heisman Trophy as the outstanding player in the nation. He was the first man picked in the NFL draft. In his first game as a pro, he led the Patriots to a season-opening 20–6 upset of the Raiders.

Now he was with them, signed at the urging of Flores, with a representative six-figure contract for a player of his experience. All through the 1978 season, he never stepped on the field during a game. "It was miserable," recalled Jim. "I practiced every day, but my mind was somewhere else. I was depressed and demoralized. I couldn't come to grips with the whole thing."

John Ralston, his college coach, said, "Jim is one of the most sensitive people I have been

Nose guard Reggie Kinlaw (62) literally hurls himself against the attack of the Eagles in Super Bowl XV. Safety Burgess Owens (44) helps.

From his post as free safety, Burgess Owens takes on Philadelphia tight end John Spagnola and holds his ground.

It's the supreme matchup—cornerback Lester Hayes, covered with stickum, sizes up his quarry, John Jefferson of San Diego.

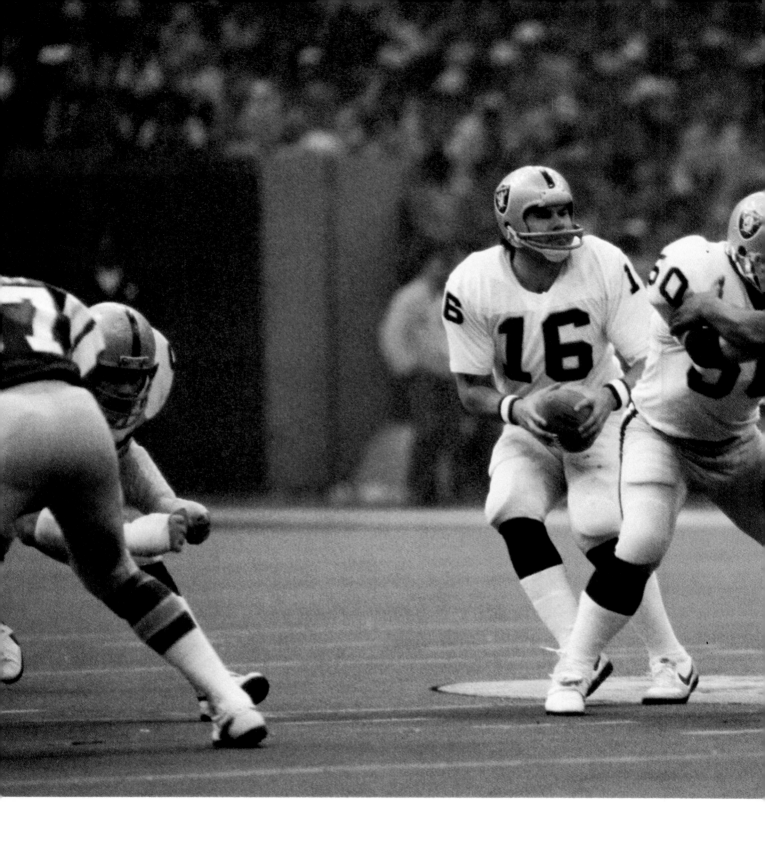

Behind the shield of center Dave Dalby (50), quarterback Jim Plunkett (16) is firmly in control of the ball and the situation as he drops back to pass against Philadelphia in Super Bowl XV.

The mobility of Jim Plunkett is a valuable asset to the Raiders in their march to the world championship.

His protection is so secure that in the game films virtually no Eagles mar the landscape as Jim Plunkett passes.

Mike Davis (36) is all over tight end Keith Krepfle of the Eagles as a Philadelphia pass attempt goes awry.

Eagle quarterback Ron Jaworski (7) is constantly aware of the movable presence of linebacker Ted Hendricks (83).

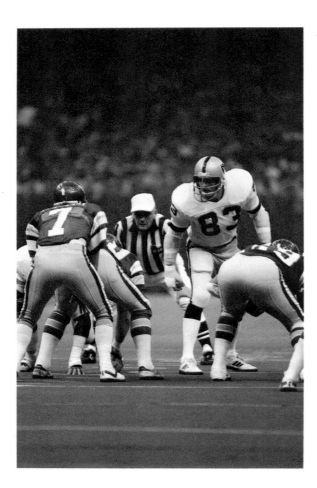

A covey of Raiderettes form a pleasant entrance archway for Jim Plunkett when he is introduced before the game.

around in my entire life. This guy wears his feelings on his sleeve, and he has both sleeves rolled down all the time."

Plunkett didn't even want to return in 1979, but once he reported to training camp, he felt comfortable playing football again. He was throwing the ball well and during the exhibition season he was even sharper than incumbent quarterback Ken Stabler. A change was delayed only because Flores had succeeded Madden as head coach and was more comfortable with the proven Snake in control, and because the Raiders were unable to trade Stabler at the time.

Plunkett threw only 15 passes in four brief appearances during the 1979 campaign, but he was ready. Getting perky, too. After a pre-season game against Washington in 1980, he asked Flores bluntly to trade him, since he was now backing up Dan Pastorini. Flores said simply that the Raiders needed a veteran like him for insurance. And sure enough, after Pastorini broke his leg in the fifth game of the season, they had a quarterback who would take them through the Super Bowl, winning 13 of the 15 games he started.

His personality didn't change. The acclaim wouldn't tilt the head of this gentle, obliging but essentially private man. He was still sensitive. You couldn't forget the slights, the skepticism, even by some teammates. But he enjoyed being a winner again. "It's a good feeling," said this born-again quarterback, "to have people saying nice things about you."

The moment of truth hit him two days after the Philadelphia conquest, when the Raiders and their huge entourage had flown home from New Orleans in two planes. On Tuesday, the city of Oakland staged a parade and civic luncheon for the Raiders. Then Plunkett and a few of his teammates zipped across the Bay to San Francisco and a Union Street boite called Perry's, where they reveled in all the good things that had happened to them. Later, Plunkett got in his car and headed south, to his house in Atherton.

"Driving home," he recalled, "I reflected on how happy and proud I was about what had happened. It hit me then more than any other time, a great feeling that caught me by surprise.

"I was really pleased. With myself. And with the Raiders."

Jim Plunkett's elusiveness in the pocket keeps the Eagles off balance.

The primer for any business dictates that the strength of an organization is the sum of its parts. The theorem pertains, too, to professional football. Obviously, the success or failure of the playing end of the operation is instantly visible. Just look at the standings at the end of the year. Other, less exposed aspects of a football team are the coaching, the scouting and the top level of management.

But even further behind the scene is the administration—the people who ensure that all the details which are integral to a smooth operation are handled capably and efficiently. There is little personal glory for the people who work in that scope of the sport. But just as an offensive lineman feels the deep gratification of having opened a wide hole through which the ball carrier ran for a touchdown, so do the men and women who function in the offices of the Oakland Raiders know the thrill of being part of a winning syndrome.

In the case of the Oakland Raiders, the vortex of their efforts was located in an industrial complex on Edgewater Drive almost within sight of the Oakland International Airport. They moved into those quarters in April, 1980. Since 1968, they had been in a silver-and-black emblazoned building on Oakport Avenue across the highway from their playing stadium. But the expiration of their lease, the tenuous nature of their situation in Oakland since the announced intention of moving to Los Angeles, the need for instant physical space dictated the move to Edgewater Drive. It did not change the nature of administering to the needs of the Oakland Raiders.

"One of the great strengths of this organization," Al LoCasale said, "is that we're football people in business—and not business people in football."

A native of Philadelphia, Pa., and honored as that city's "Man of the Year" in sports for 1978, LoCasale brought lengthy and varied football background to the business side of the Raiders.

The executive assistant to Al Davis began his coaching career with the preps in his native city,

coached while in the Navy at Bainbridge Naval Training Center and later served as an aide on the staff at the University of Pennsylvania, his alma mater. Now 29 years into his career in the sport, LoCasale served in succeedingly important positions with the University of Southern California, the San Diego Chargers and Cincinnati Bengals before joining the Raider staff in 1969. He was an original AFL man, having served with the Chargers when they were formed in Los Angeles in 1960.

After seven years with the Chargers—highlighted by the winning of five division championships and the AFL title in 1963—LoCasale became the first employee hired by Paul Brown when the latter formed the expansion Cincinnati Bengals in 1967. It was LoCasale who designed and built the player personnel system for Cincinnati, which helped provide the nucleus of talent for the Bengals' division championship season just three years later.

Name it in football, and it was a good bet Al LoCasale did it—for he also included extensive radio and television work in his background. He also was a member of the boards of directors of both NFL Properties and NFL Films, was a founder of the NFL Working Executives Group, a member of the NFL Management Council and on the *PRO Magazine* advisory committee, as well as the NFL Constitutional Revision committee.

Working from a desk piled high with books, paper, programs, etc., LoCasale seemingly was involved with almost everything but pumping up the balls on game day.

There are four areas to the structure of the Raiders: playing, scouting, coaching and business.

The latter involved LoCasale, from coordinating public relations, merchandising and ticket operations through team travel plans to overseeing the scheduling and progress of the Raiderettes and the daily activities of the front office staff.

Amidst the "controlled clutter" of his office, the constant interruption of telephone calls and discussions with department aides, he said, "Our people are generalists, not specialists. We bring

Al LoCasale, executive assistant.

Bill Glazier,
publications director.

them in because they can handle a variety of things, and they get a lot of freedom to operate and make decisions."

Many started while only teenagers, in part-time jobs, and went on to college to earn degrees in specialities they could bring back to strengthen the operation of the Raiders.

However, LoCasale was quick to admit that when it came to bottom-line decisions, he wanted to share in the input.

John Herrera, public relations director, was a teenage "go-fer" as were Steve Ballard, comptroller, and John Otten, in charge of computer operations.

Bill Glazier, 28, was publications director and, he said, "I guess I was preparing myself for the Raiders from the day my dad, Harold, took me to see them play in 1960, when I was eight years old, in Kezar Stadium in San Francisco. The only game I've missed since then was the 1974 playoff with Miami. I grew up with the Raiders like a lot of us in the organization have done, and I feel like I really do belong."

Glazier prepared for his position with the club by graduating from the University of California with a bachelors degree in journalism, and then was sports editor for three years of the Valley Pioneer newspaper in Danville, Calif.

In his four years with the Raiders, Glazier assisted in other departments and worked for a greater grasp of the overall Raider organization.

"But" he cautioned, in this world of fun and games, "I've probably wanted to quit 150 times."

The toughest part of the job, he noted, is "trying to please Al LoCasale."

"It's become a cliche, of course," said Glazier, "but he's committed to excellence and he expects the same commitment from his associates."

"I'm a football man," LoCasale declared in rebuttal. "I love the game. I'm competitive by nature, and I drive myself hard to do my best. A lot of jobs don't allow you to have that kind of competitive drive.

"Besides, how many can say they are the best in the world at what they do? The Raiders can!

"We've learned to live with controversy. But I can tell you this, though. No one is more imitated, respected or feared than the Raiders."

Director of Personnel operations Ron Wolf's daily challenge was always right in front of him, in a mountain of film and files filled with scouting reports of potential Raiders.

Wolf's office walls were lined with books of past reports, and facts and figures on every player currently active in the National Football League.

His reponsibility—with the assistance of ex-Raider performers such as Dan Conners and Kent McCloughan, plus Joe Madro and Tom Grimes and a few part-time scouts—was to look at more than 400 college teams each year and some 5,000 graduating senior players. McCloughan, a former playing great, operated as a full time scout in the Rocky Mountain area; the others were based in Oakland.

Ron Wolf, director of personnel.

With the help of his staffmates, Wolf developed reports on an estimated 3,000 seniors who see the most action. And then that number was further winnowed to about 550 of the most talented performers, with each being graded through viewing of at least five game films.

For Wolf, 42, this was his second stand with the Raiders. A native of New Freedom, Pa., he graduated from the University of Oklahoma, where he majored in history. Wolf served with Army intelligence in Europe from 1956 to 1959 and eventually found his way into football as a talent scout for the Raiders in 1963.

When Davis was named AFL commissioner in 1966, he took Wolf with him to the league office as coordinator of talent.

But when the two rival leagues called an end eight weeks later to their six-year "war," Davis resigned from his post to return to the Raiders and Wolf joined him again as director of player personnel.

With the formation of the expansion Tampa Bay Buccaneers in 1976, Wolf was the first man hired and charged with putting the pieces together. He served Tampa Bay three years as vice-president of operations.

In 1978, however, Wolf chose to return to the Raider organization. "I always have been my happiest here with the Raiders," he said. So what did he and his staff look for in the thousands of players they scouted each year? "We more or less have a Raider 'mold,'" he said, "as I'm sure other clubs have molds of their own. I personally like the guy who hits people as hard at the finish as he does at the start of a game. That's one ingredient that can't be taught or trained. You're born with it, the desire to want to hit. Of course, the athlete has to be able to run to a degree, too. Sometimes we draft one who may not be our usual type, but we draft him because he's a great player. Usually we're so far down the list when it comes our turn to draft that all we can do is take the best football player still available."

The Oakland scouts have managed to pick a nugget or two in the later rounds. "It's the players picked from the fourth through twelfth rounds who provide the nucleus for a club," Wolf said.

Among the more significant later picks were such strong contributors as Cliff Branch, Dave Dalby, Mickey Marvin and Morris Bradshaw, fourth-round selections. All-purpose lineman Steve Sylvester was a tenth round pick. Rod Martin and Reggie Kinlaw were plucked in the twelfth round.

Tom Grimes, who joined the Raiders in 1969 and served as director of public relations until moving into the personnel department six years ago, derived considerable personal pleasure out of discovering an undrafted player who can win a job with the club.

Randy McClanahan, a linebacker out of Southwest Louisiana, and fullback Booker Russell of Southwest Texas, who played two years before he was waived and signed by the San Diego Chargers, were just such undrafted "nuggets."

"If you can just find one free agent a year, you're doing super," Grimes said, "and we've had three in four years." Grimes was unique in that he left public relations for scouting.

Al LoCasale, meets frequently with Al Davis.

A one-time sports editor of the Fort Lauderdale (Fla.) *Sun-Sentinel* and a graduate of the University of Miami with a degree in education and journalism, Grimes for two years was assistant public relations director for the Miami Dolphins before joining the Raider staff.

"Harold Rosenthal," he recalled, "was then information director for the AFL, and he told me about an opening in Oakland, and suggested I give Al Davis a call. We chatted a couple times, and then on a Wednesday Al called to ask how soon I could come to work. I answered, 'How about tomorrow?' So I flew out and started the next day."

From early August, Wolf's scouting contingent began to hit the road. Each was assigned approximately 65 colleges to cover through the fall.

"Basically," Grimes reported, "We set up our own schools as best we can to work in conjunction with others so that we don't overlap in coverage. Later in the year, we crosscheck so that the club gets a second look and opinion of the same athlete."

Following the close of the regular college season, the scouts saw the All-Star games and returned with additional reports in preparation for the draft session in the spring.

John Herrera, the Raider publicity director, was another of the many in the organization who has worn other hats along the way, including that of a scout.

From a 16-year-old "go-fer" hired for training camp duties in 1963, Herrera prepared well for

*Ken LaRue,
business manager.*

future assignments. He was 19 when he was told one summer he would be administrative coordinator at the team's training facility in Santa Rosa, Calif. "It was a big deal to me," he recalled, "because I had to take care of the travel for the players when they were released, pick up their playbooks and equipment and stuff like that."

Herrera lettered four years as an end at the University of California at Davis, although he held no dreams of trying pro ball as a player, and he graduated with a degree in history.

"It was extremely helpful for me to have played football in college," he noted. "Now I see our games as a call to arms each week. I hear the bugles. It's life or death every Sunday."

Because the Raiders took such a large contingent on road trips, Herrera's job became quite an extra challenge. The club always has carried a large group of media people, plus owners and their friends and advertisers.

In fact, they took so many to Super Bowl XV they had to use two aircraft—one a giant Boeing 747, an NFL "first."

On the ownership level, the Raider organization featured an involved group of limited partners, many of them tracing back to the early days of the team when, considering the rocky days, they could have wavered but didn't. The limited partners included the following: Lou Barroero, Arnold Boscacci, Eugene Boscacci, John Brooks, Julius N. Hartman, Frank Ivaldi, E. J. McGah, Sheldon Milenbach, Gladys Sargent, Henry Trione, Ralph J. Vail and Wilfred Winkenbach.

"Getting space and credentials in our away games is like pulling teeth," Herrera said, "we bring in so many people."

Bill Glazier as director of publications worked closely with Herrera, being responsible for the media guide, programs, assisting with news releases and coordinating the club's speakers' bureau.

Ticket manager George Glace, joined the club in 1963 after three years with the Chargers. Glace followed a fast turnover of some six ticket managers the first three years of the organization.

"That was when we were $3.50 a game and $31.50 for the season ticket," he recalled. "Those

George Anderson, trainer

were the years, too, when I knew just about every ticketholder by name, and we played in Frank Youell Field.

"We sold 14,000 season tickets for our last season there in 1966, in a stadium that held about 20,000."

The Oakland Coliseum seats 54,616, and Glace said the Raiders' top season ticket sale hit 51,825 before slipping to 40,800 in 1980. The Raiders' projected move to Los Angeles may well have been responsible for the drop.

"When we moved to the Oakland Coliseum, all the season ticket buyers complained they couldn't understand why they all couldn't have seats on the 50-yard line," Glace said.

Anne Blalock was his chief assistant in the ticket department. Steve Ballard, another graduate of the ranks of "go-fers," worked closely with Glace and other department heads as the club's comptroller.

Ballard was 15 when he joined the organization as a part-time public relations department assistant. He then worked in various other departments — including extensive time with Glace while also becoming involved with club insurance matters — all the while studying for a degree in business administration at Cal State-Hayward.

Within the Raider organization, there was also responsibility for a home-away-from-home setup. "If we go some place, some hotel, and we lose the ball game that weekend we may never go back to that hotel again," said Ken LaRue, the Raiders' business manager.

"Hell, we're a very superstitious club."

Famed entertainer Bily Eckstine sang the national anthem 10 times at Raider home games, most often before must-win outings. The Raiders responded by winning all 10. Eckstine became another Raider "superstition."

Among the duties LaRue handled, travel and housing (and superstitions) were most important. He also was in charge of program advertising and sales, purchases and souvenirs sold by the club, and helped in signing players.

Lining up charter bus service to meet the team at airports, deliver the players to practices, etc., was always one of LaRue's more challenging responsibilities.

"We had this one driver in Houston," he recalled with a hearty laugh, "who didn't know how to get across the street to get us into the Astrodome.

"Another time we were at New England for a pre-season game, and we had three buses — and all of the drivers got lost in the beautiful countryside trying to take us to the Foxboro stadium. One of them was the same driver who got lost trying to get us across the river to the airport.

"We were stopped at a red light; the driver didn't know which direction to go. So I jumped out of the bus and ran over to a cab driver and told him I'd give him $10 to lead our driver to the airport!"

When the league bumped the Raiders out of a number of their reserved rooms at their league-assigned hotel in San Diego — as the big Raider entourage arrived for the 1980 playoff meeting with the Chargers — LaRue scrambled and came up with 130 rooms in another hotel.

"We've never stayed at a hotel I haven't personally visited and checked out," the Raider business manager noted.

A native of Goshen, Ind., LaRue was another who brought a football background to his job with the Raiders. He was an all-state end in high school football four years and coached at Kansas State for seven years before returning to his alma mater as director of conferences and special events.

LaRue became business manager of the Raiders in 1969 before taking the post of assistant general manager of the Tampa Bay Buccaneers in 1975. He also served a stint as a personnel scout with the Chargers. He returned to the Silver-and-Black in 1978.

Dick Romanski, equipment manager.

Menus for road trips were part of LaRue's responsibility. He saw to it that the hotel was set up to feed the athletes at a precise hour, and from a precise menu. "We always have to have grits for our pre-game meal," LaRue said. "Try to find a chef in Green Bay, Wis., who can prepare grits properly.

"On arriving in a town on Friday nights, we know we're going to eat 120 pounds of barbecued spareribs, 200 pieces of fried chicken, or 120 cheeseburgers—in addition to salad and 60 milkshakes. And there's always an open dessert bar and a contest to see who can make the most ridiculous sundae.

"Our players rank hotels at the end of the year. They rank 'em by how good the ribs were. The beds can be full of rocks, but if the ribs were good the trip was a success."

There were superstitions, too, about seating at team meals. "The players refuse to sit at tables that aren't rounds of six," he explained. "But don't ask me how that got started.

"Gene Upshaw and Art Shell always have the same seats together. For 11 years, I've been personally delivering a pitcher of grapefruit juice in the morning to Upshaw.

"Superstitious, sure, but we're winners."

If you had a youngster who made a request by mail from Raiders, it was a good bet Sandi Gardner answered the letter. If you booked Raider highlight films, it was another good bet you booked them through Sandi. The Raiders secured 80 to 100 copies of each year's highlight film, and they sent them as far away as England. "We're probably the only club working with so many films available," said Sandi. "You see we cater to our public."

Sandi joined the Raider staff in 1963 and was a secretary in the public relations department. A

From his practice field perch, Max Friedman focuses on a Raider session.

Ken Bishop helps out on the vital staff work during a Raider game.

Dr. Robert Rosenfeld ministers closely to the orthopedic needs of the Raiders.

native of Oakland, Calif., she found it a strong daily challenge to make an effective contribution in what appears to be a man's world of football. "It's always my goal," she declared, "to prove I have the ability to help the organization. And, no, I don't feel less than 'womanly' to work in the Raiders' 'man's world.' In fact, I feel it's quite the other way around, that I try to be more womanly."

Perforce, George Anderson worked solely in a man's world for the Raiders. He was their trainer. Right from the start of the team. Time was, early on in his career as an original Raider, there wasn't enough work to keep George busy year-round.

There wasn't enough money, either. So Anderson spent his off-seasons working in the jockeys' training room at Golden Gate Fields. But Anderson, the last of the 1960 charter Raiders, went full-time in 1973 and in 1980 got Rod Mar-

tin—not to be confused with the Raider linebacker and Super Bowl hero of the same name—as a full-time assistant.

Martin checked in daily at 7 a.m. for the early-bird group and Anderson arrived a couple hours later to provide training room assistance into the evening.

The players looked upon the veteran trainer as something of a Father Confessor, for they frequently told Anderson things they would share with no one else. Or they sought his advice or help on matters far removed from the world of football.

Anderson played baseball and basketball as a high school athlete in his native Vallejo, Calif., but suffered a knee injury as a sophomore to end his baseball hopes at San Jose State University. Because of his interest in his own injury, Anderson went on to graduate and serve as a high school trainer in Odessa, Tex., and then on to

Al LoCasale surrounds himself with a bevy of Raiderettes.

assignments with the University of California-Berkeley and USC. When the Raiders were being formed in 1960, Anderson applied for the trainer's job.

In the fourth game the Raiders ever played—a 1960 pre-season outing recorded as a 21–7 win over the Buffalo Bills—the players awarded Anderson the game ball out of appreciation for his tireless assistance.

Because of keen interest in knee injuries, Anderson developed and patented a knee brace that won nationwide acceptance. Twenty-six pro grid teams use Anderson's "Knee Stabler," as another piece of playing equipment.

Anderson was especially proud of the durability of Raider players and their attention to rehabilitation work following injury. The measure of a team is indicated, Anderson felt, by the willingness of players to "play hurt."

"Pete Banaszak would play with any kind of injury," the trainer said of the gutsy retired running back. "Jack Tatum and Kenny Stabler always played hurt. The same with the late Dan Birdwell. Gene Upshaw shakes off any injury; he's always ready. Dave Dalby and Matt Millen are the same."

Young Rod Martin, whose first year as Anderson's aide was a Super Bowl championship season, came to the staff following stints as a college trainer. A native of Los Angeles, and a wide receiver and defensive back in high school, Martin said he never aspired to a career as a pro gridder and was eager to settle for a sideline job as a trainer.

"I was so slow," he said, "they would time me with a calendar rather than a stopwatch."

Another locker room veteran was Dick Romanski, whose arrival on the Raider scene coincided with that of Al Davis in 1963. It was logical. He played on Davis' service teams at Fort Belvoir, Va., and also coached there under the Raider boss. Romanski came equipped with a good football background. He was a quarterback at St. Norbert College in his native Wisconsin and later coached high school football in Milwaukee.

Dr. Donald Fink, team physician.

Ed McGah, one of the original Raider owners and still influential as a general partner, clutches the supreme prize, the Super Bowl XV trophy, with the smiling approval of Ted Hendricks.

Modern technology was the reason for the presence of Max Friedman and John Otten with the Raiders. When the Raiders expanded their movie operations in 1979, Friedman, who used to film football at his alma mater, Southern Methodist University, was brought in as the team's film coordinator. His father, Bob, is the filmmaker for the Dallas Cowboys. His brother, Mitchell, handles the same role for the Chicago Bears. Otten, in charge of computer operations, had been with the organization a dozen years, starting as a field house assistant, but then put to good use his studies in computer data processing at Chabot College when Coach Tom Flores decided to modernize the statistical studies.

The jack of all trades was Ken Bishop, who joined the Raiders in 1969 and held the title of administrative assistant. He had covered the Raiders as a football writer, worked as a publicist and performed various liaison jobs within the Raider offices.

Then there were those who sat at the typewriters and maintained flow of communications. Beverly Swanson joined the Raiders in 1968 and became the secretary to Al Davis in 1975. "I enjoy," she said, "the excitement that goes along with an exciting individual." Other secretaries were Fran Bergamini, Martha Soto, Shirley Bowingon, Nina Stinson and Trish Mallick.

Finally, to ensure the good health of the Raiders, an outstanding medical staff was recruited. Team physician Donald Fink joined the team in 1977. He graduated from the University of Michigan, interned at the University of Nebraska and served two years in the U.S. Army. When not ministering to the Raider players, he practiced medicine in Castro Valley. One of the nation's outstanding orthopedic surgeons, Dr. Robert Rosenfeld of Beverly Hills, was a sideline fixture with the team since 1969. He flew in specially for all games, home and away, and over the years he was as much a fan as he was the man who dealt in the vital area of knee and shoulders and all the other parts of the body that are vulnerable to the hard contact of football play.

When the Raiders embarked for Super Bowl XV the Monday before the game, Dr. Rosenfeld was with them at the special urging of Al Davis, though he had to pull himself away from his busy practice of orthopedic medicine in Beverly Hills. it seemed that Davis wanted the good doctor there in New Orleans for the team picture the next day.

Why? Well, when the Raiders had played in Super Bowl XI, in southern California, Dr. Rosenfeld was in the team picture because it was just a short trip from his office. The Raiders won that Super Bowl, too. Al Davis wasn't taking any chance defying habit and tradition. Bob Rosenfeld had to be in the 1981 team picture, too, even if it meant leaving five days early.

As it turned out, the Raiders won again to reign as the world champions of professional football. It was due, it could be said, to a matter of organization.

Appendix

TEAM WIN-LOSS RECORDS 1960–1980 (LAST 21 YEARS)

Rank/Team	Won	Lost	Tied	Winning Percentage
1. **OAKLAND RAIDERS**	188	101	11	.651
2. Dallas Cowboys	184	108	6	.630
3. Cleveland Browns	175	116	7	.601
4. Los Angeles Rams	172	115	11	.599
5. Miami Dolphins	127	86	3	.596

TEAM WIN-LOSS RECORDS 1963–1980 (LAST 18 YEARS)

Rank/Team	Won	Lost	Tied	Winning Percentage
1. **OAKLAND RAIDERS**	179	68	11	.725
2. Dallas Cowboys	176	80	3	.686
3. Los Angeles Rams	163	86	9	.655
4. Minnesota Vikings	155	95	8	.620
5. Cleveland Browns	152	102	4	.598

TEAM WIN-LOSS RECORDS 1967–1980 (LAST 14 YEARS)

Rank/Team	Won	Lost	Tied	Winning Percentage
1. **OAKLAND RAIDERS**	148	47	7	.759
2. Dallas Cowboys	149	52	1	.741
3. Los Angeles Rams	141	54	7	.723
4. Minnesota Vikings	131	66	5	.665
5. Miami Dolphins	124	75	3	.623

RAIDER INDIVIDUAL RECORDS
SCORING

CAREER

Most Points
863 George Blanda (1967–75), 395 PAT, 156 FG
462 Fred Biletnikoff (1965–78) 77 TD

Most Touchdowns
77 Fred Biletnikoff (1965–78)
57 Cliff Branch (1972–80)

Most Extra Points
395 George Blanda (1967–75)
118 Mike Mercer (1963–65)

Most Field Goals
156 George Blanda (1967–75)
36 Errol Mann (1976–78)

Most Field Goal Attempts
249 George Blanda (1967–78)
62 Mike Mercer (1963–65)

SEASON

Most Points
117 George Blanda (1968)
116 George Blanda (1967)

Most Touchdowns
16 Art Powell (1963)
16 Pete Banaszak (1968)

Most Extra Points
56 George Blanda (1967)
54 George Blands (1968)

Most Field Goals
23 George Blanda (1967)
21 George Blanda (1968)

Most Field Goal Attempts
37 George Blanda (1969)
37 Chris Bahr (1980)

GAME

Most Points
24 Art Powell (12-22-63 vs. Houston)
18 Several players

Most Touchdowns
4 Art Powell (12-22-63 vs. Houston)
3 Several Players

Most Extra Points
7 Mike Mercer (10-22-63 vs. New York)
7 Mike Mercer (12-22-63 vs. Houston)
7 Errol Mann (11-28-76 vs. Tampa Bay)

Most Field Goals
4 Mike Mercer (11-7-65 at Houston)
4 George Blanda (12-10-67 at Houston)
4 George Blanda (12-8-68 vs. Denver)
4 George Blanda (9-23-73 vs. Miami)
4 Errol Mann (10-9-77 at Cleveland)
4 Errol Mann (10-1-78 at Chicago)
4 Jim Breech (12-9-79 vs. Cleveland)
4 Chris Bahr (10-26-80 vs. Seattle)

Longest Field Goal
54 George Fleming (10-2-61 vs. Denver)
52 George Blanda (11-8-70 vs. Cleveland)

PASSING

CAREER

Most Passes Attempted
2,481 Ken Stabler (1970-79)
2,248 Daryle Lamonica (1967-74)
1,640 Tom Flores (1960-66)

Most Passes Completed
1,486 Ken Stabler (1970-79)
1,138 Daryle Lamonica (1967-74)
810 Tom Flores (1960-66)

Most Yards Gained Passing
19,078 Ken Stabler (1979-79)
16,655 Daryle Lamonica (1967-74)
11,635 Tom Flores (1960-66)

Most Touchdown Passes
150 Ken Stabler (1070-79)
148 Daryle Lamonica (1967-74)
92 Tom Flores (1960-66)

Most Interceptions
143 Ken Stabler (1979-79)
115 Daryle Lamonica (1967-74)
83 Tom Flores (1960-66)

Best Percentage
(200 or more attempts)
59.9 Ken Stabler (1970-79)
51.3 Jim Plunkett (1979-80)

SEASON

Most Passes Attempted
498 Ken Stabler (1979)
426 Daryle Lamonica (1969)

Most Passes Completed
304 Ken Stabler (1979)
237 Ken Stabler (1978)

Most Yards Gained Passing
3,615 Ken Stabler (1979)
3,302 Daryle Lamonica (1969)

Most Touchdown Passes
34 Daryle Lamonica (1969)
30 Daryle Lamonica (1967)

Most Interceptions
30 Ken Stabler (1978)
25 Daryle Lamonica (1969)

Best Percentage
66.7 Ken Stabler (1976)
62.7 Ken Stabler (1973)

GAME

Most Passes Attempted
52 Jim Plunkett (10-5-80 vs. Kansas City)
47 Ken Stabler (10-21-79 at N.Y. Jets)
47 Ken Stabler (12-16-79 vs. Seattle)

Most Completions
31 Ken Stabler (12-16-79 vs. Seattle)
29 Ken Stabler (10-21-79) at New York Jets)

Most Yards Gained Passing
427 Cotton Davidson (10-25-64 vs. Denver)
407 Tom Flores (12-22-63 vs. Houston)

Most Touchdown Passes
6 Tom Flores (12-22-63 vs. Houston)
6 Daryle Lamonica (10-19-69 vs. Buffalo)

Most Interceptions
7 Ken Stabler (10-16-77 vs. Denver)
6 Cotton Davidson (11-1-64 at San Diego)

Best Percentage
91.7 Ken Stabler (12-21-75 vs. Kansas City)
90.9 Ken Stabler (12-17-72 vs. Chicago)

Longest Pass Play
94 George Blanda to Warren Wells, TC (11-10-68 at Denver)
93 Tom Flores to Dobie Craig, TD (10-20-63 vs. New York)

RUSHING

CAREER

Most Rushing Attempts
1,436 Mark van Eeghen (1974-80)
1,133 Clem Daniels (1961-67)
963 Pete Banaszak (1966-78)

Most Touchdowns Rushing
47 Pete Banaszak (1966-67)
33 Mark van Eeghen (1974-80)
30 Clem Daniels (1961-67)

Best Average Per Rush
(150 or more attempts)
4.8 Marv Hubbard (1969-76)
4.5 Clarence Davis (1971-78)
4.5 Clem Daniels (1961-67)

Most Yards Rushing
5,757 Mark van Eeghen (1974-80)
5,103 Clem Daniels (1961-67)
4,399 Marv Hubbard (1969-76)

SEASON

Most Rushing Attempts
324 Mark van Eeghen (1977)
270 Mark van Eeghen (1978)
233 Mark van Eeghen (1976)

Most Yards Rushing
1,273 Mark van Eeghen (1977)
1,100 Marv Hubbard (1972)
1,099 Clem Daniels (1963)

Most Touchdowns Rushing
16 Pete Banaszak (1975)
9 Mark van Eeghen (1978)

Best Average Per Rush
6.0 Charlie Smith (1968)
5.9 Clarence Davis (1971)

GAME

Most Rushing Attempts
36 Mark van Eeghen (10-23-77 at N.Y. Jets)
31 Mark van Eeghen (10-30-77 at Denver)
31 Clem Daniels (11-18-63 at Kansas City)

Most Yards Rushing
200 Clem Daniels (10-20-63 vs. New York)
187 Clem Daniels (12-9-62 at Houston)
187 Hewritt Dixon (9-29-68 at Houston)

Most Touchdowns Rushing
3 Tony Teresa (11-4-60 vs. Boston)
3 Pete Banaszak (11-23-75 at Washington, 12-21-75 vs Kansas City)
3 Mark van Eeghen (10-14-79 vs. Atlanta)
3 Booker Russell (10-25-79 vs. San Diego)

Best Average Per Rush
13.0 Charlie Smith (12-8-68 vs. Denver)
11.8 Tony Teresa (11-30-60 vs. Buffalo)

Longest Run From Scrimmage
89 Kenny King (10-12-80 vs. San Diego)
87 Jack Larscheid (10-16-60 vs. Boston)

PASS RECEIVING

CAREER

Most Pass Receptions
578 Fred Biletnikoff (1965-78)
364 Cliff Branch (1972-80)
254 Art Powell (1963-66)

Most Yards Gained
8,974 Fred Biletnikoff (1965-78)
6,378 Cliff Branch (1972-80)
4,491 Art Powell (1963-66)

Most Touchdown Receptions
76 Fred Biletnikoff (1965-78)
57 Cliff Branch (1972-80)
50 Art Powell (1963-66)

Best Average Gain Per Catch (50 or more receptions)
23.3 Warren Wells (1967-70)
17.7 Art Powell (1963-66)
17.5 Cliff Branch (1972-80)

SEASON

Most Pass Receptions
76 Art Powell (1964)
73 Art Powell (1963)

Most Yards Gained
1,361 Art Powell (1964)
1,304 Art Powell (1963)

Most Touchdown Receptions
16 Art Powell (1963)
14 Warren Wells (1969)

Best Average Per Catch (14 or more receptions)
26.8 Warren Wells (1969)
24.2 Cliff Branch (1976)

GAME

Most Pass Receptions
12 Dave Casper (10-3-76 at New England)
11 Art Powell (10-8-65 at Boston)

Most Yards Gained
247 Art Powell (12-22-63 vs. Houston)
206 Art Powell (10-8-65 at Boston)

Most Touchdown Receptions
4 Art Powell (12-22-63 vs. Houston)
3 Art Powell (12-8-63 vs. San Diego)
3 Fred Biletnikoff (12-7-69 vs. Denver)
3 Warren Wells (12-7-69 vs. Cincinnati
3 Warren Wells (10-11-70 vs. Denver)
3 Raymond Chester (10-25-70 vs. Pittsburgh)
3 Cliff Branch (11-30-75 vs. Atlanta)
3 Bob Chandler (10-26-80 vs. Seattle)

Best Average Gain Per Catch (3 or more receptions)
57.3 Clem Daniels (3 for 172) (9-15-63 vs. Buffalo)
38.7 Mike Siani (3 for 116) (10-22-73 at Denver)

PUNT RETURNS

CAREER

Most Punt Returns
168 Neal Colzie (1975-78)
148 George Atkinson (1968-77)

Most Yards Returned
1,747 Neal Colzie (1975-78)
1,247 George Atkinson (1968-77)

Most Touchdowns
3 Claude Gibson (1963-65)
3 George Atkinson (1968-77)

Best Average Per Return (20 or more returns)
12.6 Claude Gibson (1963-65)
11.9 Ron Smith (1974)

SEASON

Most Punt Returns
48 Neal Colzie (1975)
48 Ira Matthews (1980)

Most Yards Returned
655 Neal Colzie (1975)
612 Rodger Bird (1967)

Most Touchdowns
2 Claude Gibson (1963)
2 George Atkinson (1968)

Best Average Per Return (14 or more returns)
14.4 Claude Gibson (1964)
13.6 George Atkinson (1968)
13.6 Neal Colzie (1975)

GAME

Most Punt Returns
9 Rodger Bird (9-10-67 vs. Denver)
8 Neal Colzie (10-5-75 at San Diego)

Most Yards Returned
205 George Atkinson (7-15-68 at Buffalo)
143 Rodger Bird (9-10-67 vs. Denver)

Most Touchdowns
1 Claude Gibson (11–3–63 vs. Kansas City)
1 Claude Gibson (12–22–63 vs. Houston)
1 Claude Gibson (9–12–65 vs. Kansas City)
1 George Atkinson (9–15–68 at Buffalo)
1 George Atkinson (10–13–68 vs San Diego)
1 Alvin Wyatt (9–20–70 at Cincinnati)
1 George Atkinson (9–16–73 at Minnesota)

Best Average Per Return (3 or more returns)
42.3 Neal Colzie (11–2–75 at Denver)
41.0 George Atkinson (9–15–68 at Buffalo)

Longest Punt Return
86 George Atkinson (9–15–68 at Buffalo)
85 Claude Gibson (11–3–63 vs. Kansas City)

KICKOFF RETURNS
CAREER

Most Kickoff Returns
113 Bo Roberson (1962–65)
79 Clarence Davis (1971–78)

Most Yards Returned
2,791 Bo Roberson (1962–65)
2,140 Clarence Davis (1971–78)

Most Touchdowns
1 Bo Roberson (1962–65)
1 Jim Smith (1960)
1 Harold Hart (1974–75, 1978)
1 Ira Matthews (1979–80)
1 Arthur Whittington (1978–80)
1 Derrick Jensen (1979–80)

Best Average Per Return (20 or more returns)
28.4 Jack Larscheid (1960–61)
27.1 Clarence Davis (1971–78)

SEASON

Most Kickoff Returns
38 Bo Roberson (1963)
36 Bo Roberson (1964)

Most Yards Returned
975 Bo Roberson (1964)
873 Ira Matthews (1979)

Most Touchdowns
1 Jim Smith (1960)
1 Bo Roberson (1962)
1 Harold Hart (1975)
1 Ira Matthews (1979)
1 Arthur Whittington (1980)
1 Derrick Jensen (1980)

Best Average Per Return
30.5 Harold Hart (1975)
28.4 Jack Larscheid (1960)

GAME

Most Kickoff Returns
7 Bo Roberson (10–27–63 at San Diego)
7 Bo Roberson (12–22–63 vs. Houston)

Most Yards Returned
180 Ira Matthews (10–25–79 vs. San Diego)
171 Bo Roberson (10–27–63 at San Diego)

Most Touchdowns
1 Jim Smith (10–9–60 at Dallas Texans)
1 Bo Roberson (9–30–62 vs. San Diego)
1 Harold Hart (9–22–75 at Miami)
1 Ira Matthews (10–25–79 vs. San Diego)
1 Arthur Whittington (11–9–80 vs. Cincinnati)
1 Derrick Jensen (12–21–80 at N.Y. Giants)

Best Average Per Return (3 or more returns)
53.0 Harold Hart (9–22–75 at Miami)
45.0 Ira Matthews (10–25–79 vs. San Diego)

Longest Kickoff Return
104 Ira Matthews (10–25–79 vs. San Diego)
102 Harold Hart (9–22–75 at Miami)

INTERCEPTIONS
CAREER

Most Interceptions
39 Willie Brown (1967–78)
30 George Atkinson (1968–77)

Most Yards Returned
636 Jack Tatum (1971–79)
624 Dave Grayson (1965–70)

Most Touchdowns
4 Dave Grayson (1965–70)
3 Dan Conners (1964–73)
3 Lester Hayes (1977–80)

SEASON

Most Interceptions
13 Lester Hayes (1980)
10 Tommy Morrow (1962)
10 Dave Grayson (1968)

Most Yards Returned
273 Lester Hayes (1980)
195 Dave Grayson (1968)

Most Touchdowns
2 Dave Grayson (1965)
2 Gus Otto (1965)
2 Warren Powers (1965)
2 Jimmy Warren (1971)
2 Lester Hayes (1979)

GAME

Most Interceptions
3 Tommy Morrow (9–7–63 at Houston)
3 Dave Grayson (10–26–69 at San Diego)
3 Willie Brown (10–29–72 vs. Los Angeles)
3 George Atkinson (10–6–74 at Cleveland)
3 Charles Phillips (12–8–75 vs. Denver)

Most Yards Returned
96 Tommy Morrow (10–63–64 at Buffalo)
91 Fred Williamson (9–30–62 vs. San Diego)

Most Touchdowns
1 by 20 players

Longest Interception Return
91 Fred Williamson (9–30–62 vs. San Diego)
82 Phil Villapiano (10–29–72 vs. Los Angeles)

PUNTING

CAREER

Most Punts
558 Ray Guy (1973–80)
364 Mike Eischeid (1966–71)

Most Yards Punting
24,067 Ray Guy (1973–80)
15,380 Mike Eischeid (1966–71)

SEASON

Most Punts
81 Ray Guy (1978)
79 Mike Eischeid (1970)

Most Yards Punting
3,462 Ray Guy (1978)
3,364 Mike Eischeid (1967)

Best Average Per Punt
45.3 Ray Guy (1973)
44.3 Mike Eischeid (1967)

GAME

Most Punts
11 Wayne Crow (9–11–60 vs. Houston)
11 Mike Mercer (9–12–63 vs. Boston)
11 Mike Eischeid (11–20–66 at Denver)
11 Ray Guy (11–18–73 vs. Cleveland)

**Best Average Per Punt
(3 or more punts)**
55.3 Mike Mercer (9–19–65 vs. San Diego)
54.8 Ray Guy (11–5–78 vs. Kansas City)

Longest Punt
77 Wayne Crow (10–29–61 vs. New York)
74 Ray Guy (10–30–77 at Denver)

RAIDER SUPERLATIVES

SEASON

1,000 YARDS RUSHING

Yards	Name	Year
1,273	Mark van Eeghen	1977
1,100	Marv Hubbard	1972
1,099	Clem Daniels	1963
1,080	Mark van Eeghen	1978
1,012	Mark van Eeghen	1976

1,000 YARDS RECEIVING

Yards	Name	Year
1,361	Art Powell	1964
1,304	Art Powell	1963
1,092	Cliff Branch	1974
1,037	Fred Biletnikoff	1968
1,026	Art Powell	1966

3,000 YARDS PASSING

Yards	Name	Year
3,615	Ken Stabler	1979
3,302	Daryle Lamonica	1969
3,245	Daryle Lamonica	1968
3,227	Daryle Lamonica	1967

SINGLE GAME

300 YARDS PASSING

Yards	Name	Game
419	Cotton Davidson	10–25–64 vs. Denver
407	Tom Flores	12–22–63 vs. Houston
368	Daryle Lamonica	10–27–68 at Cincinnati
364	Daryle Lamonica	10–11–70 vs. Denver
360	Ken Stabler	10–21–79 at N.Y. Jets
358	Cotton Davidson	11–22–64 vs. N.Y. Jets
354	Daryle Lamonica	12–8–68 vs. Denver
349	Daryle Lamonica	12–3–67 at San Diego
344	Daryle Lamonica	9–21–68 at Miami
343	Ken Stabler	9–16–79 at Seattle

100 YARDS RUSHING

Yards	Name	Game
200	Clem Daniels	10–20–63 vs. N.Y. Jets
187	Clem Daniels	12–9–62 at Houston
187	Hewritt Dixon	9–29–68 at Houston
167	Clem Daniels	10–25–64 vs. Denver
164	Hewritt Dixon	10–19–70 vs. Washington
158	Clem Daniels	12–22–63 vs. Houston
151	Mark van Eeghen	9–17–78 at Green Bay
149	Larry Todd	11–7–65 at Houston
146	Charlie Smith	11–12–72 at Cincinnati
144	Clem Daniels	12–20–64 vs. San Diego

100 YARDS RECEIVING

Yards	Name	Game
247	Art Powell	12-22-63 vs. Houston
206	Art Powell	10-8-65 at Boston
198	Warren Wells	10-11-70 vs. Denver
181	Art Powell	9-7-63 at Houston
172	Clem Daniels	9-15-63 vs. Buffalo
167	Cliff Branch	10-10-76 at San Diego
163	Warren Wells	12-8-68 vs. Denver
163	Cliff Branch	11-7-76 at Chicago
158	Fred Biletnikoff	11-23-78 at Kansas City
156	Cliff Branch	9-12-79 at Seattle

CAREER TOTAL
100-YARD RUSHING GAMES

No.	Name	Years
14	Clem Daniels	1961-67
10	Marv Hubbard	1969-75
8	Mark van Eeghen	1974-80
5	Clarence Davis	1971-78
4	Hewritt Dixon	1966-70

100-YARD RECEIVING GAMES

No.	Name	Years
21	Fred Biletnikoff	1965-78
19	Cliff Branch	1972-80
17	Art Powell	1963-66
13	Warren Wells	1967-70
6	Dave Casper	1974-80

300-YARD PASSING GAMES

No.	Name	Years
10	Daryle Lamonica	1967-74
8	Ken Stabler	1970-79
4	Cotton Davidson	1962-69
2	Tom Flores	1960-66
1	Dan Pastorini	1980

HISTORICAL HIGHLIGHTS

1959

August 14—First organizational meeting held under leadership of league founder Lamar Hunt. **August 22**—American Football League chosen as official name. **November 22**—First draft meeting held, with first round choices composed of: Boston—Gerhard Schwedes; Buffalo—Richie Lucas; Dallas—Don Meredith; Denver—Roger Le-Clerc; Houston—Billy Cannon; Los Angeles—Monty Stickles; Minneapolis—Dale Hackbart; New York—George Izo. **November 30**—Joe Foss named league commissioner.

1960

January 26—Lamar Hunt of the Dallas Texans named first AFL president. **January 27**—First fourteen game home-and-home schedule adopted. **January 30**—Oakland awarded former Minneapolis franchise. **February 9**—Eddie Erdelatz appointed as first head coach of Raiders. **June 9**—AFL signs five-year contract with ABC for network televising of games. **July 30**—First pre-season game held: Boston defeats Buffalo, 28-7, before 16,000 at Buffalo. **September 9**—First league game held: Denver defeats Boston, 13-10, before 21,597 at Boston. **September 11**—Raiders open at home, losing to Houston, 37-22.

1961

January 1—First championship game held: Houston defeats Los Angeles, 24-17, before 32,183. **January 16**—E. W. McGah named president of Raiders.

1962

January 7—First AFL All-Star game held: West defeats East, 47-27, before 20,973 at San Diego.

1963

January 15—Al Davis named head coach and general manager of Raiders. **February 8**—Dallas Texans announce move of franchise to Kansas City, becoming the Chiefs. **March 28**—New York Titans sold to group headed by David (Sonny) Werblin. Club becomes the Jets. **December 22**—Raiders down Houston 52-49 to finish one game out of playoffs with 10-4-0 record, first winning season in club history.

1964

January 17—AFL owners vote to recognize AFL Players' Association, formed just three days earlier. **January 29**—AFL and NBC sign a five-year, $36-million television contract to begin with 1965 season.

1965

February 1—Construction started on 54,000-seat Oakland Coliseum; completion date set for Aug. 25, 1966. **July**—AFL announces intention to place a franchise in Miami, Fla., for 1966 season.

1966

April 8—Al Davis, general manager and head coach of Oakland Raiders, is named second Commissioner of American Football League, succeeding Joe Foss. **June 8**—American Football League and National Football League agree to an alliance that includes common draft and Championship Game. **July 25**—Al Davis resigns as League Commissioner. Milt Woodard appointed President of the American Football League. **September 18**—Oakland Raiders open 54,000-seat Oakland-Alameda County Coliseum against Kansas City Chiefs.

1967

January 15—First World Championship Game played at Los Angeles. National Football League champion Green Bay Packers pull away from American Football League champion Kansas City in second half to win, 35-10. **January 21**—AFL All-Star Game held in Oakland. East posts first series win, 30-23. **March 14-15**—First AFL-NFL common draft held. **August-September**—First pre-season games between AFL and NFL held, including Sept. 3 meeting between Oakland Raiders and San Francisco 49ers. **December 31**—Raiders rout Houston, 40-7, to win AFL Championship.

1968

January 15—Super Bowl—Green Bay pulled away from AFL champions, the Oakland Raiders, to win 33-14. **December 22**—Raiders wallop visiting Kansas City 41-6 to capture Western Division Playoff. **December 29**—Raiders fall to New York Jets 27-23 in AFL championship game at Shea Stadium before 62,627.

1969

January 12—Jets defeat heavily-favored Baltimore Colts in Super Bowl, 16-7, in Orange Bowl. **February 4**—John Madden appointed Raiders head coach to replace John Rauch, who left to go with Buffalo Bills. **May 10**—Pro football realignment finds Cleveland Browns, Baltimore Colts and Pittsburgh Steelers moving to American League (Conference) in 1970. Colts join Boston, Buffalo, Miami and New York in one division, Browns and Steelers join Houston and Cincinnati in another and Kansas City, Denver, San Diego and Oakland remain together in third division. **June 1**—Veteran AFL player personnel director and administrator Al LoCasale named Executive Assistant for the Raiders. **June 26**—ABC acquires rights to televise NFL regular season Monday night games. **October 19**—Raiders quarterback Daryle Lamonica sets a pro record with six touchdown passes in first half to direct a 50-21 victory over Buffalo. **October 26**—Raiders defeat San Diego 24-12 and equal the AFL record for unbeaten games at 15. **December 21**—Raiders defeat Kansas City 10-6 in regular season finale and capture record-tieing third straight AFL Western Division title. **December 21**—Raiders win playoff and set club scoring mark in 56-7 triumph over Houston.

1970

January 4—Raiders bow to Kansas City 17-7 in AFL Championship game before record Oakland Coliseum crowd of 54,544. **January 11**—Super Bowl: Kansas City upsets favored Minnesota Vikings 23-7 in New Orleans. **March 16-21**—Pro football owners meet in Honolulu. Uniform rules adopted, including discarding of AFL's two-point conversion option in favor of the one-point kick; acceptance of the NFL game ball; and use of players' names on the back of team jerseys. **December 12**—Raiders become first American Football Conference club ever to capture four consecutive Western Division crowns with a 20-6 triumph over the Kansas City Chiefs. **December 27**—Raiders win third straight playoff by defeating AFC Eastern Conference runner-up Miami Dolphins 21-14 at the Oakland Coliseum.

1971

January 3—Baltimore Colts defeat Raiders 27-17 in AFC title game at Baltimore's Memorial Stadium. **January 17**—A 32-yard field goal by Jim O'Brien gives Baltimore a 16-13 Super Bowl victory over National Conference champion Dallas Cowboys in Miami. **September 26**—Raiders commence nine-week unbeaten string by blanking Chargers 34-0 in San Diego. **December 12**—Jan Stenerud's field goal with 1:34 left provides Chiefs 16-14 victory over visiting Raiders to end Oakland string of four division championships.

1972

January 16—Dallas captures Super Bowl 24-3 over Miami in New Orleans. **March 20-24**—Owners move the in-bounds markers in to 23 yards, 21 inches from each sideline. Former location was 20 yards in from sideline. **December 3**—Raiders return to glory by capturing fifth AFC Western Division championship in six seasons with a 21-19 victory against the Chargers in San Diego. **December 17**—Raiders boast winningest record of 1963-72 10-year period (94-36-10) with 10-3-1 finish. **December 23**—Controversial pass deflection on fourth down in final 22 seconds provides Pittsburgh Steelers with a 12-7 playoff decision over Raiders, who had taken 7-6 lead with 1:13 left to play.

1973

January 14—Miami completes first modern perfect season (17-0) by defeating Washington 14-7 in Super Bowl VII in Los Angeles Coliseum. **September 23**—Largest Bay Area crowd to attend a pro game (74,121) fills California Memorial Stadium as Silver and Black stun Super Bowl Champion Miami 12-7 on four George Blanda field goals. Dolphin win streak stopped at 18. **December 16**—Raiders down Denver Broncos 21-17 to capture third consecutive AFC Western Division championship and sixth in seven seasons. **December 22**—Oakland returns to AFC Championship Game with 33-14 playoff triumph against Pittsburgh. **December 30**—Miami wins third consecutive AFC title, topping Raiders 27-10.

1974

January 13—Miami successfully defends Super Bowl title with 24-7 win against Minnesota Vikings in Rice University Stadium. **April 25**—Rules changes, culminating three years of study, are announced at NFL Owners' meeting in New York. Pre-season and regular season games tied after regulation time will be allotted a single 15 minute or sudden death overtime. Goal posts were moved to the end line; kick-offs from scrimmage (punt or field goal) cannot cross line of scrimmage until ball is kicked. Wide receivers are afforded better opportunity to go downfield by elimination of roll blocking and cutting of receivers and by restricting extent of downfield contact defenders will be permitted to have with eligible receivers. Offensive holding penalty, illegal use of hands and tripping infractions occurring in area of line of scrimmage and three yards beyond are reduced from 15 to 10 yards. Wide receivers blocking back toward the ball three yards from line of scrimmage cannot block below the waist. Tampa was awarded

NFL franchise. **June 4**—Seattle awarded NFL franchise. **September 22**—Raiders begin nine-game winning streak with 27-7 victory over rival Kansas City Chiefs. **November 18**—Oakland captures seventh AFC Western Division championship after only 10 regular season games as Kansas City topples Denver in Monday night clash, following Raiders' 17-10 Sunday victory over San Diego. **December 14**—Raiders complete 1974 campaign with 27-23 victory over Dallas and best won-loss record in NFL (12-2). **December 21**—Miami's bid for fourth consecutive Super Bowl appearance is ended as Raiders defeat the World Champions 28-26 at the Oakland Coliseum in AFC Playoffs. **December 29**—Pittsburgh defeats Oakland 24-13 and advances to Super Bowl.

1975

January 12—Pittsburgh defeats Minnesota 16-6 in Super Bowl IX at Tulane Stadium in New Orleans. **February 7**—Long Island Athletic Club selects Al Davis NFL Executive of the Year. **March 17**—Pro football owners meet in Honolulu. Rule changes include: penalties for having an illegal player downfield and offensive pass interference were reduced from 15 to 10 yards. **September 3**—Jim Otto, last original Raider, retires after 15 years as the Raiders' starting center. **September 22**—Raiders snap Miami's 31-game Orange Bowl winning streak with a 31-21 Monday night victory. **November 3**—Raiders become pro football's all-time winningest team since 1960 with a victory over New Orleans to up its all time record to 129-77-11, a winning percentage of .626. **November 23**—Raiders go into overtime for the first time in history, defeating the Washington Redskins 26-23 at 7:13 of the extra period. **November 30**—Raiders cinch eighth AFC Western Division Championship in past nine seasons with a 37-34 overtime victory over the Atlanta Falcons. **December 21**—George Blanda's second of four extra-point kicks against Kansas City made the 26-year veteran the first player in pro football history to score 2000 points. **December 28**—Raiders advance to AFC Championship game with 31-28 win over Cincinnati at home.

1976

January 4—Raiders bow 16-10 at Pittsburgh in AFC Championship game. **January 18**—Pittsburgh successfully defends its Super Bowl title with a 21-17 victory over Dallas at the Orange Bowl in Miami. **March 15**—Pro football owners meet in Coronado, California. Rule changes adopted, include: official coin toss moved to three minutes before kickoff; two 30-second time clocks will be placed in each end zone so fans can see how long it takes offenses to put ball in play; **March 30**—Tampa Bay Buccaneers and Seattle Seahawks complete their selection of veteran players in NFL Expansion draft. Raiders losing Bob Moore, Harold Hart and Louis Carter. **November 21**—Raiders clinch ninth Western Division Championship in 10 years with 26-7 win over the Eagles in Philadelphia. **December 12**—With 24-0 victory over San Diego, Raiders conclude league season with 13-1 record, the best in pro football. **December 18**—Raiders defeat New England, 24-21, in AFC Playoff to advance to Conference Championship. **December 26**—Raiders win AFC Championship with impressive 24-7 win over Pittsburgh at home.

1977

January 9—Raiders defeat the Minnesota Vikings 32-14 in Super Bowl XI at the Rose Bowl in Pasadena before a record crowd of 103,424, plus a world-wide television audience of over 130 million. **January 10**—Over 20,000 fans turn out at the Coliseum to greet World Champions on their return to Oakland. **January 29**—Raider Head Coach John Madden named the Washington Touchdown Club's Coach of the Year. **March 5**—Al Davis, Raiders' managing general partner, named NFL Executive of the Year. **March 29**—At NFL meetings in Phoenix, owners vote to go to 4 pre-season, 16 regular season game schedule in 1978; Seattle assigned to the AFC Western Division. **June 8**—Raiders' players and staff receive World Championship rings . . . **October 9**—Raiders down Cleveland 26-10 to win 17th consecutive game, a record topped only twice in 58 years of NFL play. **December 11**—Raiders clinch 10th playoff appearance in 11 years with 35-13 win over Minnesota in Coliseum. **December 18**—Raiders beat Kansas City 21-20 to become first NFL team to win 150 league games since 1960. **December 24**—Raiders defeat Colts at Baltimore, 37-31, in second overtime period to win AFC Playoff and advance to Conference Championship. At 75 minutes and 43 seconds this game is longest in Raider history and third longest played in NFL to date.

1978

January 1—Raiders lose 20-17 at Denver in AFC Championship Game. **January 15**—Dallas defeats Denver 27-10 in Super Bowl XII at Superdome in New Orleans. **March 13**—NFL owners meet in Palm Springs. Rule changes adopted include: liberalized pass protection blocking, elimination of defenders bumping eligible pass receivers more than five yards downfield and the addition of a seventh game official. **June 7**—NFL owners vote to increase active rosters in 1978 to 45 players. Teams will still have to cut to 43, then can add two players. **October 1**—Raiders record in overtime game goes to 4 and 0 with 25-19 fifth-quarter win over Bears in Chicago. **November 5**—Raiders' John Madden becomes 13th coach in NFL history to win 100 games as Oakland wins in Kansas City, 20-10. **December 17**—Raiders beat Minnesota Vikings in Coliseum, 27-20, to wrap up 14th consecutive winning season.

1979

January 4—John Madden retires from football coaching after 12 years with Raiders—two as linebacker coach and 10 as head coach. **January 21**—Pittsburgh defeats Dallas 35-31 in Super Bowl XIII At Orange Bowl in Miami. **February 8**—Tom Flores named as head coach of the Oakland Raiders by Managing General Partner Al Davis. **March 1**—KGO Radio awarded broadcast rights to Raider games for 1979 through 1981. **March 12**—NFL owners meet in Honolulu. Rule changes adopted include: eliminating blocking below the waist on punt and kickoff returns, officials instructed to blow the play dead as soon as the quarterback is in the grasp of any tackler, active roster for 1979 will be 45 players. **May 11**—Pete Banaszak retires after 13 seasons at running back for the Raiders. **July 1**—Cornerback Willie Brown retires after 12 seasons with Raiders and 16 seasons in the league. **July 9**—Raiders close season ticket sales at an all-time high of 51,825. **July 28**—Raiders play in Pro Football Hall of Fame Game for first time in Canton, Ohio, defeating Dallas Cowboys 20-13. **September 2**—New Head Coach Tom Flores gets his first league win as Raiders down the Rams 24-17 in Los Angeles Coliseum. **October 14**—Raiders score 50 points fifth time in team history, defeating Atlanta 50-19. **December 3**—Raiders run Monday Night record to 13-1-1 with great comeback win against Saints in New Orleans 42-35. **December 9**—Win over Cleveland, 19-14, earns Raiders 15th consecutive winning season, tying all-time NFL record set 35 years ago by Chicago Bears. **December 16**—Raiders complete 1979 season, having scored in 198 consecutive games.

1980

January 20—Pittsburgh defeats Los Angeles 31-19 in Super Bowl XIV at Rose Bowl in Pasadena. AFC now leads Super Bowl series 10 wins to 4. **April 29**—Raiders select BYU quarterback Marc Wilson, nation's leading passer, in first round of college draft. **August 2**—Original Oakland Raider Jim Otto, starting center for 210 consecutive league games from 1960 through 1974, is inducted into Pro Football Hall of Fame in Canton, Ohio. **September 7**—Ray Guy punts seven times for 51.8-yard average in season-opening 27-14 victory in Kansas City. **October 5**—Dan Pastorini, secured in trade with Houston for Ken Stabler, breaks leg against Chiefs and is succeeded at quarterback by Jim Plunkett. **October 12**—Longest run from scrimmage in Raider history, 89 yards by Kenny King (another ex-Oiler), enables Raiders to beat San Diego, 38-24, and evens season record at 3-3. **November 14**—Raider winning streak stands at six straight with 19-17 victory over Seattle, first win ever for Raiders in the Kingdome. **December 1**—Monday night record of Raiders stands at phenomenal 16-1-1 with 24-21 triumph over Denver. **December 21**—Raiders close out regular season at 11-5 and make playoffs as wild card team. Their 16th straight winning season is a new NFL record. Lester Hayes leads NFL in pass interceptions with 13, just one short of record. **December 28**—Homecoming of Ken Stabler, Jack Tatum to Oakland is spoiled by Raiders' 27-7 victory over Houston in First Round Playoffs.

1981

January 11—Raiders qualify for third Super Bowl appearance by beating San Diego, 34-27, as Jim Plunkett completes 14 of 18 passes. **January 25**—Raiders win world championship with convincing 27-10 defeat of Philadelphia Eagles in Super Bowl XV. Plunkett voted most valuable player. His 80-yard touchdown pass to Kenny King is longest play in Super Bowl history. **April 28**—Defensive back Ted Watts of Texas Tech picked by Raiders in first round of NFL draft. **May 11**—Suit of Raiders against NFL for right to move franchise to Los Angeles Coliseum starts in Federal District court in Los Angeles.

RAIDER LEADERS BY YEARS

PASSING

		Atts.	Comp.	Yds.	Pct.	TD	Int.
1960	Tom Flores	252	136	1738	.540	12	12
1961	Tom Flores	366	190	2176	.519	15	12
1962	Cotton Davidson	321	119	1977	.370	7	23
1963	Tom Flores	247	113	2101	.457	20	13
1964	Cotton Davidson	320	155	2497	.484	21	19
1965	Tom Flores	269	122	1593	.453	14	11
1966	Tom Flores	306	151	2638	.494	24	14
1967	Daryle Lamonica	425	220	3227	.518	30	23
1968	Daryle Lamonica	416	206	3245	.495	25	15
1969	Daryle Lamonica	426	221	3302	.519	34	25
1970	Daryle Lamonica	356	179	2516	.503	22	15
1971	Daryle Lamonica	242	118	1717	.488	16	16
1972	Daryle Lamonica	281	149	1998	.530	18	12
1973	Ken Stabler	260	163	1997	.627	14	10
1974	Ken Stabler	310	178	2469	.574	26	12
1975	Ken Stabler	293	171	2296	.584	16	24
1976	Ken Stabler	291	194	2737	.667	27	17
1977	Ken Stabler	294	169	2176	.575	20	20
1978	Ken Stabler	406	237	2944	.584	16	30
1979	Ken Stabler	498	304	3615	.610	26	22
1980	Jim Plunkett	320	165	2299	.516	18	16

RUSHING

		No.	Yds.	Avg.	TD	LR
1960	Tony Teresa	139	608	4.4	6	83
1961	Wayne Crow	119	490	4.1	2	62
1962	Clem Daniels	161	766	4.7	7	72
1963	Clem Daniels	215	1099	5.1	3	74
1964	Clem Daniels	173	824	4.7	2	42
1965	Clem Daniels	219	953	4.0	5	57
1966	Clem Daniels	204	801	3.9	7	64
1967	Clem Daniels	130	575	4.4	4	52
1968	Hewritt Dixon	206	865	4.2	2	28
1969	Charlie Smith	177	600	3.4	2	23
1970	Hewritt Dixon	197	861	4.4	1	39
1971	Marv Hubbard	181	867	4.8	5	20
1972	Marv Hubbard	219	1100	5.0	4	39
1973	Marv Hubbard	193	903	4.7	6	50
1974	Marv Hubbard	188	865	4.6	4	32
1975	Pete Banaszak	187	672	3.6	16	27
1976	Mark van Eeghen	233	1012	4.3	3	21
1977	Mark van Eeghen	324	1273	3.9	7	27
1978	Mark van Eeghen	270	1080	4.0	9	34
1979	Mark van Eeghen	223	884	4.0	7	19
1980	Mark van Eeghen	222	838	3.8	5	34

RECEIVING

		No.	Yds.	Avg.	TD	LR
1960	Billy Lott	49	524	10.7	1	28
1961	Doug Asad	36	501	13.0	2	51
1962	Max Boydston	30	374	12.4	0	58
1963	Art Powell	73	1304	17.8	16	85
1964	Art Powell	76	1361	17.9	11	77
1965	Art Powell	52	800	15.4	12	66
1966	Art Powell	53	1026	19.4	11	46
1967	Hewritt Dixon	59	563	9.5	2	48
1968	Fred Biletnikoff	61	1037	17.0	6	82
1969	Fred Biletnikoff	54	837	15.3	12	53
1970	Fred Biletnikoff	45	768	17.1	7	51
1971	Fred Biletnikoff	61	929	15.2	9	49
1972	Fred Biletnikoff	58	802	13.8	7	39
1973	Fred Biletnikoff	48	660	13.8	4	32
1974	Cliff Branch	60	1092	18.2	13	67
1975	Cliff Branch	51	893	17.5	9	53
1976	Dave Casper	53	691	13.0	10	30
1977	Dave Casper	48	584	12.2	6	27
1978	Dave Casper	62	852	13.7	9	44
1979	Cliff Branch	59	844	14.3	6	66
1980	Bob Chandler	49	786	16.0	10	56

PUNT RETURNS

		No.	Yds.	Avg.	TD	LR
1960	Jack Larscheid	12	106	8.8	0	41
1961	Charles Fuller	4	52	13.0	0	25
1962	Bob Garner	20	162	8.1	0	25

		No.	Yds.	Avg.	TD	LR
1963	Claude Gibson	26	307	11.8	2	85
1964	Claude Gibson	29	419	14.4	0	58
1965	Claude Gibson	31	357	11.8	1	58
1966	Rodger Bird	37	323	8.7	0	42
1967	Rodger Bird	46	612	13.3	0	78
1968	George Atkinson	36	490	13.6	2	86
1969	George Atkinson	25	153	6.1	0	30
1970	Alvin Wyatt	25	231	9.2	1	63
1971	George Atkinson	20	159	8.0	0	34
1972	George Atkinson	10	33	3.3	0	8
1973	George Atkinson	41	336	8.2	1	63
1974	Ron Smith	41	486	11.9	0	55
1975	Neal Colzie	48	655	13.6	0	64
1976	Neal Colzie	41	448	10.9	0	32
1977	Neal Colzie	32	334	10.4	0	23
1978	Neal Colzie	47	310	6.6	0	24
1979	Ira Matthews	32	165	5.2	0	20
1980	Ira Matthews	48	421	8.8	0	34

		No.	Yds.	Avg.	TD	LR
1973	George Atkinson	3	48	16.0	0	36
1974	Alonzo Thomas	6	70	11.7	1	34
1975	Alonzo Thomas	6	86	14.3	0	48
1976	Monte Johnson	4	40	10.0	0	22
1977	Jack Tatum	6	146	24.3	0	41
1978	Charles Phillips	6	121	20.2	1	42
1979	Lester Hayes	7	100	14.3	2	52
1980	Lester Hayes	13	273	21.0	1	62

KICKOFF RETURNS

		No.	Yds.	Avg.	TD	LR
1960	Jack Larscheid	30	852	28.4	0	78
1961	George Fleming	29	588	20.3	0	36
1962	Bo Roberson	27	748	27.7	1	87
1963	Bo Roberson	38	809	21.2	0	58
1964	Bo Roberson	36	975	27.0	0	59
1965	Larry Todd	20	461	23.1	0	50
1966	Pervis Atkins	29	608	21.0	0	35
1967	Dave Grayson	19	405	21.3	0	29
1968	George Atkinson	32	802	25.1	0	60
1969	George Atkinson	16	382	23.9	0	39
1970	George Atkinson	23	574	25.0	0	62
1971	Clarence Davis	27	734	27.2	0	44
1972	Clarence Davis	18	464	25.8	0	49
1973	Clarence Davis	19	504	26.5	0	76
1974	Harold Hart	18	466	25.9	0	67
1975	Harold Hart	17	518	30.5	1	102
1976	Rick Jennings	16	417	26.1	0	55
1977	Carl Garrett	21	420	20.0	0	31
1978	Art Whittington	23	473	20.6	0	34
1979	Ira Matthews	35	873	24.9	1	104
1980	Ira Matthews	29	585	20.2	0	45

PASS INTERCEPTIONS

		No.	Yds.	Avg.	TD	LR
1960	Eddie Macon	9	105	11.7	1	42
1961	Joe Cannavino	5	14	2.8	0	9
1962	Tom Morrow	10	141	14.1	0	36
1963	Tom Morrow	9	104	11.5	0	35
1964	Fred Williamson	6	40	6.7	0	28
1965	Warren Powers	5	56	11.2	0	12
1966	Warren Powers	5	88	17.6	0	35
1967	Willie Brown	7	33	4.7	0	25
1968	Dave Grayson	10	195	19.5	1	54
1969	Dave Grayson	8	132	16.5	1	76
1970	Kent McCloughan	5	5	1.0	0	5
1971	Nemiah Wilson	5	70	14.0	0	22
1972	Jack Tatum	4	91	22.8	0	56

PUNTING

		No.	Yds.	Avg.	LP
1960	Wayne Crow	76	2958	38.9	72
1961	Wayne Crow	61	2613	42.8	77
1962	Cotton Davidson	40	1569	39.2	64
1963	Mike Mercer	75	3007	40.0	53
1964	Mike Mercer	58	2446	42.1	67
1965	Mike Mercer	75	3079	41.1	70
1966	Mike Eischeid	64	2703	42.2	56
1967	Mike Eischeid	76	3364	44.3	62
1968	Mike Eischeid	64	2788	43.6	72
1969	Mike Eischeid	69	2944	42.7	58
1970	Mike Eischeid	79	3121	39.5	57
1971	Jerry DePoyster	57	2013	39.4	56
1972	Jerry DePoyster	55	2031	36.9	57
1973	Ray Guy	69	3127	45.3	72
1974	Ray Guy	74	3124	42.2	66
1975	Ray Guy	68	2979	43.8	64
1976	Ray Guy	67	2785	41.6	66
1977	Ray Guy	59	2552	43.3	74
1978	Ray Guy	81	3462	42.7	69
1979	Ray Guy	69	2939	42.6	71
1980	Ray Guy	71	3099	43.6	66

SCORING

		TD	PAT	FG	Total
1960	Tony Teresa	10	0	0	60
1961	George Fleming	1	24	11	63
1962	Clem Daniels	8	0	0	48
1963	Art Powell	16	0	0	96
1964	Mike Mercer	0	34	15	79
1965	Clem Daniels	12	0	0	72
	Art Powell	12	0	0	72
1966	Mike Eischeid	0	37	11	70
1967	George Blanda	0	56	20	116
1968	George Blanda	0	54	21	117
1969	George Blanda	0	45	20	105
1970	George Blanda	0	36	16	84
1971	George Blanda	0	41	15	86
1972	George Blanda	0	44	17	95
1973	George Blanda	0	31	23	100
1974	Cliff Branch	13	0	0	78
1975	Pete Banaszak	16	0	0	96
1976	Cliff Branch	12	0	0	72
1977	Errol Mann	0	39	20	99
1978	Errol Mann	0	33	12	66
1979	Jim Breech	0	41	18	95
1980	Chris Bahr	0	41	19	98

(Turn page for identification of world champion Oakland Raiders)

OAKLAND RAIDERS, winner, Super Bowl XV, left to right:

Front row—Marc Wilson, Ray Guy, Chris Bahr, Malcolm Barnwell, Leo Gray, Jim Plunkett, Cliff Branch, Arthur Whittington, Tom Flores.

Second row—Lew Erber, Odis McKinney, Keith Moody, Mark van Eeghen, Derrick Jensen, Kenny King, Dwayne O'Steen, Mike Davis, Lester Hayes, Monte Jackson, Ray Willsey, Joe Madro.

Third row—Charlie Sumner, Ira Matthews, Burgess Owens, Todd Christensen, Kenny Hill, Dave Dalby, Bob Nelson, Mario Celotto, Rod Martin, John Adams, Matt Millen, Jeff Barnes, Sam Boghosian, John Herrera.

Fourth row—Steve Ortmayer, Randy McClanahan, William Bowens, Reggie Kinlaw, Gene Upshaw, Mickey Marvin, Steve Sylvester, Henry Lawrence, Lindsey Mason, John Matuszak, Dave Browning, Dave Pear, Phil Livingston, Joe Campbell, Willie Brown.

Fifth row—Earl Leggett, Chet Franklin, Art Shell, Bruce Davis, Morris Bradshaw, Ted Hendricks, Derrick Ramsey, Bob Chandler, Cedrick Hardman, Raymond Chester, Rich Martini, Willie Jones, Bob Mischak, Dick Romanski.

Sixth row—Donald Fink, H. Rod Martin, John Otten, George Anderson, Al LoCasale, Bob Rosenfeld, Mike Gonzalez, Pete Eiges, Al Degler, George Jones, Ken Bishop, Max Friedman, Bob Romanski, Tom Grimes, Bill Glazier.

1980 OAKLAND RAIDERS: That Championship Season
(home team in bold)

September 7, 1980

| Oakland | 27 |
| **KANSAS CITY** | 14 |

September 14, 1980

| Oakland | 24 |
| **SAN DIEGO** | 30 |

September 21, 1980

| **OAKLAND** | 24 |
| Washington | 21 |

September 28, 1980

| Oakland | 7 |
| **BUFFALO** | 24 |

October 5, 1980

| **OAKLAND** | 17 |
| Kansas City | 31 |

October 12, 1980

| **OAKLAND** | 38 |
| San Diego | 24 |

October 20, 1980

| Oakland | 45 |
| **PITTSBURGH** | 34 |

October 26, 1980

| **OAKLAND** | 33 |
| Seattle | 14 |

November 2, 1980

| **OAKLAND** | 16 |
| Miami | 10 |

November 9, 1980

| **OAKLAND** | 28 |
| Cincinnati | 17 |

November 17, 1980

| Oakland | 19 |
| **SEATTLE** | 17 |

November 23, 1980

| Oakland | 7 |
| **PHILADELPHIA** | 10 |

December 1, 1980

| **OAKLAND** | 9 |
| Denver | 3 |

December 7, 1980

| **OAKLAND** | 13 |
| Dallas | 19 |

December 14, 1980

| Oakland | 24 |
| **DENVER** | 21 |

December 21, 1980

| Oakland | 33 |
| **NEW YORK GIANTS** | 17 |

Playoffs

December 28, 1980

| **OAKLAND** | 27 |
| Houston | 7 |

January 4, 1981

| Oakland | 14 |
| **CLEVELAND** | 12 |

January 11, 1981

| Oakland | 34 |
| **SAN DIEGO** | 27 |

SUPER BOWL XV
(New Orleans):

January 25, 1981

| Oakland | 27 |
| **PHILADELPHIA** | 10 |